Tierge

P9-CSU-124

9/17 $14-

619-238-5100

1075 11th Avenue

San Diego CA 92101

Peasants against the State

Stephen G. Bunker

Peasants against the State
The Politics of Market Control in Bugisu, Uganda, 1900-1983

UNIVERSITY OF ILLINOIS PRESS

Urbana and Chicago

This book has been brought to publication with the generous assistance of the Department of Sociology of the University of Illinois at Urbana-Champaign and of the Faculty of Arts and Sciences of the Johns Hopkins University.

This book is printed on acid-free paper.

LIBRARY OF CONGRESS CATALOGING-IN-PUBLICATION DATA

Bunker, Stephen G., 1944-
  Peasants against the state

  Bibliography: p.
  Includes index.
  1. Peasantry—Uganda—Bugisu (District)—Political
activity. 2. Agriculture—Uganda—Bugisu (District)—
Societies—Political activity. 3. Agriculture and
state—Uganda—Bugisu (District). 4. Coffee trade—
Uganda—Bugisu (District). I. Title.
HD984.Z8B843   1987   306'.3   85-20894
ISBN 0-252-01288-7 (alk. paper)

Contents

Acknowledgments

Many people have helped and encouraged me in the researching and writing of this book. That my greatest debt is to the Bagisu is amply evident in the pages that follow. Conversations and correspondence with Robert Bunker have influenced and clarified the ideas that have given shape to this study. Crawford Young's work on Uganda and on Bugisu gave me new insights on my own research there; the present form of this book owes much to the acute critical review he provided of an earlier draft. Frank Holmquist has inspired, encouraged, and criticized at crucial moments over many years.

Linda Seligmann provided advice, encouragement, solace, and close critical attention during the long process of revision. I did most of the writing in the single room we lived and worked in while she did research in a remote Andean village. It is a tribute to her tolerance and patience that we managed on a single table with a single kerosene lamp and a single typewriter.

David W. Cohen, Joan Sokolovsky, and Melvin L. Kohn all made extremely useful comments on what were getting close to final drafts. Jane Mohraz provided useful editorial advice while I was trying to put a first draft together, and Susan L. Patterson's expert copyediting helped to make the book more readable. Sheila Welch, once again, typed many drafts and did many revisions with the patience, good humor, and skill that have always characterized her work. I owe her special thanks.

Different parts of the research were funded by the Rockefeller Foundation (1969-70), a Shell Foundation International Fellowship (1970-71), and a Hewlett Fellowship (1983). Additional funds for special projects were provided by the African Studies Program and by the International Agriculture Program of the University of Illinois. The Center for Advanced Study there provided a fine work environment at a very opportune point in the writing.

I worked out early forms of some of the arguments presented here in articles in the *British Journal of Sociology* (1983a), *American Ethnologist* (1983b), *Africa* (1984b), and the *Canadian Journal of African Studies* (1985a). I am grateful to the editors of all of these journals, and especially to Norman E. Whitten, Jr. (*American Ethnologist*) and to J. D. Y. Peel (*Africa*), for the challenging criticisms and comments their review processes provided. Donald Crummey's editorial exigencies and suggestions (1985b) taught me a lot about writing history, even as they left me doubtful about my ability to satisfy his high standards.

List of Abbreviations Used in the Text

ACO	Assistant cooperative officer
BCMA	Bugisu Coffee Marketing Association
BCMCo.	Bugisu Coffee Marketing Company
BCS	Bugisu Coffee Scheme
BCU	Bugisu Cooperative Union
BNA	Bugisu Native Administration
CCD	Commission for Cooperative Development
CMB	Coffee Marketing Board
DC	District commissioner
DCD	Department of Cooperative Development
DP	Democratic party
GCS(s)	Growers' cooperative society(ies)
MP	Member of Parliament
RDP	Rural Development Program
UPC	Uganda People's Congress

Glossary of Lugisu Words Used in the Text

bagasya	plural of umugasya
bagoosi	plural of umugoosi
baguga	plural of guga
bakhulu	plural of mukhulu, senior men in lineage
baraza	meeting or council
biguga	plural of kiguga
gombolola	subcounty (administrative unit)
guga	ancestor, grandfather
inda	womb, smallest level of kiguga
Kabaka	monarch (Luganda)
kiguga	clan, lineage
Lukhobo	council, Bugisu District Council
miluka	plural of muluka
mitongole	plural of mutongole
mugasya	see umugasya
muluka	parish (administrative unit)
mutongole	subparish (administrative unit)
saza	county (administrative unit)
umugasya	leader of major level lineage
umugoosi	leader of minor level lineage
umusakhulu	preeminent elder, ritual head of lineage

Introduction

"Africa's history raises the insistent question whether its common people have not been better able than most of their kind around the world to resist the demands of those who exploit them." So wrote John Lonsdale (1981:167) in a long review essay on states and social processes in Africa. In a similar vein, in another review essay prepared as part of the same project, Frederick Cooper (1981a) discussed the ways that African peasantries have limited the manner and extent of their incorporation into the world economy. Lonsdale's and Cooper's general conclusions contrast sharply with the assumptions of many recent analysts of East African politics who argue that national states there have increased political control and economic exploitation of the peasants who make up much of their population. With a few exceptions (e.g., Brett, 1973; Hyden, 1980; Holmquist, 1977, 1980; Vincent, 1982) they treat national peasantries as passive victims (Leys, 1975; Mamdani, 1976; Shivji, 1976). Lonsdale and Cooper correctly criticize these ideas, but their emphasis on resistance to exploitation and on capital's incomplete domination precludes considerations of how some of Africa's common people have achieved constructive programs aimed at establishing local control over vital economic and political processes. In this history of the ways that one African peasantry engaged the state directly, I argue that freeholding peasants who produce valuable export crops can sustain effective challenges to central state power.

These challenges are usually stimulated by local leaders in pursuit of their own political goals. The use and manipulation of peasant protest against the state raises the question of who benefits and who loses in these struggles. Peasant protest often provides crucial leverage in struggles to open political space for locally based power groups, which are usually more sensitive to peasant demands than are power-holders in the central state. On the other hand, their stimulation of peasant protest may seriously disrupt local economies and politics in ways that impose heavy costs on the peasants.

I examine these issues in this study of how peasants who grow coffee in Bugisu, Uganda, protested against crop prices and marketing conditions and how local aspirants to representative positions in government and in the local crop-marketing cooperative manipulated these protests in their struggles to achieve autonomy from the central state and in their competitions with each other. I argue that these struggles represent essential determinants of local and national social and political organization that dependency, world-system, and many orthodox Marxist analyses ignore in their assumptions that capitalism or a capitalist world market can restructure noncapitalist societies and economies. Peasant resistance to the state is rooted in political and economic processes that straddle autochthonous social organization and national crop-marketing systems, but the economic interests and the social power that drive these processes are profoundly local and must be studied at the local level.

Peasants have seldom been seen as an effective political force. Karl Marx's (1963) analysis in *The Eighteenth Brumaire* of peasants mobilized behind a revolution that ultimately consumed them sets the tone for other studies of peasant political participation. Observers have described peasants as the backbone and also as the final victims of Latin American independence movements and of the Mexican Revolution (see, e.g., Hamnett, 1978). They imply that peasants react to and advance new economic and political arrangements in which they only partially participate. In this view peasants may be essential to the establishment of new regimes, but they finally succumb to new forms of exploitation under the regimes they help establish (Anderson and Cockcroft, 1966; Cockcroft, 1972). Analysts of peasant rebellion and resistance explain that peasants are too bound to the soil and to its seasonal routines, live and work in excessive isolation, and are too much subject to manipulation by "Kulak" members of their own class with compromising ties to urban and national life to sustain their own political impetus (Wolf, 1969).

These notions about the peasantry's liminal political status are replicated in discussions of the peasantries' economic position. This "awkward class" (cf. Shanin, 1972), caught between modes of production but having none of its own, is seen by many as producing values and reproducing labor essential to a capitalist mode of production that increasingly smothers it but finally maintains it in order to exploit it (de Janvry, 1981).

These same themes appear in the long and complex debate about the articulation of modes of production in Africa. Ideas that started with Lenin's (1939) and Rosa Luxemburg's (1951) rather different notions about capitalism's need for primitive accumulation and new markets at its own fringes continue with Claude Meillassoux's (1973) statements that noncapitalist forms survive because capitalism needs them and Charles Bettelheim's (1972) thesis that capitalism partially dissolves but finally conserves elements of the other modes of production that it encounters. By attributing the existence and the persistence of African peasantries to capitalism, authors reify and attribute intentionality to capitalism and ignore the autonomous role of peasant societies in reproducing themselves.

Without denying the tremendous impact that penetration by capitalist regimes of exchange, labor recruitment, and production has had on the development of peasantries in Africa, I insist that Africans actively participated in the shaping of their own economic and social organization. Africans resisted the pressures imposed by colonial and capitalist agents, and they took advantage of new opportunities that those agents provided. Their response to these pressures and opportunities engendered new forms of power based on new alliances and new conflicts within their societies (see Palmer and Parsons, eds., 1977; Cooper, 1981a, 1981b). These new groups struggled against the colonial state and against each other for control of key political and economic resources. I believe that it is in these struggles, rather than in the abstract notion of capitalism, that we must search for the dynamics that molded colonial and postcolonial society in Africa. In this sense, we must see peasantries as actively participating in the formation, reproduction, and conservation of their own societies.

I will show in this study that the Bagisu acted collectively to resist exploitation by the state and to retain control over their own labor. They used the state's dependence on their crops to increase their own influence on local economic and political processes and institutions. Each resolution of their protests or resistance against the state changed the economic and political environment in which they acted and thus established the conditions in which subsequent protest occurred.

New ascendant groups and political institutions emerged from this struggle. Only a privileged few could enter or participate directly, but because the economy depended on peasant production and because political change was driven by peasant protest, the Bagisu peasants achieved and maintained considerable political power. This power, however, was not of the type that a conventional analysis of legislative and executive institutions would illuminate. Peasants do not appear clearly in the available documentary evidence. Rather, the power of the peasantry and the political centrality of their protest can only be deduced from the political actions and statements of the holders of official positions and writers of reports and memoranda whose names and words fill the archives.

Perspectives on Peasant Politics

World-system, dependency, and more orthodox Marxist analysts have all exaggerated the potential of capitalism as a mode of production and exchange to restructure other modes of production and extraction. Immanuel Wallerstein's (1974) and Andre Gunder Frank's (1967) affirmations that the entire system is capitalist, Bettelheim's (1972) assertion that capitalism shapes other modes of production to its own ends, and Meillassoux's (1973:89) refusal to attribute any autonomous capacity for self-reproduction to noncapitalist modes of production ignore the facts that locally based dominant groups enter into world market exchanges according to their own perceived opportunities, that they themselves may reorganize local modes of production and exchange, and that the opportunities to which they respond are frequently ephemeral, while the reorganization of local modes of production may have enduring local consequences (see, e.g., collections by Palmer and Parsons, 1977, and McCoy and de Jesus, 1982). Acknowledgment of the specific characteristics of precolonial social formations, and of their persistence over time, is crucial in this regard. The human groups that enter and depart from this exchange network are responding to changing market opportunities (see Stavenhagen, 1966-67); they maintain and reproduce themselves not because capitalism needs them nor because they themselves have become capitalist. Rather, they persist as human groups always have, by adapting to their own environments, of which international exchange opportunities form a highly variable part, but which are also structured by the organization of earlier modes of production and extraction (see also Bunker, 1984a).

   The self-maintenance of such groups and the rates of exchange which they achieve for their production depend on their own power. The articulation of particular modes of production results not only from the exchange of goods, but also from the relative political strength of the groups and classes in various interacting social formations (see Lonsdale and Berman, 1979). A focus on specific modes of production and specific social formations allows us to consider these forms of power, but in order to understand the particular position of specific social formations within a world-system, we must develop models of power that can be applied simultaneously to the organization (its capacity for mobilization and its control over economic and political resources) within a particular social formation and to the conflicts and struggles between it and other social formations.

Some recent studies of the formation of African peasants (see especially Palmer and Parsons, eds., 1977; Vincent, 1982) have emphasized the ways that indigenous social organization, relations of authority, trade, and warfare, and the ecology of the areas they inhabited influenced the ways that different African societies responded to contact with commercial capitalism and later to incorporation into colonial regimes. Rather than locating all determinants in the colonizing societies, these studies have shown how different groups of Africans responded to—both resisting and exploiting—new market, employment, and political opportunities. They acted in their own interests. They adjusted to changes in their social, political, and economic environment in ways that maintained their own societies in the face of powerful external forces.

This perspective is particularly useful for analyses of peasant political action against the state in much of Africa. The ways in which Africans entered into the world economy gave the freeholding peasant societies that emerged in many African countries political leverage denied to peasants in other parts of the world, who till fields owned by large landowners. These freeholding peasants produce the great bulk of the commercial crops on which the national economy and the national state depend, and they can grow what they choose on their lands. In Tanzania and Uganda, for example, freeholding peasant households predominate in production for both local consumption and international markets (Young, 1971:141; Brett, 1973:217-34; Hyden, 1980:9-28; Young, Sherman, and Rose, 1981:54). This means that if they are not satisfied with the prices export crops bring or the conditions in which they must sell them, they can produce other crops for domestic markets or for their own subsistence. In these nations the dispersion and fragmentation of economic control within and among numerous freeholding peasant communities counterbalance the political control of the state.

States that derive most of their revenues from freeholding peasants' production are susceptible to sustained local challenge.[1] Freeholding peasants can withdraw into subsistence production if the state attempts to appropriate too much of their labor or products. The state's expansion and its ability to transform economic, political, or social arrangements are therefore subject to an economic veto. The "exit option" provides local groups who can mobilize and direct freeholding peasants' significant bargaining power against the more centralized and wider rang-ing power of the state apparatus (Brett, 1973:245).[2]

Indirect rule, which incorporated autochthonous organization into wider administrative structures, enhanced this economically based bar-gaining power. In Uganda the colonial state assigned members of local communities to administrative positions, which gave them authority over larger areas than had been possible in precolonial societies. Their expanded power disrupted previous socioeconomic arrangements (Brett, 1973:1), but this disruption was only partial (Brett, 1973:300-310). The resulting administrative structure, devised to permit control of local societies at minimal cost to the state, could also be used by local power groups to stimulate and coordinate local resistance to the state (La Fontaine, 1969:185-91; Brett, 1973:262; Bunker, 1981:91-5; Vincent, 1982:247-58). This resistance generally corresponded to what Jeffrey Paige (1975:45-48, 70) calls commodity reform movements, that is, struggles of a cultivating class dependent on land against a class de-pendent on commercial capital, aimed at limited market reform rather than at revolutionary change.

In Uganda, however, the state, rather than a dominant commercial class, depended on agricultural commerce for its income. Because the state apparatus was largely staffed by members of local communities whose interests partially, but importantly, coincided with those of the peasant farmers, continuity of autochthonous organization and state dependence on locally recruited staff provided a firmer and more ef-fective organizational basis for peasant mobilization and protest than Paige suggests. The state's nearly total dependence on agricultural rev-enues meant that effective movements to raise prices or reduce pro-cessing costs to farmers or to relax onerous quality controls seriously threatened state revenues. As such movements were supported and directed by the same groups the state employed for local administration, they also threatened public order. National states are highly vulnerable to threats against their revenues or against public order and therefore tend to make concessions to groups that can manipulate these threats (Block, 1977).

Direct repression of commodity reform movements supported by a freeholding, economically predominant, and locally administered peas-antry would disrupt both the administration, which maintains order, and the production from which the state appropriates its revenues, and so is generally used as a last resort (Bunker, 1981). Instead, the state is likely to attempt to coopt the leaders or groups that oppose it; that is, it will extend recognition, formal position or office, powers, re-sponsibilities, and privileges to these leaders or groups in return for their participation in officially sanctioned, supervised, formal organizations through which it can regulate their actions (see, e.g., Selznick, 1966). I will show that where indirect rule and peasant economic predominance coincide, such cooptation provides local leaders with additional organizational and economic resources that they can manipulate both as reward and as threat to mobilize the peasants even more effectively behind their demands to expand local autonomy.

Thus, where freeholding peasants produce most of a nation's marketable goods, the state faces a difficult dilemma. It must derive most of its revenues from the peasants' cash crops, but if it appropriates too much, it will drive the peasants away from the cash market and into subsistence agriculture, the products of which the state can neither sell nor tax (Hyden, 1980; Bunker, 1983b). Many African states have attempted to assure their revenues through direct control of crop markets (Bates, 1981). Market control in peasant economies, however, usually offers the major means to wealth and power, so local groups attempt to seize control of the state's marketing apparatus (Saul, 1969; Hyden, 1970a, 1973). Their success depends on their ability to convince the state that the peasants will indeed reduce their cash crops if the state refuses to allow more local control over marketing. Their ability to convince the state that they can reduce cash crops, in turn, depends on their ability to mobilize the peasants. Local leaders must therefore attempt to satisfy peasant demands, usually for higher crop prices, less onerous quality controls, and more convenient marketing procedures, all of which threaten to reduce the surplus that the state can appropriate. The state will devolve market control on local actors only insofar as its agents believe that popular resistance would reduce its revenues and political power even more than local control. This means that the state will allow local groups to control crop markets only if they can organize peasant production and sale in such a way that the state can continue to appropriate revenues from the peasants' crops. Even then, power-holders in the state often perceive local autonomy as threatening to their own political control. They may attempt to restrict local power even when this entails economic costs or social disorder.

Successful leaders of resistance to the state are thus coopted into serving the state even while they work against its interests. These leaders attempt to satisfy partially the demands of both the peasants and the state—and to derive economic and political advantages for themselves. They must constantly balance their own aspirations to power and wealth against the danger that the state will remove them from their positions if they try to reward the peasants too well or if they themselves become too powerful. The resulting arrangement is so complex that no resolution is possible; the political powers of the state, of local leaders, and of the peasants themselves remain in flux, and the economic and political condition of all three remains highly unstable.

The Mobilization and Manipulation of Peasant Protest in Bugisu

I have spent parts of the last fifteen years trying to sort out the dynamics of struggles for market control in Bugisu District, a fertile, mountainous area on the Kenyan border of Uganda. I first went to Bugisu in 1969. Fifteen years earlier, Bagisu leaders had won a long struggle to establish a cooperative that took over crop marketing functions that the central state had controlled since 1933. I was allowed access to the files and archives of their organization, the Bugisu Cooperative Union (BCU), as well as those of the state's Department of Cooperative Development and of the Bugisu District Council. I interviewed all surviving leaders of the popular campaign against state market control as well as all the men who had served on its representative committee or on its staff. Almost without exception, these men talked extensively about their work with the BCU, about their farms and other economic activities, about their other political involvements, about the kin and affinal alliances that supported their political campaigns, and about the rewards and frustrations of their work with the cooperative. Some of these men also became close friends and wise advisers. They understood, sometimes better than I, what I was trying to do, and from more than one I was given pointed lessons in how to do fieldwork. One of the most powerful and controversial politicians in the district, for example, warned me one day that it had become too easy for me to talk to him, and that I'd better be sure to give his enemies equal time.

I used the archival and interview material to piece together a history of the struggle to gain, maintain, and expand local power against the state, and of the struggles between different groups of Bagisu to control and exploit the resources that the state's concessions to their demands made available. I also collected career biographies of all of these men and conducted a survey in four areas to collect parallel information from nonleaders.

During the time I was in Bugisu, and even more acutely when I started to analyze the information I had gathered, I was troubled by what seemed to me then two irreconcilable sets of attitudes and outcomes in these leaders' political activities. On the one hand, these men were proud of the BCU and of the services it provided for the Bagisu.

They, and most of the other Bagisu I spoke to, saw the union as an essential part of the Bagisu's ability to prosper, as a crucial lever obliging the government to provide necessary social and economic services, and as a symbol of Bagisu competence to participate in the national economy and politics. Various leaders also emphasized the egalitarian aspects of the cooperative ideology of popular control. On the other hand, most of the BCU leaders and officeholders also perceived and used the union as a source of power, privilege, and wealth for themselves. In the course of pursuing their own individual and factional strategies for upward mobility, they had on various occasions disrupted the functioning of the union, provoked destructive power struggles within it, and used the cooperatives' resources extravagantly or, more rarely, dishonestly. Their power struggles against the state and against each other depended on their mobilizing the peasants, and the extension of their own fights had also greatly exacerbated hostilities between different factions, lineages, and regions and had occasionally provoked violence and property destruction.

The stories the Bagisu leaders told me were fascinating, and I enjoyed the challenge of checking the oral against the written record and of using each to flesh out what I learned from the other. The Bagisu's generosity in explaining endless details of their lives, work, and politics was a pleasure in itself. The natural beauty of the lush, rugged, densely cultivated, volcanic formation where I was given hospitality and friendship heightened the excitement and happiness I felt. The men who had been most intensely involved in and committed to the cooperative knew the most about its history and about its workings, and their enthusiasm made them eager to talk. It was not by accident that the man I became closest to and told me the most about the union had been its most powerful and ambitious president. I worried then, and still do, about how much all of this warmth and interest biased my perceptions of the leaders. I was afraid of becoming too much a BCU partisan.

I was somewhat reassured, however, by the frankness with which many of the men I interviewed told me about their own and their allies' mistakes, peculations, and power strategies. The intense conflicts that had emerged in the district also assured that I got more than one side of any important story.

Finally, I was after a time simply allowed to be around when important political strategies were discussed, and I had ample opportunity to learn about the less honorable parts of these plans. On one such occasion in 1970, one of Bugisu's MPs and a cabinet minister joined a group of local Uganda People's Congress (UPC) officials and seven officers of the Department of Cooperative Development (DCD) to discuss strategies for the national elections. I joined the group before the visitors arrived. I had talked to the Mugisu MP twice, both times in English, and I had never met the minister. They came in, and started to discuss, in Lugisu, ways that the DCD officers could manipulate local cooperative society elections to assure that the MP's political allies were elected. The cabinet minister spoke Lugisu incorrectly but fluidly; he clearly would have done better in Luganda or English. After the two dignitaries left, everyone in the room had a good laugh about the trick they'd played by letting the visitors plan illegal political schemes without knowing I understood what was being said, even though the local politicians and DCD officers themselves were clearly included in the political dirty work.

I was also present at numerous elections in the smaller cooperative units where I heard heated arguments, debates, accusations, and defenses of various political leaders. The correspondence I read in DCD and BCU files gave me ample evidence that various cooperative leaders were using their powers in ways that at least some of their neighbors thought were illegal or unethical.

It is a testimony to these leaders' openness and acceptance of my work that despite the intensity of factional conflict, no one I interviewed objected to the time I spent with his opponents. The only difficulty of this sort that I experienced resulted from the antagonism between the north, central, and southern regions of Bugisu. Though mutually intelligible to the familiarized ear, there are distinct dialectal differences between the regions. I learned Lugisu in a northern village, but then spent most of the next three months working in the south. When I returned to the north, my friends were furious that I was speaking like a "cowardly dog from the south." The Bagisu leaders used contacts and alliances across the entire district and did not seem worried about my accent, but I endeavored when talking to other Bagisu, who had little experience outside their lineages' territories, to sound like them.

Idi Amin's coup of January 1971 put a terrifying end to the atmosphere of optimistic prosperity and energetic politics that I so enjoyed in Bugisu. Various leaders disappeared into unknown prisons or out of the country. Soldiers roamed the streets, demanding free food and drink and beating anyone who objected with their rifle butts.

I witnessed several brutal arrests, one of a district agricultural officer I was talking to at his own desk. There were rumors that various Bagisu were settling old scores by accusing their enemies of opposition to the soldiers, and reports of torture and mutilation. Most Bagisu, and I, were constantly frightened and constantly watching for the soldiers.

I was particularly worried because so much of the information I had recorded was about high-ranking members of the local branch of the UPC, the deposed party whose officers were bearing the brunt of the military repression. I took what I thought were the most compromising of these records over the back road to Kenya and sent them home from there.

My friends were as worried for me as for themselves, and we were all careful not to be seen together except in trusted company — usually in their home areas. Remarkably, many of them expressed an urgency to give me as much information as quickly as possible. This urgency extended to several district administration officers, who gave me access to files they had previously said were confidential. One of them expressed explicitly what many had said indirectly when he told me that he wanted me to see the files so that people would know what had really been going on in Bugisu before Amin changed both its present and its history.

I stayed on, perhaps foolishly, for another five months, but decided I had to leave after two North American researchers were tortured, killed, and burned in army barracks south of Kampala. I smuggled what I still had of my notes and records through the seven heavily armed military roadblocks between Bugisu and Kampala. A friend arranged with an expatriate air-freight agent to smuggle my files out of Uganda.

I left Bugisu weighing thirty pounds less than I had five months before. My earlier enthusiasm had turned to a fairly abject disillusionment, and I found it very difficult to think, talk, or write about Uganda. I also knew that I could not, in good conscience, publish most of what I knew about Bugisu as long as Amin was in power. I was not particularly happy in the United States either, and I continued to worry that the experience I had had in Bugisu had given me a distorted view of dependent agricultural economies. I became especially concerned that the relatively even distribution of land in Bugisu had enhanced the potential for effective peasant organization in ways I would never understand until I had comparable experiences in less egalitarian societies. I decided to take a job in a Guatemalan university, where I did research on peasant cooperatives. After two years there, I taught and did research on cooperatives, colonization, agricultural development, and peasant organization for three years in the Brazilian Amazon.

I started to compare abstractly the political potential for peasant organization and influence on state policy in Brazil and Uganda (Bunker, 1981). In comparison with the rural inequalities I saw in Latin America, the extra powers, privileges, and wealth of the Bagisu leaders seemed far less significant than they had when I was in Uganda. My central question about these leaders slowly changed from the simple and rather naive worry about how the cooperatives had heightened social differentiation to the more complex issue of how the Bagisu peasants provided the leverage that local leaders manipulated against the state and against each other to gain power and wealth even while their dependence on the peasants' continued support and on the continued tolerance of the state restricted the degree of social differentiation they could achieve.

Only after Amin was finally overthrown in 1979 did I feel I could start to write about the contradictions between peasant mobilization as a means to better the peasantry and as a means to enhance their leaders' upward mobility. I went back to Bugisu during the summer of 1983 and saw the effects of both the Amin regime and of the second Obote regime that replaced it—the decline in agricultural production, the decay of economic infrastructure, and the demoralization of what I had known as an energetic, dynamic, and highly aggressive organization. This experience strengthened my conviction that however volatile peasant organization may make local politics, it is essential to the promotion and coordination of commercial agricultural production, because it provides the only effective means of communication between the state and the vast majority of direct producers. When the state suppresses local organization for political reasons, it ultimately undermines its own economic base. Struggles between national-level politicians, bureaucrats, and soldiers to capture and control the state by reducing local autonomy may produce economically irrational results that further weaken the state.

I have had to wrestle during this writing with my own sorrow about the effects three different centralizing regimes (Obote, Amin, Obote) have had on Bugisu. I have attempted to remain true to my own data, and to the contradictions they imply. I cannot pretend, however, that this is a dispassionate book. I am firmly convinced that peasants must organize to defend themselves, even though I realize that their mobilization may unleash violent and destructive political forces. The problem is to keep these forces within constructive limits and to convince national states whose revenues depend on peasant production that they ignore or suppress peasant organization and the leaders who direct it at their own risk.

The Analysis of Peasant Political Space

My perspective on the struggle between the peasants and the state focuses on the theoretical space and practical issues defined by two recent pioneering studies of state-peasant relations. Robert Bates (1981) has shown that many African states, including Uganda, have used market control to increase the rate at which they appropriate revenues from the peasantry. He demonstrates that these states use these revenues in favor of urban and industrial investment and to strengthen their political alliances with nonpeasant groups. He implies, however, that peasant small-holders are politically and economically defenseless against the state. Goran Hyden (1980) has shown that freeholding peasants maintain an "exit option," which allows them to veto unpopular state programs by withdrawing from cash cropping. Hyden was particularly concerned with the weakness of a state that depends primarily on peasant production and with the distortions of state policy that occur when local peasants "capture" the state's bureaucratic agents. He maintained that the peasants refuse to use their political "voice" to influence state policies directly, and that, because the peasants' exit option weakens the state, the state must somehow contrive to capture the peasants (1980:139-40 and passim).

I generally agree with Bates on the motives and consequences of state control of markets, and I believe that Hyden's notion of the exit option is extremely useful, but I also believe that they are both too pessimistic about the potential for and effects of peasant political organization and participation. In this study I show that through symbolic manipulation of the threat to exit, the Bagisu gained and used voice to expand the local political arena and their autonomy within it. Their effective use of voice created space within which they could form their own associations and organizations and use them to bring direct pressure on state policies. In this sense, I follow more closely Albert Hirschman's (1970:82-85) assertions that the exit option does not necessarily atrophy voice, but can in fact be used as a lever to strengthen it.

The Bagisu valued and depended on the goods and services they could purchase with the cash they received for their crops. They preferred not to withdraw from the market, and as individuals would only withdraw or reduce their production if low prices and unfavorable marketing conditions made these goods and services too costly. Bagisu peasants, however, learned to form and participate in organizations that created the threat of collective withdrawal from cash-cropping and communicated it to the state in ways that allowed the state to confront the threat symbolically, that is, before prices and marketing conditions deteriorated to the levels at which peasants would implement the threat on the basis of individual or household decisions. The Bagisu's experience provides the basis of my argument that the mobilization of peasant protest and the manipulation of the threat to reduce cash crops or withdraw from the market can be used constructively to moderate the state's exploitation of the peasants. Peasant-based organizations can effectively communicate their needs and demands to the state at the same time that they coordinate crop production, sale, and processing more efficiently than the state can manage. Symbolic, political use of the peasants' exit option, however, requires that local leaders focus and direct this threat in such a way that it becomes a bargaining lever rather than just a veto against the state. Once the threat of crop withdrawal is actually implemented, it cannot serve any effective political purpose. Rather, it directly reduces both state revenues and peasant cash income. Used symbolically, however, it can force the state to allow the peasants to keep a greater part of their surplus production and to conserve their own social forms. Hyden argued that this protection against exploitation also reduces the state's ability to accumulate the capital necessary for social and economic development. I believe that I can demonstrate, however, that the state's attempts to increase its exploitation of the peasants will provoke a total reduction of cash cropping, so that both the state and the peasants lose. Effective communication and increased production, therefore, depend on local organization sufficient to force the state to listen to and accommodate peasant demands (see also Holmquist, 1980).

State, Class, and Dependency: Latin American Models and Their Application in East Africa

A direct focus on the conflict between the peasants and the state, and on the ways that local power groups can both take advantage of and positively direct this conflict, resolves some of the major limitations of the dependency perspective that has framed many recent studies of East African politics and class relations. These studies have tended to treat peasants as the passive victims of national states that are themselves totally subordinate to the dictates of international capital. They thus ignore the ways in which peasant organizations can exploit the national state's dependence on them. This means that the political activities of the vast majority of the population are simply assumed away.

Latin American scholars first developed dependency theories in response to economic, social, and political problems that accompanied rapid industrialization after World War II. They were particularly concerned with the political and economic consequences of government and business policies designed to attract international capital and to manage the subsequent problems of foreign indebtedness. Their models also reflected the extreme polarization of social classes typical of most Latin American societies. The Latin American dependency theorists emphasized the associations between dominant class interests, international capital, and the state's economic policy. They saw dependence on international capital as an option that strengthened certain class fragments; these classes promoted foreign control of the economy and of the state in the pursuit of their own interests (Cardoso and Faletto, 1979).

The various theories within the dependency perspective differ considerably in their explanations of underdevelopment, despite a general agreement that a nation's position in an international system of unbalanced or dependent exchange affects its developmental potential. Some theories attribute underdevelopment to the production and exchange systems that colonizing metropoles imposed on their satellites to maximize their own accumulation of capital (Frank, 1969). Others stress the composition of trade, especially in terms of the relative value of raw and processed exports and imports (Galtung, 1971). Many consider the composition of foreign trade and the historic experience of colonial conquest and administration as context for, rather than determinant of, class structure and political processes within dependent countries (Chilcote, 1974, 1978; Bath and James, 1976; Portes, 1976; Cardoso, 1977). This perspective emphasizes the partial autonomy of internal economic and political processes from a nation's position within the world economy. It clearly cautions against direct extension of dependency analysis to class analysis. The actions of national states and domestic dominant classes and the relations between them must be dealt with as particular historical cases of self-interested decisions within situations of dependency rather than as direct outcomes of dependency.

A growing interest in the dependency and world-system perspectives has stimulated a number of cross-national comparative studies that further extend and refine the Latin American dependency models (Galtung, 1971; Chase-Dunn, 1975; Bornschier, Chase-Dunn, and Rubinson, 1978; Bornschier and Ballmer-Cao, 1979). These studies suggest that both the fiscal and political autonomy of the state and the levels of social and economic inequality vary significantly with the type and degree of a nation's dependency, particularly as a function of its penetration by multinational corporations.

These refinements of the earlier, Latin American–based dependency theories are especially important for application of the dependency perspective to East African societies. Unlike the Latin American situations from which contemporary dependency theories emerged, indigenous African social organization significantly influenced the ways that individual colonies were incorporated into systems of world trade (see, e.g., Palmer and Parsons, eds., 1977; Cooper, 1981a). In many of these African colonies imperialist adaptations to local social organization in the form of indirect rule and the exploitation of peasant economies for agricultural exports restricted social differentiation and class formation. The extraordinary degree of land-tenure concentration and peonage and the creation of a landless rural mass that followed the capitalist penetration of agriculture in much of Latin America (see de Janvry, 1981) did not occur in most of Africa. The colonial state emerged in Africa as the predominant political and economic force, unchallenged and unaided by autonomous land- or capital-owning classes. Local communities continued as viable political and economic structures from which members of ethnically defined groups could challenge the colonial and later the national state (Hyden, 1980). The state remained predominant but was constrained to take the local bases of political and economic power into account (Lonsdale, 1981).

Locally ascendant groups adapted, manipulated, and extended autochthonous organizational forms, both to satisfy the exigencies of the colonial state and to exploit the opportunities it offered. These groups adopted some European forms and ideas into their own expanded social organization. These changes and adaptations served to preserve the continuity of local organization and the ways that it could be used against the state. Because the state was the unit of incorporation, these struggles mediated the participation of each local economy in the world-system. Any study of the role of the state within the world-system, or the ways that the state appropriates value to itself or to a bureaucratic class, must therefore take local power bases, and their evolution through struggles against the state, into account. Analyses that simply assume that situations of dependency, loosely defined as parallel to those of Latin America, create a strong central state supported by international capital ignore crucial limits to the powers of national states confronted by viable local organization.

In contrast to Latin America, the much less industrialized East African nations depend little on foreign capital. They are dependent only in the sense that their specialized agricultural economies were originally imposed by external forces and are still highly susceptible to fluctuations in international markets and to the extent their states make political concessions in return for foreign aid. Uganda, for example, consistently enjoyed positive trade balances until Amin began to exploit the agricultural economy to expand and strengthen his army. Only in the current economic and political crisis has the state become dependent on foreign capital, but this dependency is still quite different from Latin America's (see Chapter 9).

The social and economic distances between classes are much smaller in East Africa than they are in Latin America. This is especially so in Tanzania and Uganda, where colonial administrative and economic policies impeded the formation of national dominant classes. Thus, the defining characteristics of Latin American dependency do not occur in these East African countries. A number of recent authors, however, have adopted the Latin American dependency perspective as a context for class analysis in East African society without incorporating the refinements and qualifications suggested by dos Santos (1970) and Cardoso (1977) or by the recent cross-national extension of earlier dependency models (see Lonsdale, 1981; Cooper, 1981a).

Various recent studies of the Tanzanian and Ugandan political econ-omies have used dependency perspectives to posit two related trends: first, a unilinear tightening of state control over national populations and production (see Holmquist, 1980:157-59), and second, the emer-gence and growing power of an internally hegemonic bureaucratic class that closely identifies its own interests with those of international capital (Mamdani, 1976; Shivji, 1976).[3] They are correct in identifying state attempts to tighten control, and there is clear evidence that the state bureaucracy has increased in size, privilege, and consequently in the share of nationally produced value that it appropriates to itself. Their rather mechanical incorporation of the assumptions of dependency theory, however, leads them to ignore and implicitly deny the weakness of the state in relation to the peasant economy. They seriously under-estimate the economic and political limits to the power of both the state and its bureaucracy. These limits include: (1) the dispersal of economic power, or control of the means of production, among and within numerous freeholding peasant communities; (2) the ability of these communities to withdraw from cash cropping to subsistence; (3) the continued basis of local administration in the autochthonous social organization and authority structures that were originally coopted into the state apparatus; and (4) the ability of locally based power groups to exploit this dispersed economic control and administrative decen-tralization in their challenges to central state power.

Because these studies ignore these limits, they misinterpret the evo-lution and growth of both the colonial and the independent African state. As the colonial state grew, it became increasingly dependent on revenues from crop exports and thus more susceptible to challenge by the ever larger, ever more complex African-staffed systems of agricul-tural extension and crop marketing it had erected. The independent state was forced to expand even more rapidly, both to satisfy the developmental aims that it espoused and to provide the spoils that successful claimants to state control distributed to gain and keep political and military support.

To satisfy its growing needs, the state sought simultaneously to stimulate greater production of crops and to increase its rate of appropriation. I have already explained why these two goals are incompatible. The state's failure to realize both imperatives threatened its own control over production and marketing systems *and* individual power-holders' control over the state. As control became more tenuous, the hypertrophied state resorted to violence.

The independent state's expanded scope and its increasing use of violence against its own subjects created a superficial impression of heightened political control and economic exploitation, but, as Lonsdale's (1981) review essay correctly points out, the violence and the forceful appropriation of surplus shattered the bonds between society and state. Lonsdale does not clearly indicate, however, how definitively this rupture weakened the state. Nor does he specify the ways in which the state's needs for increased revenues impelled the holders of state power to try to increase simultaneously agricultural production and the rate of appropriation. The costs of the bureaucratic expansion that the state initiated to increase its control over appropriation further weakened it by heightening its dependence on a peasant agriculture that was both fragile and recalcitrant.

Gerd Spittler (1983:131), in a brief essay comparing eighteenth- and nineteenth-century European and twentieth-century African peasant states (which he defines as territorial and political organizations based on peasant input), expresses the dilemma precisely. "To the superficial observer, nothing seems to be easier than to rule over the homogeneous and passive peasantry of the agrarian state. But the reality is quite different. There is nothing more difficult than to build up an administration covering millions of partly self-sufficient peasant households. It is not only the great number of widely dispersed households which makes this task so intractable. Even more important are the implications of self-sufficiency. The greater the autarky of households, the less can they be controlled from the outside. Due to the lack of information and means of exerting pressure the administration often relies on physical force." Spittler argues that the use of physical force is a sign of weakness and not of power. He shows how the state bureaucracy cannot apply its general, abstract rules to the diversity of peasant communities and their economic strategies. The only way that the bureaucracy can function at all is through local intermediaries who do not perform according to the bureaucracy's abstract rules. I extend Spittler's logic, arguing that if the state, through this bureaucracy, attempts to increase its control, or to increase rates of appropriation, by subordinating these intermediaries to its own rules, it either provokes their resistance or undermines their local efficacy. The bureaucracy thus collapses; this collapse intensifies the use of violence. Violence becomes, not just a sign of weakness, but a major factor in the collapse of the state itself.

When the state begins to use violence against local organizations, the peasants no longer attempt to bargain with it. Instead, they withdraw from controlled crop markets as much as possible to avoid forced appropriation and because any contact with the state is dangerous. Violence thus reduces the state's access to revenues. At the same time, the reliance on violence increases the claims that the military can make on the state's shrinking revenues. This means that the state diverts to the military the monies necessary to maintain the organizational and physical infrastructure of its crop marketing systems. The progressive deterioration of this infrastructure further reduces the state revenues. With its economic base in shambles, the state disintegrates politically, becoming merely a prize to be won, and kept, in increasingly violent contests.

The state initiates its own inexorable decline by attempting to control and to appropriate more than the peasant economy will allow. I use the political history of the Bagisu to argue, however, that viable local peasant political associations can forestall this process. Relatively autonomous local organizations can provide the mediation between bureaucracy and peasants that the state needs to survive. Whether independent African states have the political security and discipline necessary to permit such local autonomy is, unfortunately, another matter.

The assumption of a unilinear trend to centralized control by a strong national state can be falsified by an examination of the ways that local-level organization articulates with national power structures through the various levels of bureaucratic and political organization that mediate national-local power relations. As I explained above, the potential self-sufficiency of a freehold peasant economy, from which the state extracts most of its revenues, and the relative autonomy of a decentralized administrative structure profoundly rooted in autochthonous social organization combine to offset the central powers of the state and limit the potential for class formation and differentiation. Uganda provides a vivid example.

Indirect Rule and the Weak State

C. C. Wrigley (1959) and E. A. Brett (1973) have both shown how colonial strategies in Uganda combined with pressure from textile mill interests in Britain to prevent the emergence of either a plantation-owning expatriate class or a large landowning Ugandan class. In the absence of such classes the state had to appropriate its revenues directly from the producers, who were primarily peasants. Hence Mahmood Mamdani's (1976) perceptive observation that the state acted as a surrogate dominant class. The state is not a class, however, even though a state must act very differently where there is no dominant class. Peasants may form a class, and they may struggle against the state, but again, both class and action are very different where there is no dominant class. The processual class analysis that Cooper (1981a) calls for must take these differences into account.

Central to both Wrigley's and Brett's analyses is the fundamental weakness of an understaffed, underfinanced colonial state that depended on autochthonous local organization for both political and economic administration. Lacking access to the credit necessary to establish plantations, the state stimulated and used peasant cash cropping to satisfy British industrial and consumer demand and to finance its own administration. Its dependence on freehold peasant production and autochthonous local organization, however, severely limited both its control over production and its ability to appropriate surplus. This state was overdeveloped only in the sense of exceeding in complexity the economic bases on which it rested (see Leys, 1976). Its primary strength came from the failure of the different ethnically and regionally based peasantries and local rural power groups to coordinate their political activities and economic interests across district boundaries. African politicians, bureaucrats, and soldiers inherited both the strengths and weaknesses of this state when Uganda achieved formal political independence. Eventually, they turned even the state's relative strength into weakness, as their struggles to control a hypertrophied state ruined both economy and polity.

The state's dependence on peasant agriculture and on autochthonous organization emerged from early colonial government attempts to satisfy British textile manufacturers' demands for a cheap, elastic supply of cotton and its own need for revenues. It had to satisfy these needs within the limits imposed by a tight credit market, opposition within the colonial office to the establishment of a rentier or large landowning class, a limited budget, a very small European staff, and a tenuous political control frequently threatened by rebellion (Wrigley, 1959:20-

43; Brett, 1973:217-34; Mamdani, 1976:128). Plantation agriculture expanded rapidly, with considerable state encouragement, until prices declined after World War I. The competitive advantages of peasant agriculture, both because of its reduced labor and overhead costs and because of the peasants' ability to weather price declines by retreating into subsistence, became especially apparent in the economic crisis of 1921-22. This advantage stimulated both colonial and textile manufacturing support for small-scale cotton cultivation. The subsequent decline of plantation agriculture left the Ugandan economy primarily dependent on peasant cultivation of cotton (Mamdani, 1976:40-61). Rapid expansion of peasant-grown coffee, which by the 1950s had replaced cotton as Uganda's principal export, left the peasantry firmly in control of the bulk of export crop production (Young, 1971:144; Uganda Republic, 1966a:55, 1966b).

The colonial state in Uganda used local authorities to introduce cash crops in ways that reduced both its own administrative costs and the danger of social disorder or rebellion. The extension of political control and of cash cropping through coopted indigenous authority structures, however, left the colonial state directly dependent on local authorities who were themselves dependent on popular support, first, to achieve compliance, and second, to expand their own powers and the benefits that could be derived from them.

In order to expand the volume and the value of the cash crops on which it depended, the colonial state had to increase the number of local authorities and assign them increasingly complex functions within the export economy. This deepened the state's dependence on local organization at the same time that it created new groups whose upward mobility depended on their ability to demand more jobs at higher bureaucratic levels. Local groups achieved power over marketing by mobilizing peasants to threaten commercial crop reduction. They then used their formal powers over crops to enhance the peasants', and their own, bargaining position against the state. They strengthened peasant support by demanding higher prices for crops, less onerous quality controls, and lower taxes, and then used this support and the threat of crop reduction or withdrawal to demand more autonomy from the state. All of these demands threatened the state's fiscal base.

The state, however, controlled and regulated access to the bureaucratic positions that the new groups strove to enter and so could use the threat of removing each group's members from office. The state also could attempt to strengthen the position of the older established groups that were least dependent on peasant support, such as chiefs and civil servants, against popular representatives and leaders. The popular leaders' formal power, moreover, was conditioned by their need to win elections. This made them accountable to their followers, heightened their competition with each other, and made their tenure less secure.

Various local power groups competed among themselves, and some allied themselves with the state when new groups threatened their own power bases. The tensions between these groups, the power of the state to remove individuals from office, and the instability of elected office all restricted the potential for any of these groups to achieve independent power or to accumulate significant amounts of wealth or property. The state's dependence on the peasants for production and on local leaders for order thus both created and limited social differentiation at the local level and left local power bases intact. Local leaders could use these power bases to challenge the state and to defend the local economy and society against exploitation, but the state retained the capacity to restrict these power bases directly and to exclude particular individuals from access to them.[4]

Peasant Protest and Local Power in Bugisu: A Special Case?

The Bagisu provide a particularly interesting and vivid case of the ways that local power groups can use the autochthonous social organization that controls administration and cash cropping both to take advantage of and to resist the needs and demands of the states that mediate between them and world capitalist markets. Mount Elgon, whose western slopes the Bagisu occupy, provides the fertile soils, rain, and elevation needed to cultivate the high-priced Arabica coffee. In all but very small areas of the rest of Uganda, only the much poorer Robusta variety was grown. By the 1950s Bugisu was consistently supplying over 10 percent of the total value of the coffee exports, which contributed over half of Uganda's foreign revenues (Uganda Republic, *Statistical Abstracts*, 1969).[5] Except for Mengo, the peri-urban district around Kampala, Bugisu had the highest per capita income in Uganda. Its location on the Kenya border gave the Bagisu access to other markets than those in Uganda and allowed them to avoid officially controlled crop-purchase by smuggling during the Amin regime.

Bugisu's prosperity and the high value of its coffee enhanced the political leverage that the peasants' exit option gave local power groups. At the same time, this prosperity intensified the state's desire to control their crops. As a result, the struggles for local autonomy were more intense than they were in the rest of Uganda. The BCU was by far the richest, strongest, and politically most active of Uganda's cooperatives. National cooperative legislation was revised in 1959 specifically to allow state intervention in its operations, but the resulting opposition in Bugisu was explosive, destructive, and violent. The BCU was also the first Uganda cooperative subjected to state intervention a second time. In an interview in 1970, the minister of cooperatives and marketing told me that the BCU was Uganda's most important and most difficult cooperative.

Remarkably, despite their prosperity and number (over half a million), the Bagisu were little represented in national ministerial positions or in the national civil service. This was partially a reflection of their educational patterns. Their attendance through the beginning of secondary school compared favorably with that of other ethnic groups, but then dropped sharply. This may be because the arduous circumcision rituals, which occurred for boys between the ages of sixteen and twenty-five, interrupted their time, concentration, and health (see La Fontaine, 1957).

Bugisu was well represented, however, and the BCU was very powerful, at the national levels of the various cooperative apex organizations established after 1962. Indeed, most of the Bagisu's considerable political energy was directed to the politics of market control, both at the national and at the local level. This preoccupation with the politics of marketing generally overrode the ethnic and religious divisions and rivalries that marked much of local and national politics in the rest of Uganda (see Saul, 1976; Young, 1976; Young, Sherman, and Rose, 1981). While the identification of various political parties with different religious denominations did occur in Bugisu as well, even party politics revolved primarily around issues of who would control crop sales. Religious organizations were important in the defense of Bagisu rights prior to the establishment of the BCU, and many of the first cooperative leaders had worked as catechists and religious teachers. Both Catholic and Protestant leaders used the prestige of their religious work in the common cause of organizing the Bagisu peasants.

Ethnic identity was an important part of the campaign to establish the cooperative, but more as the basis of local rights against the state than against other ethnic groups (Bunker, 1984b). There was, however, considerable ethnic conflict with the Sebei, the Bagisu's poorer and weaker neighbors to the north, ten years after the BCU was founded. The Bagisu's encroachment on Sebei territory and their desire to keep the Sebei as a small and subordinate part of the BCU membership eventually provoked extensive violence, which led to the formation of a separate Sebei cooperative. The Sebei protested that the Bagisu exploited their cooperative's continued dependence on the BCU coffee mill, but this conflict had little effect on the BCU. That the vast majority of the BCU's members and of Bugisu's inhabitants all identified themselves as members of a single, powerful, proud, and important ethnic group meant that ethnicity per se was not an important factor in the BCU's and the district's factional struggles. Ethnicity is, of course, more likely to emerge and to be identified as an issue in national politics than in the local politics of an ethnically homogeneous district. Antagonisms between the different regions of Bugisu and recrimination about the predominance of certain lineages in the BCU did contribute to the intense struggle for power within the union, however. To the extent that the regional antagonisms were culturally based, they created conflicts analagous to those between ethnic groups.

The Bagisu's and the BCU's economic strength and importance to the national state, the intensity and effectiveness of their political activities, their strategic geographical location, and the relative insignificance of religious and ethnic divisions in their internal power struggles all distinguish the Bagisu from other Ugandan ethnic groups. Other, poorer ethnic groups in Uganda did, however, organize and use their contribution to the national economy to resist the state's pressures and demands (Wrigley, 1959; Brett, 1970, 1973; Kasfir, 1970; Young, Sherman, and Rose, 1981; Vincent, 1982). The Bagisu provide an opportunity to examine the potential and the limitations of peasant organization against the state precisely because their political activities were so intense. The salience of these activities in the district's economic and social organization allow a detailed study of the processes that gave rise to new political and economic institutions, and of the struggles to control them.

The history of the Bagisu's struggle against the state, and the careers of the men who stimulated, directed, and profited from this struggle, cannot inform us directly about the conditions and political opportunities of the rest of Uganda's peasants, much less those of other African nations. I believe that they can, however, tell us a great deal about how to examine peasants' struggles against the state. The conversations I had with various Bagisu about their experiences under and responses to colonial and national rule convinced me that we must consider peasants as active participants in their own fate.

The Bagisu learned enough about the state's needs and about its ideologies and weaknesses and about their own social and economic organization to use the state's dependence on them in their struggles for local power.[6] They combatted the state on its own ground, often using both bureaucratic forms and Western ideological principles against the colonizers who had imported them (Bunker, 1984b). What they learned and how they used it were particular in many respects to their own situation, but the process of their learning and the ways that the outcome of each struggle against the state changed the environment in which the peasants, the state, and local power groups acted can tell us what to look for and what to compare with when we examine peasant political organization in other places.

We need detailed case studies of local politics. Most analyses focus directly on the central state without examining the local processes that limit and structure its powers and policies. This facilitates analysis; in Uganda and in other countries of different ethnic composition and characterized by uneven economic development, the central state is single and unitary, while the bases of opposition to it are multiple and diverse. Convenient research and elegant analysis must not lead us to ignore local systems. Understanding national politics requires a series of detailed historical and processual studies of local political systems and of their relations to the central state.

Outline of the Study

In the chapters that follow, I will show how chiefs, civil servants, and politicians in Bugisu have used the essential functions they served for the state and their ability to mobilize peasants against the state in their struggles for power. In Chapter 1, I trace first the growing power of the colonial chiefs who took advantage of their obligation to enforce commercial crop cultivation and then the ascendancy of the civil servants the colonial state employed to manage the rapidly expanding crop sales. Chapter 2 recounts how these civil servants allied themselves with an emergent group of local leaders to mobilize the peasants behind their demands for greater responsibility in, and later control of, coffee sales. This chapter ends with an analysis of the ways the state contrived to control the cooperative union that the Bagisu had organized. Chapter 3 interrupts the chronology of events to describe the ways that the BCU and other representative institutions opened new avenues to wealth and power for Bagisu politicians. The purpose of this chapter is to explain why Bagisu leaders struggled so hard to maintain and expand BCU autonomy against the state and to safeguard their positions in competitions with each other. I also use this chapter to consider the extent to which the powers, privileges, and wealth of the chiefs, civil servants, and politicians distinguished them as separate status groups or as a single social class.

I return to the questions of class and power in chapters 4-7; these chart the chronology of struggles between the state and different groups for control over the BCU from 1954 until the Amin coup in 1971. Chapter 8 recounts the ways that the Amin regime suppressed local organizations and how the Bagisu responded by implementing their long-standing threat to withdraw from officially controlled export markets. It also explains how the centralizing tendencies of the second Obote regime prevented the reemergence of viable local organization and why this impeded the revitalization of coffee and cotton exports. This chapter addresses an issue that emerges implicitly in the preceding four chapters: that is, the ways that different groups' strategies to capture the state and to extend its powers beyond its precarious economic capacities actually weakened the state and undermined both social order and economic production.

Before proceeding, however, I should explain why I have retained the prefixes of ethnic group names in this study. Most studies of Bantu groups drop these prefixes; the Bagisu, for example, become the Gisu. This is only a part of their name in their own language. The British imposed the name Bagisu on them when they created a district out of acephalous lineages that called themselves by many different names. The Bagisu have, over time, developed an ethnic identity and call themselves by this name, although they also call themselves Bamasaaba, after the apical ancestor they all recognize. I do not think it my place to rename them, so I have kept the prefixes in this text; Bugisu is the district,[7] Mugisu is one member of their ethnic group, Bagisu are two or more. Lugisu is the language they speak. There are at least twenty-six other sets, singular and plural, of noun classes with corresponding prefixes, but I have conformed to English usage in all but the cases that name human beings.

NOTES

1. See Uganda Protectorate (1955c, 1956), Gayer (1957), and Brock (1969) on de facto and de jure freehold in Uganda and Bugisu.

2. Domar's (1970) point that free land and free labor imposed limitations on accumulation by a landowning class can be extended in this case to accumulation by the state. See Blau (1964) on resource control, bargaining, and power.

3. Samoff (1979) correctly argues that this approach ignores crucial elements of class conflict, but does not explore the power bases for peasant organization against a bureaucratic class or the state that maintains it. See also Saul (1976) for a critique of Mamdani and Shivji. Saul acknowledges the weakness of the state but sees it as the result of conflict between fractions of the bourgeoisie. He, too, ignores the crucial role of peasant organization and politics in limiting the power of the state.

4. The resulting distribution of power between local and central systems directly affected two important variables in different theories of national development. The first of these variables, the ability of the national government to implement and coordinate coherent national development programs, informs both modernization (see Higgott, 1980) and Marxian (e.g., Hyden, 1980) arguments that a strong state is necessary for national development. The second of these variables, the capacity of the state to exploit the direct producers of exportable commodities, informs dependency and Marxian arguments that East African states control and appropriate increasing proportions of nationally produced surplus (Saul, 1972, 1974; Cliffe, 1973; Mamdani, 1976; Shivji, 1976; Samoff, 1979; see also Holmquist, 1980:157-59).

Despite the significant impact that successful local demands for power can have on both of these variables, there has been remarkably little analysis of local challenges to state power in the freeholding peasant societies of East Africa. The few studies that recognize the phenomenon interpret it either as a reflection of temporary political uncertainty or instability at the national level (Leys, 1967; Young, 1979); as transitory local movements whose leaders and organizations are soon suppressed or coopted by the central state (Mamdani, 1976; Shivji, 1976); or as an impediment to the efficient management of the agricultural cooperatives that handle local crop collection and processing (Saul, 1969). Other studies have acknowledged organizational and leadership roles of local elites in economic and social change (Hyden, 1973), even while admitting that such leadership was selective (Vincent, 1971) or even corrupt (Hyden, 1969) in the defense of elite interests, but they have ignored the fundamental conflict between these groups' interests and those of the state. Hyden's (1980) study of Tanzania is exceptional in its recognition of both the endogenous bases and the persistence of local challenges to central authority, but its primary focus is on the limitations these impose on the central state's developmental capacity. This study focuses on both the limitations and the contributions to social and economic development that peasant mobilization and organization may produce.

5. The coffee crop's importance to the district administration, an arm of the central state, dated back to the early 1930s. Much of the Bagisu's protest against the state was focused at the district level, and the sensitivity of locally based state agents to this protest strengthened popular movements.

6. The Bagisu's ability to learn to bargain with the state in this way provides, at the very least, a limiting case for Wolf's (1969) assertions that peasants cannot understand the complexities of the state.

7. Amin renamed the district Mbale, after its urban center. This was still its official name in 1983, but nobody seemed to be calling it that.

1

The Changing Ecology of Power, 1900-1940

The dynamic links between the different (social, political, and economic) institutions are best seen when one follows the careers of successful men.
—Vansina, 1973:18

The metropolitan demand for raw materials and the colonial state's need to reduce production and administrative costs led the British to introduce cash cropping into indigenous subsistence and land-tenure systems and to coopt indigenous authorities into colonial administration. Subsistence horticulturalists became market-oriented peasants, and lineage heads became colonial chiefs. The state's need to expand export crop production, improve crop quality, and assure efficient marketing required it to recruit increasing numbers of Bagisu into the administration of the rural development amd marketing programs. Increased Bagisu employment in the administration of the cash crops heightened the state's dependence on local organization and strengthened the position of groups that were crucially situated to mobilize peasants and to negotiate for greater Bagisu participation and representation in local administration and crop marketing. Each of these groups used the state's dependence to enhance its own powers and to demand more autonomy from state control. They also created upward pressure on crop prices and administrative costs, thus threatening state revenues.

The state's dependence on peasant production forced it to take peasant demands into account both in its administrative organization and in its economic development policy. It was particularly susceptible to such demands in Bugisu, because the valuable Arabica coffee grown there provided a disproportionate share of Uganda's exports, eventually reaching nearly 10 percent of total coffee export values, while coffee supplied about 50 percent of Uganda export revenues (Uganda Republic, 1969). Thus, the threat that the Bagisu might withdraw from market production into a subsistence economy provided a strong counter to the ampler powers of the state. The bargaining between the state and the Bagisu was particularly delicate because of the nature of coffee cropping. Cotton farmers who resisted by neglecting their crops could be persuaded, or coerced, to return to their crops the next year. Coffee farmers who destroyed their trees effectively withdrew from production for at least four years, the time needed for new plantings to reach production. Reestablishment of coffee plantations required considerable capital. The destruction or neglect of coffee trees, therefore, was a potent threat. Reduction of coffee production, however, also reduced peasant income, so it usually occurred only when other forms of bargaining failed. Bagisu leaders and the peasants themselves had to learn to use the threat of coffee reduction symbolically, to convince the state to accede to their demands without always having to damage their economy.

The administrative arrangements that evolved out of the state's dependence on locally controlled administration, locally controlled crops, and an international market favored different groups of Bagisu at different times. The growth of cash cropping stimulated new demands and protests against the state. New ascendant groups emerged out of local protest movements and the state's response to them. The relations of each ascendant group to the preceding groups, to the rest of the Bagisu, and to the state created new forms of political and economic organization and so changed the available avenues to power and wealth. In order to understand the processes and consequences of economic growth, social differentiation, and struggles over crop surplus, it is necessary to follow these changes from the time of colonial conquest. These processes were deeply rooted in autochthonous social organization, which in turn was much affected by the ecology of the region.

Physical Ecology and Social Organization

Mount Elgon, a volcanic cone with ridges radiating out to twenty miles from its crater, rises to 14,000 feet from a wide, 4,000-foot high plain which lies south, west, and north of it. Eighty miles north of the equator, it straddles the Kenya-Uganda border. Its steep slopes are covered with rich soil, which allows intensive cultivation of subsistence crops and Arabica coffee on the mountain itself and which has run off to enrich the surrounding flatlands, where cotton is the main crop. At its summit, the mountain receives almost twice as much rainfall as the surrounding area, about 90 inches a year, tapering down to 60 inches on the lower

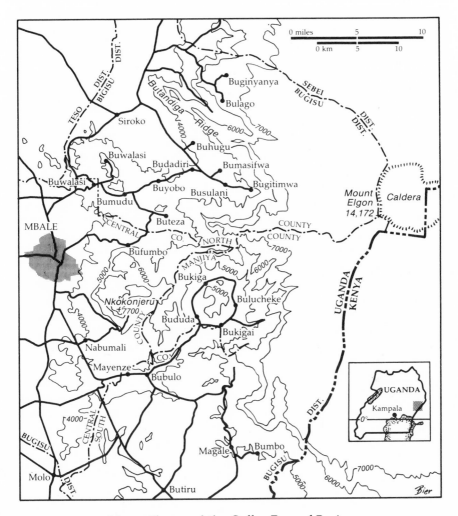

Mount Elgon and the Coffee Zone of Bugisu

foothills and 50 over the plain itself (Uganda Republic, 1967). Rain normally falls throughout the year, but there are usually marked dry and rainy seasons. Almost 80 percent of the rainfall occurs in the six months between April and September, and 5 percent occurs in December and January. This cycle is not altogether reliable, and there are periodic droughts of sufficient severity to cause famine in what is otherwise a reasonably prosperous farming area. These droughts are sometimes followed by storms violent enough to ruin crops and cause disastrous landslides on the heavily tilled and populated ridges.

The Bagisu, a Bantu people numbering over 500,000, occupy Bugisu District, which covers 1,170 square miles of eastern Uganda and includes the western and southern slopes of Mount Elgon. The earliest Bagisu settlements were on the mountain, but during the last century many of the Bagisu moved down onto the plains. They first located in the southwest and then moved around the mountain to settle the central and later the northern areas. To the north live the non-Bantu Sebei, on whose lands the Bagisu have steadily encroached, and over the border in Kenya live the closely related Babukusu, whose language and customs parallel those of the Bagisu.

The mountain itself has changed little over the past century, but the Bagisu's relations to the mountain, to each other, and to the world beyond it have changed drastically. John Roscoe (1909, 1915, 1924), a British missionary who used his vacations for exploration and ethnography, toured the area soon after an army of Baganda, backed by the British and led by the freebooter Semei Kakungulu, had conquered it. He described a people living in territorially defined clans, bounded by such natural landmarks as rivers and ridges, with no central organization between them. Each clan defended its own boundaries by force. Safe conduct beyond the territory of one's own clan was possible only at certain ritually specified times, and then only into the areas of related clans. The widest level of authority was the influence of prominent men within their own clan; only in time of a defensive or offensive alliance would a military leader emerge, possibly directing the operations of related minor clans (see also Weatherby, 1962).

Roscoe's observations are particularly interesting because they occurred so soon after the Bagisu were conquered. Jean La Fontaine's ethnographic work has contributed to a more systematic description of precolonial kinship and authority systems. It has also shown that there was as well a coordination of the biennial circumcision rituals, which provided an anterior basis for an ethnic identity that included all of the Bagisu.

La Fontaine (1957, 1959a) described Bagisu kinship as a four-layered segmentary lineage system. In her scheme, each maximal lineage contained a number of major lineages; the major lineages contained a number of minor lineages, each of which was made up of a number of minimal lineages (Figure 1). I found this description fit best in the mountainous regions, but that lineage levels were fewer in the more recently settled plains. La Fontaine's maximal lineage is best called a clan as there is no consistent recognition of consanguineal links beyond that level. Descent is generally traced back between nine and eleven generations to the apical ancestor of each clan.

Precolonial systems of authority traditionally followed closely the divisions of kinship, and personal power was automatically limited by the narrow boundaries of kin solidarity. The Bagisu chose different categories of leaders according to different criteria, such as wealth, prowess in war, ability to talk and to arbitrate disputes, and honesty and generosity. All of them ruled more through influence than through formal authority. The most important single individual leader was the *umugasya*, who La Fontaine (1959b:270) says "was consciously chosen for his wealth." Standards of wealth, which was measured primarily in cattle, varied between the south, with its great expanses of open

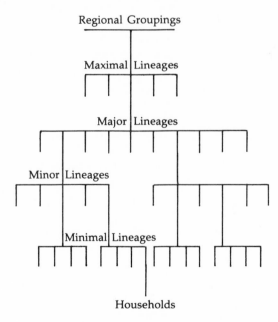

Figure 1. Bagisu Lineage Structure

land, and the mountainous north. Wealth alone was not sufficient to gain leadership, however. Rather it was a necessary condition of being chosen *umugasya* and for carrying out the necessary mediation between related minor lineages.

Each minimal lineage chose its own *bagoosi*. These leaders dealt with conflict internal to the minimal lineage. Like the *umugasya*, they were chosen from among the wealthier men for their generosity in helping their kin and for their capacity to settle disputes between them. The *bakhulu*, the older men in the lineage, served as an advisory council on the basis of their seniority and wisdom. In addition to giving advice in matters of internal conflict or external aggression and defense, these men performed ritual functions, especially important during the periods of circumcision. One of the *bakhulu*, the *umusakhulu*, ideally the senior male of the senior minimal lineage, served as ritual leader and chief mediator to the *baguga*, the ancestors.

In addition to wealth, an aspirant to leadership needed crucially placed affinal relationships. Men dominated the positions of authority and the ownership of wealth, but women provided the crucial links between families and lineages. They exercised a limited degree of political influence, as they were able to mediate between their husbands and their brothers. Affinity created strong bonds of cooperation among the Bagisu. The wife-taker was obliged to provide a large brideprice and to continue fulfilling his affines' requests for both material and physical assistance, and his affines were expected to provide him with political and defensive assistance. Affinal terms applied to all members of both spouses' minimal lineages, and rights and obligations were similarly extended. Affinity was an important part of the maintenance of good relations and the settlement of disputes between minor lineages. Men who could control the relations between lineages tended to have more power within their own lineage, and wealthy men tended to have more wives (La Fontaine, 1962:111). La Fontaine (1967:254) has explained that the wealthier and more powerful families in each lineage chose wives of similar social standing and wealth from other lineages whose locations made them economically or defensively important. Politically powerful families, therefore, tended to have more, and more widely spread, affinal ties. This, in turn, enabled them to maintain their authority across generations.

Conquest and the Imposition of the Baganda Administrative System

When the British-backed expeditionary force of Baganda,[1] led by Semei Kakungulu, arrived to conquer the area west of Mount Elgon in 1900, the resistance it encountered was based on the temporary alliances between small lineages. The conquest was slow, as each lineage had to be separately subordinated.

By 1902 Kakungulu had founded his own "kingdom" in Bugisu with himself as *Kabaka* or monarch. He established a hierarchical system of chieftaincies based on the Baganda model, appointing his own followers as chiefs at the higher levels (i.e., *saza* and *gombolola*). The Baganda appointed Bagisu of already established influence, usually the *bagasya* (plural of *umugasya*), as subchiefs over the lineages they subordinated. In some cases, however, particularly if resistance had been fierce, the old *umugasya* either fled or was killed. A less influential man was then appointed, but then had to deal with the resentment and opposition of the family of the former *umugasya*, who often regarded him as an usurper.

Kakungulu ruled Bugisu from his "capital" in the foothills through a series of forts until 1904, when the British, uneasy about his growing power in the area, followed him there and replaced him with a British administrator. They claimed that his rule had been too harsh, but they continued to use the administrative structure that he had established, in most cases with the same personnel. Certainly the British were no less harsh until they had finally subdued the last rebellion in 1912 (Gale, 1959). Kakungulu was given a twenty-square-mile tract in freehold a little north and east of the present site of Mbale. He died there a few years later, bitter and disappointed at his treatment by the British, for whom he had conquered most of the land between Buganda and Bugisu (see Twaddle, 1966; Vincent, 1982).

It was some years before the actual administration bore any resemblance to the Baganda model of a four-level hierarchy. The Baganda had conquered individual lineages one at a time, so local chiefs initially had to be given equal status and independent command whether they had 500 or 5,000 followers (Entebbe Secretariat Archives E.S.A. B10).[2]

The first Bagisu chiefs ruled with the assistance and advice of Baganda agents. Their armed but unpaid followers maintained a forcible reminder of the ultimate authority of the British. Between 1907 and 1915 these Bagisu chiefs became subcounty or *gombolola* chiefs under the overall direction of a Muganda county, or *saza*, chief. By 1924 the number of these subcounties had been reduced considerably and the Baganda model of lower-level authority firmly established. Two grades of chiefdom were recognized below the *gombolola* level: the parish, or *muluka*, and the subparish, or *mutongole*. Amalgamation of the subcounty chiefdoms generally followed the death of a chief, so the process was slow and uneven. In 1925 subcounties still ranged in size from

500 to over 3,000 adult men and parishes from 200 to 500 (Uganda Protectorate, 1925). These were eventually consolidated into twenty-four subcounties (see also Heald, 1982:77-78).

Nevertheless, especially in the mountainous north, the administrative system as it finally evolved strongly reflected the concessions to individual lineages on which the eventual consolidation of colonial rule depended. The territorial boundaries of the Bagisu's maximal, major, and minor lineages generally formed the limits of subcounties, parishes, and subparishes. The counties followed overarching geographical, cultural, and dialectal divisions. Lower-level chiefs had to legitimize themselves and their rule to groups whose kinship provided an anterior base for solidarity and traditional expectations of leaders' behavior (La Fontaine, 1962:90). The higher-level chiefs were obliged to manipulate lineage and affinal relations to exercise their authority. They depended extensively on the collaboration of lower-level chiefs and lineage leaders and so used traditional strategies for binding alliances across the new, much broader scope of unified authority. That is, high-level chiefs developed affinal networks with strategically placed lower chiefs' families. Later, as the chiefs became more conscious of the ways they could increase their own powers within the colonial administration, and as they worked to find employment there for their sons, these affinal networks spread across county boundaries. The resulting "status group" of chiefly families protected its own members' privileges but was also crucial in forming a district-wide ethnic consciousness (La Fontaine, 1969), which became a major factor in local challenges to colonial rule (Bunker, 1984b).

Thus, the chiefly system of rule established by the colonialists did not displace, and in some ways extended, the older arrangements and strategies of authority in the lineages. The coopted lineage heads who became chiefs could only fulfill colonial demands by manipulating autochthonous kin and authority structures. Even though many of the functions of the *bagasya* were taken over by the official chiefs, most minor lineages continued to recognize this position. The *bagasya* still served as arbitrators in disputes that could be settled without recourse to official authority. They were often the source of important help to kinsmen who needed bridewealth or other material goods. They also served as their lineages' intermediary to the chiefs. They carried complaints and requests to the chiefs. The chiefs relied on them to communicate orders to the lineage and to provide the necessary organization for carrying out work projects. The *bagoosi* continued to fulfill similar functions at their own level of authority. The *bakhulu* had never had any direct authority, and their roles continued with little change.

All three of these positions were changed beyond the simple imposition of higher authority, however. A chief was also a wealthy and useful kinsman and so could become influential in lineage matters. This detracted from the authority of the traditional roles. Nevertheless, these roles remained important both for the internal organization and stability of the lineages. They persisted in part because the chiefs relied on traditional organization to mobilize the Bagisu to carry out the tasks that the colonial state required and in part because of their importance to the Bagisu themselves.

The system of indirect rule implemented in Bugisu had a series of consequences that would later affect the potential for and the forms of political organization against the state. First, colonial administrative boundaries coincided with lineage organization and so tended to reinforce autochthonous bases of solidarity. Second, autochthonous patterns of authority were incorporated into colonial administration either directly, as with the chiefs, or indirectly, as with the persistence of informal positions and roles that articulated with those of the chiefs. Third, the establishment of an administrative district allowed the extension of autochthonous patterns of alliance and affinity and the eventual emergence of an ethnic self-consciousness fostered by district-wide communication about common interests and concerns. Colonial dependence on local authorities to introduce and supervise cash crops enhanced all three of these effects and greatly increased the powers of the chiefs and their families.

Cash Crops and Chiefly Powers

The British introduced coffee and cotton in Bugisu in 1912 to provide an economic basis for the collection of taxes, to stimulate sufficient commerce to support a broader administrative system, and to stem the out-migration triggered by a tax burden heavier than the available resources or the available labor market would support (Haydon, 1953). Both crops were forcibly introduced; the British imposed fines and penal labor for not growing them.

Cash cropping was not at first popular with the Bagisu, and there was considerable resistance to it. Cotton spread fairly rapidly, however, because it is easier to cultivate and because it was grown on the plains, in areas more susceptible to colonial supervision. Because the areas suitable for coffee cultivation were on the mountain itself, and because coffee trees require four years of considerable care before they start to yield, the Bagisu's lack of enthusiasm was much more difficult to overcome. It was some years before coffee cultivation became widespread; and even then, problems of neglect or inappropriate procedures continued.

The coffee growers on the mountain proved to be very sensitive to low prices or unfavorable marketing conditions. The British investment in and commitment to Bugisu's Arabica coffee were high, and the district administration responded quickly to these farmers' complaints and to any signs of withdrawal from coffee production and sale. The coffee growers quickly earned a reputation with the colonists as being "difficult" (Haydon, interview, Mbale, 1970; R. Woods, interview, Nairobi, 1970). On the basis of interviews with some of the early chiefs and other old men, I suspect that the British unwittingly taught the Bagisu that they could gain major concessions by threatening to withhold their coffee or neglect their trees.

The most immediate effect of the new crops, however, was to increase greatly the chiefs' responsibilities, powers, and wealth. The chiefs were crucial in the introduction of both coffee and cotton. They were put in charge of enforcing cultivation. The British encouraged them to cultivate extensively so that they would set an example for the rest. Because they were far more susceptible to colonial pressure than were their subjects, they were the first to grow significant amounts of either crop.

Both the Baganda and the Bagisu chiefs had nearly despotic powers during the early years. As elsewhere in Uganda, these chiefs received a commission on the taxes they collected, and they were also allowed to exact tribute such as meat, other foods, and beer from their subjects. Another form of tribute, which was even more important in their eventual accumulation of wealth, was their right to demand free labor. This right was augmented by their power and duty to call on their subjects for community work projects, such as building roads, schools, and churches. There was often little distinction made between work to which the chief had a right as tribute and work he could claim for community projects, so the chief often disposed of a huge work force that he could use for his personal advantage. Many chiefs, taking advantage of this free labor, were soon cultivating coffee or cotton or both on a large scale. Because of their greater wealth and the need for the rest of the Bagisu to pay taxes, and because very few Bagisu at first saw that land was both scarce and important, the chiefs were able to acquire relatively large areas of land. In some cases they took land away from subjects who had broken a law or otherwise left themselves vulnerable. Thus the chiefs' power and wealth became much more significant as cash cropping increased in the district. In later years the

Bagisu's resentment of the chiefs and of their abuses of power facilitated and intensified their mobilization against the state.

Some early chiefs also commanded their own "armies," perhaps no more than several men with guns, but nonetheless a highly superior firepower. Their authority to punish was formally reinforced in 1919 and 1925 by ordinances giving them jurisdiction over their own courts. They had the power to arrest for all offenses under protectorate or customary law and to enforce the decisions of the courts. The rest of the Bagisu had very little recourse against the chiefs. Contact between the early chiefs and the European district commissioner was often minimal, and in most cases the Bagisu's only channels of communication to higher authority were the chiefs themselves.

The unchecked power of the chiefs led to fairly widespread abuses; they commandeered property and livestock, demanded special privileges (such as still notorious cases of some chiefs insisting that they be carried by one of their subjects when they went about their areas), arbitrarily punished or discriminated against members of other families or lineages under their jurisdiction, and in some cases abused other men's wives. Nevertheless, they were forced to respect the traditional expectations that a leader should be generous with his food and drink and should help his kinsmen with brideprice and other necessities. It is true that this tradition continued without the force that loss of influence had previously entailed, but the chiefs still needed the collaboration of lineage leaders to administer their areas (compare La Fontaine, 1959b; Gluckman, 1963; Fallers, 1955, 1964).

As the British colonial government became more firmly established, and as new roads facilitated communication between the administrative headquarters and the rural areas, the chiefs came under more direct government control, and some of the worst abuses diminished. The chiefs' formal powers and political strength, however, were enhanced. In 1927 their positions became secure posts in an official bureaucracy. The chiefs were defined as civil servants with salaries and, at the higher ranks, pensions. A *baraza,* or council, of the chiefs had been established in 1925 to discuss administrative business among themselves and with the district commissioner. The *baraza* increased official contact with the colonial government. It also contributed to the formation of collective strategies and alliances by which the chiefs could present requests and demands to the government. It served to sharpen ethnic identity and to define common interests at the same time that it heightened the powers of the chiefs and their families as a powerful status group.

The colonial creation of a district administration and the imposition of cash cropping gave rise to a powerful new group of chiefly families.

The entire colonial economy, however, depended on peasant agriculture. In order to expand this economy, the state had to mobilize and control peasant production. This required an expanded and more specialized civil service. The group the state recruited for this task was closely related to and allied with the chiefs. Over time, however, the civil servants' own interests led them into alliances with the peasantry that they had been recruited to administer. These alliances gave rise to peasant political participation and eventually to new institutions over which the peasants had more direct influence than they had over either the civil servants or the chiefs.

Chiefly Families in an Expanding District Administration

The initial close identity between chiefs and civil servants emerged from the chiefs' own position in the colonial administration. The chiefs' families were the first to receive Western education (La Fontaine, 1959b), and chiefs used their influence to get their sons jobs in the colonial administration.

European missionaries, both Catholic and Protestant, had arrived in Bugisu while Kakungulu was still in control. He had helped them establish their missions and had directed his chiefs to provide labor to build their schools. The missionaries recruited and trained Baganda teachers. By 1916 the Protestants had established a boarding high school in Nabumali in central Bugisu, and in 1923 they established another in Buwalasi, a large hill area at the foot of the longest and widest valley in the north.

The British insisted that each chief send at least one son to school. There was some resistance, as the chiefs were afraid of losing their sons. Some chiefs, for example, sent the sons of other men. A growing number of chiefs, however, influenced by their contact with the Baganda, who had eagerly accepted and profited from European training, saw the advantages of Western education.

The chiefs were able to pay the fees for education up to higher levels. Their families therefore constituted a disproportionate number of the educated Bagisu for many years. Because of their fathers' influence with the Europeans, and because they were the most educated Bagisu, chiefs' sons were chosen almost exclusively to fill their fathers', or in some cases brothers', positions as the latter died or retired. More important, they were appointed to replace the Baganda county chiefs. In 1934 the last Muganda *saza* chief was replaced by a Mugisu. He was the son of an early chief, brother of a powerful *gombolola* chief, and one of the first Bagisu to finish Nabumali High School.

The early education of chiefs' sons and their succession to their fathers' positions gave the chiefship a hereditary character that lasted through independence. This pattern continued; in an unpublished survey conducted by Suzette Heald in 1969, 60 percent of the higher (*saza* and *gombolola*) chiefs interviewed were themselves the sons of chiefs.

Chiefly families benefited even more from the expansion of specialized civil service positions. The number of chieftaincies was fixed, but as cash cropping grew, and as the colonial administration took on more marketing and rural extension functions, the number of paid positions available for Africans within the Bugisu Native Administration (BNA) and within the local departments of the protectorate government also increased. Due to both education and family influence, the chiefs' sons had favored access to these jobs. The British need for inexpensive administration and for a profitable export crop thus opened a whole new set of formal positions. This strengthened the positions of the chiefs and of their families.

This group actively enhanced its delegated powers by manipulating traditional patterns of alliance. The Bagisu chiefs and their families used traditional strategies of marriage alliances between prominent families, but across a much wider scope of social organization and at higher levels of power than were possible before the establishment of a unified district administration. Sons of chiefs tended to marry the daughters of equally powerful chiefs, in some cases from different counties. Traditional rights to political help from affines gave the chiefly families widespread networks of highly placed supporters. As the civil service grew and was filled with the sons of chiefs, this network grew larger and more powerful. This completed the creation of a district-wide status group bound by kin and official networks (see Fallers, 1959:12; Weber, 1958:180-94) with extensive cooperation between its members. Sons of chiefs could expect assistance not only from their own lineage but also from highly placed affines, and through them from the whole status group of high-level chiefs and civil servants.

In Pursuit of Peasant Production

The BNA depended on the chiefly families, who were able to articulate their demands through their direct participation in the colonial administration. The BNA was ultimately even more dependent on the Bagisu peasants than on Bagisu administrators. The chiefs and their families wanted more participation in and control of district agencies and of the local departments of national bureaucracies that controlled crop marketing. The Bagisu peasants wanted higher crop prices and the relaxation of labor-absorbing quality controls. Over time, the chiefly families and the peasants learned how to form alliances and to exploit the state's dependence on the first group for cheap administration and on the second for profitable crops.

The coffee crop increased from 11 tons in 1915 to 50 tons in 1925. It reached 260 tons by 1930 and over 4,000 tons in 1940. An agricultural officer was appointed to instruct in the cultivation of the crop in 1925, and a field staff was gradually built up to help him. As the size and economic importance of the crop increased, the Bugisu were able to strengthen their demands for higher prices by threatening to reduce production and withdraw into subsistence cultivation (Haydon, 1953).

As early as 1926, and again in 1929, Bagisu peasants withheld coffee for sale and allowed their crops to deteriorate to protest low prices (Kerr, 1947). The state responded to this threat very rapidly. When indirect attempts to raise prices failed, the BNA attempted to boost prices by purchasing coffee in competition with other buyers and then started to buy coffee on a regular basis. This policy further increased its need to hire Bagisu and so strengthened the position of the chiefly families. It also created direct peasant interest in BNA organization and decisions and gave them their first experience of colonial sensitivity to crop reduction.

Although the BNA was responsible for promoting the cultivation of coffee, it exercised no control over its marketing until 1927. The buying and selling of coffee were left entirely to private entrepreneurs, mostly Asian small businessmen, who bought the coffee and then sold it to one of three large companies. The coffee sold by the farmers was generally of poor quality and badly processed; it was frequently delivered before being completely dried. The Asian traders had no experience or knowledge of coffee grading or handling, nor did they have the proper equipment, so the coffee that the large companies bought had frequently deteriorated from an already poor condition. The BNA tried to promote the reputation of the Bugisu crop to British buyers, but the continued bad quality of the coffee made the crop very difficult to sell. The farmers, who were receiving very low prices for their coffee, threatened to reduce cultivation, so the BNA's campaign to promote cultivation was seriously endangered.

In 1927 the BNA intervened to establish quality control on the coffee bought from the farmers, especially stipulating that wet coffee would be refused. The traders, brought together by the government to facilitate control, formed a buying ring and depressed the prices even further. The Bagisu, caught between the BNA's quality control and the traders' conspiracy to hold down prices on what they were allowed to sell, were further embittered. In order to break up the buying ring, the BNA started to buy coffee directly from the growers in 1930. The buyers responded by paying more than the BNA at the beginning of the season and then dropping their prices down to less than two-thirds of what the BNA was paying. The BNA bought only one-fourth of that season's crop. In 1931 the protectorate government licensed the BNA to buy coffee on a regular basis with the understanding that the organization set up for this purpose, the Bugisu Coffee Scheme (BCS), would be turned over to the farmers as a marketing cooperative "at the earliest opportunity" (Haydon, 1953:5).

Buying licenses for coffee were still issued freely to private dealers, and the BCS found that it was not competing successfully with the private traders. In order to promote coffee quality, the BCS had erected pulping stations and an expensive drying factory. The private dealers were still buying wet coffee, as they were paid per pound of coffee delivered. They were still outbidding the BCS at the beginning of the season and then cutting their prices back as soon as they had control of the market. In order to protect its investment in the pulpers and drying factory, and in order to stop the sale of wet coffee, the central government passed the Native Produce Marketing Ordinance in 1932. This gave the BCS exclusive rights to purchase all Bugisu coffee except that produced in the north Bugisu lowlands area, to which the private buyers successfully demanded continued access. The BCS claimed, though, that it was operating at a disadvantage, as the north Bugisu lowlands were closer to the railheads than the restricted buying areas were. In 1936 it gained exclusive buying rights for the whole district.

This first competition for control of coffee sales in the district took place between the BNA, a district-level institution which derived all of its power directly from the protectorate government, and a district-level interest group made up of Asian traders and the companies they sold to. The BNA and the buyers were trying to achieve contrary goals: the first was aiming to establish a permanent and profitable cash crop that would help the district pay its own way in the British colonial scheme, while the latter was attempting to maximize the immediate profits of its members. The success of the BNA's program depended on the good will and efforts of the Bagisu coffee growers. The goal of the traders was not nearly as dependent on the Bagisu as was that of the BNA. It is, of course, possible that if the BNA had not intervened, coffee production would have decreased to the point that the traders would have started to compete among themselves, pushing prices back up. On the other hand, it is also possible that the trees would have been abandoned altogether if the prices to the farmers—who were still not particularly interested in growing coffee—had continued low. In this case the BNA's investment in establishing the coffee crop would have been lost.

The administration's sensitivity to the threat of Bagisu withdrawal from cash cropping appears clearly in both BCS and BNA records from this period. The BCS was an onerous burden for an understaffed and penurious BNA (Haydon, 1953). Except for two seasons (1933-34 and 1936-37), it operated at a loss, but the BNA considered it essential to the district's economy.

In addition to assuring the smooth collection and controlled processing of coffee, BCS managers spent a great deal of time responding to growers' complaints about falsification of weights and low quality classifications that BCS agents used to underpay growers. BCS documents also reflect a concern with Bagisu demands from chiefs and lineage leaders to include more Bagisu on the BCS staff.

Bagisu were trained and employed in the various processing centers, and some—those few with secondary education—became buyers. Most of the supervisory and thus more remunerative positions continued to be dominated, though, by Baganda, Asians, and a few Europeans.

A five-man board that included two Bagisu—a county chief and a civil servant—appointed by the district commissioner (DC) had been established in 1933 to advise the BCS's European managers. The Bagisu representatives to the board kept demanding more employment for Bagisu in the BCS. These men did not argue from an independent power base; they were appointed by the DC and were subject to removal by him. Their demands were consistent with the BNA's stated goal of involving the Bagisu in the market, however, and so were not themselves subject to sanctions.

The BNA program to improve quality involved heavy capital investment, primarily through loans from the protectorate government and other district administrations. The expansion of coffee cultivation required high prices to farmers. The BCS suffered considerable trading losses in its first years and was heavily in debt by 1936. Its ability to continue crop purchases depended on protectorate government guarantees of bank loans. In order to protect its growing investment, the protectorate government appointed three upper-level government officers to sit on the BCS committee. Thus control of BCS policy passed in large measure to a higher domain and was less responsive to Bagisu demands.

The outstanding debts to the protectorate government and the Busoga Native Administration[3] were a persistent embarrassment. In 1938 the BNA decided to turn over the collection of coffee to an independent trading company. The four major trading companies then operating in Bugisu combined for this purpose to form a single unit, the Bugisu Coffee Marketing Company (BCMCo.), which undertook all the risks and expenses of the collection, processing, and marketing of coffee. It rented the BCS's equipment and properties, paid coffee prices set by the BCS committee to the farmers, and received a standard commission on everything it sold. Profits remaining after this commission accrued to the BCS, to be held in trust for the Bagisu.

The BCS continued only in its supervisory role as the BNA's representative. Under this arrangement, the BCS earned a steady profit, which clearly benefited the BNA. The Bagisu chiefs and civil servants, however, protested that their positions in the BNA had given them greater influence over the management of the BCS than they now had over the more autonomous BCMCo. They also believed the new company was less likely to include them as employees or eventually be turned over to them (Haydon, interview, Mbale, 1970). In fact, the continued growth of coffee production opened more employment opportunities in the BCMCo. and in the BNA (especially in agricultural extension), but the rate and rank of recruitment generated more contention as the number and technical capacity of Bagisu employees increased (Haydon, 1953:21).

By 1940 at least fifteen Bagisu with secondary education had experience in at least one, and often more, of the technical and administrative aspects of the coffee and cotton trades, either as extension agents in the Department of Agriculture or as buyers, graders, and drying center technicians in the BCS and BCMCo. Three of them eventually became high-level chiefs, but those who did not soon discovered that the channels of promotion were quite limited, as all "responsible" civil service positions were still held by Europeans.

The chiefs had used their influence in the BNA to increase the number and rank of civil service positions open to Bagisu, but the chiefs' dependence on the colonial administration prevented them from making militant demands to accelerate local control. The Bagisu civil servants' most useful allies, therefore, were the peasants who could be persuaded that the colonial administration was not paying them adequate prices for their crops and was excluding the Bagisu from due participation in marketing. The civil servants started to question publicly the distribution of coffee revenues and to accuse the BNA of ethnic discrimination. Because they occupied positions that put them in direct contact with the peasants, and because they usually enjoyed high status within their clans, they were well situated to stimulate opposition to the European control of crop marketing. They also played a crucial role in creating and diffusing the political consciousness necessary to mobilize the peasants.

The civil servants' ability to integrate concepts that they had learned in their formal Western-style education with their extensive knowledge of colonial economic and administrative practices and with their deeper knowledge of and participation in Bagisu ideas and values about social organization, wealth, and authority allowed them to become effective ideological innovators. They could take European ideas about democratic representation, fair returns to labor, equivalent values in monetary exchange, and the rights of ownership and recast them in forms that both reflected the Bagisu's experience in the recently imposed production and marketing of cash crops and simultaneously resonated with autochthonous notions of leaders' obligations to redistribute wealth and to make decisions based on consultation, mediation, and arbitration. The civil servants were also able to stimulate nascent ideas of ethnic unity and identity that extended the principles of loyalty, trust, and mutual obligation beyond the boundaries of the lineage to include all Bagisu. These ideas could never be as powerful at their wider levels as they were within lineages, and suspicion and jealousy between lineage and regions always lay close to the surface of Bagisu ethnic unity, but these new principles were essential to later campaigns based on beliefs that Bagisu control over crop sales would assure fair prices and honest commercial practices (see also Bunker, 1984b). None of these ideas would have had any relevance to the Bagisu's forms of life and social organization before they were colonized. The civil servants were able to incorporate exogenous ideas appropriate to the Bagisu's new experience of markets and submission to a widened scope of authority into autochthonous systems of values and expectations and then to communicate these new principles to the rest of their recently formed ethnic group. They thus contributed directly to the Bagisu's consciousness and interpretation of their new situation.

The peasants themselves had developed a much greater propensity for political action and economic demands. Most of them were now growing cash crops extensively enough that coffee prices and marketing conditions had considerable impact on their levels of subsistence and shelter. Coffee production, for example, had risen from 260 tons in 1931, the year the BCS was established, to 4,144 tons in 1939-40 (Table 1). The peasants' growing reliance on the market made them sensitive not only to prices, but also to questions of taxes, the condition of warehouses, roads, and bridges, and the procedures followed at the buying stations. They were also increasingly concerned with the availability of education and medical attention in the rural areas. In all of

Table 1. Arabica Coffee Production in Bugisu/Sebei, 1930-42

Season	Tons	Season	Tons
1930-31	260	1936-37	1,321
1931-32	264	1937-38	2,079
1932-33	734	1938-39	1,822
1933-34	964	1939-40	4,144
1934-35	1,378	1940-41	2,165
1935-36	2,034	1941-42	3,010

NOTE: See Appendix 1 for production figures between 1915 and 1982.

these ways the expanding cash economy changed the alignment of political interests and the potential for political action in the district. The civil servants were able to manipulate the peasants' concerns to gain more power, but they could only do so by espousing policies that benefited the peasants.

The civil servants' alliance with the peasants and their positions in the expanding cash economy and increasingly complex administrative structure put them in competition with and opposition to the chiefs. Though the chiefs were legally defined as civil servants, their administrative tasks were too diffuse and their ties to lineage organization too important for them to develop the specific disciplines and technical qualifications that characterize civil service in Western bureaucracies. The state needed specialists in health, education, construction, pest control, agricultural extension, crop processing, and accounting to achieve further increases in crop volume and quality and to respond to the demands of the Bagisu growers for improved social services.

The Bagisu civil servants who were trained for and later performed these tasks needed the chiefs' cooperation to assure the peasants' collaboration, but they identified themselves as more highly qualified and therefore as having more rights and powers than the chiefs. In order to achieve what they thought their own rights should be, they attempted to establish their own relations and authority with the peasants.

Thus, though most of the civil servants were from chiefly families, and had depended in part on pressure from the chiefs to move up the administrative hierarchy, their ascent eventually diminished the power of the chiefs. Early chiefly functions had covered the entire range of administrative needs in the rural areas—from tax collection to agricultural extension, road and school building, the maintenance of law and order, and even the prosecution and punishment of certain crimes. The growth of the local civil service and its assumption of a widening range of specific functions undercut the power of the chiefs and frequently brought the more specialized civil servants into conflict with them.

The civil servants could present their criticisms of European control over crop buying and processing from a basis of direct familiarity with and specialized knowledge of administrative and marketing procedures. Kin and affinal ties still bound individual civil servants to the chiefs, but as a power group with its own interests, the civil servants started to make more effective alliances with the informal leaders who could mobilize the Bagisu against European control of the marketing apparatus. They started to attack the chiefs as the complacent tools of the British. They proclaimed the rights of the Bagisu as an ethnic group to benefit from their own labor. Their demands for a fair return to labor and resources included control over the marketing of the crop and decisions about how to use the surplus from the sale (Bunker, 1984b). The demands for market participation were thus linked to the campaign for more effective popular representation in the district council, where issues of public expenditures and social welfare could be debated. Popular representation in the district council necessarily meant a displacement of the chiefs who still constituted most of its membership.

The growth of coffee production ultimately undermined the chiefs' power in other ways as well. Arabica coffee requires intensive care, so the absence of a disciplined labor force effectively limited coffee plantations to sizes that permitted the owners' direct supervision. This restriction affected the higher-level chiefs most directly; their greater powers had enabled them to accumulate land, but they were the most likely to be posted outside their own lineage areas. Colonial sanctions against neglect or inappropriate cultivation of coffee trees tended to favor small holdings. The chiefs were held responsible for these functions and could themselves be fined or fired if the coffee in their areas was not properly tended. The growing interest of the rest of the Bagisu in cash cropping—and in the industrial commodities they could buy—further limited the chiefs' ability to acquire land. Finally, traditional inheritance patterns restricted chiefly accumulation of land. Chiefs, like other wealthy Bagisu, tended to polygamy. As most chiefs had numerous sons, their holdings, though large, tended to be fragmented fairly rapidly. As the rest of the Bagisu expanded cash cropping, the dispersion of chiefs' land holdings contributed to creating a smoother gradient of holding size than had existed during the height of the chiefs' ascendancy.

To summarize, in less than forty years the Bagisu had changed their economy and their politics from a series of acephalous segmentary lineages organized around subsistence agriculture and hunting to an administratively unified district organized around cash cropping, complemented by subsistence farming. In the process a small group of local chiefs had risen to power and had helped in the formation of a larger group of Western-educated civil servants whose powers eventually overshadowed their own. The political activities of these civil servants had combined with the growing market participation of the Bagisu peasants to generate increasing political consciousness and ethnic identity among them. Baganda conquerors and colonial agents and British administrators had imposed both the administrative structures and the commercial crops that were the catalysts for these changes, but it was the Bagisu themselves—chiefs, civil servants, and peasants—who grew the crops, administered the rural areas, and learned to use the state's dependence to demand more direct control over their own economy and politics. Britain's entry into World War II would force her to involve her colonies in the war, both as soldiers and suppliers. The Bagisu turned the extra pressures and needs of the British war effort to their own advantage. In the next chapter I will explain how they used the political knowledge and the economic importance they had gained over the previous four decades to heighten their demands for greater participation in and control over the ways the British tied them to the world economy.

NOTES

1. The British presence in Uganda was formally predicated on treaties with the *Kabaka,* or monarch, of Buganda. The Baganda used British arms to conquer other parts of what became Uganda, while the British used the Baganda as their subimperialist agents, first for conquest and later for administration. For some of the consequences of this unholy alliance, see Young (1976).

2. I am grateful to Suzette Heald for much of the information about early chiefs in Bugisu.

3. Busoga is another district, located closer to Buganda.

2

The Campaign for Control of the Local Market, 1940-55

The actions of the protectorate government during World War II to assure an adequate and uninterrupted supply of coffee and to control inflation provoked widespread discontent among the Bagisu and greatly accelerated and facilitated their mobilization against central control of the coffee crop. In 1940 an all-European board was appointed to oversee the operations of the BCMCo., making the original board merely an advisory committee to the new board and removing the only agency with any African representation one step further from actual power (Haydon, 1953). Bagisu chiefs and civil servants protested vigorously. Further conflict arose during the following years, when much of the crop was sold directly to the British Ministry of Food. Coffee prices were high, and imported goods were scarce (Wrigley, 1959:68-73). The board decided to withhold part of the price for the peasants' coffee in order to prevent inflation, putting the money withheld into a fund to be held in trust for the Bagisu coffee growers. This fund had grown to £280,000 by 1946 and to £500,000 by 1948; half of this was eventually transferred to a price stabilization fund (Haydon, 1953:15-21). The British invested most of these funds outside the district; the rest were used as a development fund within the district.

The allocation of these funds became a major focus of contention. The Bagisu resented their diversion into development projects that would ordinarily fall within the purview of the BNA. This breach of prior assurances by the British-dominated board that these monies would not be used for such projects heightened Bagisu distrust of the board and the BNA (BCS, Minute 3(7)45; Haydon, 1953:23-27). Moreover, the price assistance fund was never activated. In 1946 a coalition of Bagisu civil servants, lineage leaders, and political activists began a concerted campaign to establish cooperative marketing of the crop.

They pointed to the existence and size of the fund as evidence that they were not receiving their rightful share from the Bugisu Coffee Scheme.

Political Representation and Shifting Power Bases

The Bagisu's campaign to control their own crops coincided with the move toward more popular representation in the district council. From 1934 onward, the chiefs' council (*baraza*) had been gradually expanded to include other Bagisu. At first these were simply a few "professionals," mostly teachers and clergymen, appointed by the district commissioner. By the mid-1940s, these "nonofficials" included some local representatives as well as employees from other government branches, such as the Commission for Cooperative Development and the Department of Agriculture. The Bagisu were able to use the district council to support their demands for greater market control and participation.

The Bagisu civil servants gained greater participation in the running of the BCS after 1944, when a third Mugisu member, an agricultural assistant, was added to the advisory committee, joining the secretary general of the African Local Government and county chief of north Bugisu (BCS, 1944). In 1949 a fourth Mugisu, Paulo Mugoya, son of a *saza* chief and later chairman of the district council, was appointed to the advisory committee (BCS, 1949). As minority members of an advisory committee, these Bagisu could only make recommendations on the running of the BCS. As they were all appointed members, their positions on the committee depended on the government. They were effective, however, in bringing some of the growers' complaints and problems about weighing, collection, and sale to the attention of the Scheme. They also maintained pressure on the board to increase the employment of Bagisu. As members of the district council, they were able to act as liaison between the council and the board. The board eventually bowed to district council pressure and delegated limited executive powers to the advisory committee, but all of its executive decisions remained subject to the board's approval.

Although the number of Bagisu hired for senior positions did increase during these years, the rate of increase was a frequent source of conflict. In 1946, for example, there were complaints to the committee that the district council had been assured that the European BCS supervisor for north Bugisu would be replaced by a Mugisu. Instead, another European was appointed. The British attempted to meet Bagisu demands by creating new posts, such as buying overseers (BCS, Minute 36(6)46).

The British found themselves in a difficult dilemma. The BNA depended almost entirely on revenues from the marketing systems that the Bagisu were demanding to control. Bugisu's marketing system also provided a significant share of the central state's revenues. Furthermore, the rest of the state's revenues depended on similar marketing systems in other parts of Uganda; decisions made in Bugisu had to be compatible with legislation and administrative practice governing the rest of the protectorate, and concessions made to Bagisu might inspire pressures for similar concessions elsewhere. Some form of continued control was imperative for the state, but direct control was becoming politically and economically dangerous. The state attempted to deal with this dilemma in a series of rapid organizational changes, each of which first included more Bagisu representation in the agencies that controlled crop marketing and then changed the composition or hierarchy of these organizations to reduce the influence of the Bagisu who had been admitted to formal positions of power. The Bagisu responded by opposing organizational recomposition and by attempting to increase the autonomy of the agencies that they could control or influence. Even when the Bagisu were successful, however, the state could, and did, change other parts of the system, creating new agencies as fast as it abolished old ones and redefining competencies and powers of the ones that remained.

Each such change required the Bagisu leaders to revise their strategies, and these new strategies frequently required communicating with and coordinating the political activities of the widely dispersed peasantry. The state's greater flexibility frustrated the Bagisu leaders and greatly complicated their task of mobilizing the Bagisu against specific policies and programs, but it also reinforced their perception of the state as basically duplicitous. They were able to invoke autochthonous ideals of generosity and honesty to enhance popular indignation against an authority that blatantly violated these precepts, and were thus able to maintain pressure against the state's agencies even during the mystifying and rapid changes in their composition. I can only hope that the readers who find the plethora of new organizations and laws described in this chapter irritating and confusing will be able to imagine the effort that the Bagisu had to make to understand and then learn to deal with them.

Legitimation and Cooptation of the Cooperative Movement

Three sources of pressure for more Bagisu participation in coffee processing and marketing combined with and strengthened each other after World War II. First, the growing number of Bagisu civil servants were increasingly vociferous in their denunciations of the BCMCo. (BCS, 1945-50; Haydon, 1953; BNA, 1946-50). Second, the district council, which was becoming more representative and less dependent on the BNA (Uganda Protectorate, 1955b), opposed the BCMCo. and demanded more posts for Bagisu (BCS, 1945, 1950; Lukhobo, 1946-50). Third, various major lineages were organizing behind political leaders who were becoming more effective at coordinating their efforts and demands for participation in both the BCS and the district council across lineage boundaries (Bunker, 1975:210-40).

District council members, Bagisu civil servants, and lineage-based leaders formed alliances that were strengthened by kin and affinal ties and by overlapping memberships in these groups. The popular movement against the BCMCo. gained strength, and local demands for greater participation in coffee marketing threatened to disrupt the district's economically vital coffee production and collection. In 1946, under the threat of violence, destruction of coffee trees, and a decline in crop quality, the colonial government agreed to establish formal Bagisu control of coffee production, processing, and sale (BCS, 1946). The rapidity and extent of this formal transfer became the focus of new conflict.

The Bagisu leaders were able to take advantage of the new legislation that authorized the establishment of agricultural cooperatives and provided a government agency to help organize them. The colonial state had adopted these measures in response to serious peasant unrest and rioting throughout Uganda (Brett, 1970:110-11; Mamdani, 1976).

Starting in 1946, the colonial government directed its newly formed Commission for Cooperative Development (CCD) to promote the establishment of primary growers' cooperative societies (GCSs) in the villages, with the aim of eventually incorporating these into a union to succeed the BCS. As in the Department of Agriculture, the heads of this commission were Europeans, but a number of young, secondary-school–educated Bagisu were hired and trained to work with them. These civil servants worked closely with the lineage-based leaders of the opposition to the BCS and the BCMCo. to organize viable cooperative societies in their own areas. At least twelve of these leaders, including Samson Kitutu, who was eventually the Bugisu Cooperative Union's first president, had already worked in politics and as catechists, were known and trusted in lineages other than their own, and were able to coordinate the plans and demands of lineages over a wide area. Most were themselves the sons of lower-level chiefs or wealthy men; some were already members of the district council. Many of the leaders came from the higher parts of south Bugisu, where both coffee and cotton were grown. Through them, cotton growers also joined the cooperative movement. The campaign thus included the entire district.

A number of chiefs encouraged and assisted the organization of GCSs in their areas. The structure of local administration and the activities of the Bagisu who held positions and could communicate within it—chiefs, civil servants, and politicians—had become crucial in the campaign to achieve local control of crop marketing. The central state had effectively created the organizational base for opposition to its own central power.

BCS managers and the board acted to slow the advance of Bagisu control. The British agents invoked principles of management efficiency, bureaucratic qualification and specialization, and public service ethics to justify their continued control of key positions in the BCS. Obversely, they implied that Africans were incapable of competent and honest management. For example, in 1947 the BCS board acquiesced to Bagisu pressure to allow the district council to appoint a Mugisu to supervise the collection of coffee from central Bugisu. The board agreed, however, that as this was a step toward Bagisu control of crop sales, any loss incurred through embezzlement or mismanagement would be paid for out of BCS funds, which nominally were held in trust for the Bagisu, rather than out of the BCMCo.'s funds as would normally have been the case (BCS Advisory Committee, Minute 2(7)48). The Mugisu appointed was in fact removed from his post after charges of theft and forgery were brought against him, and the BCS refused to appoint other Bagisu until 1949.

Bagisu leaders claimed that the BCS and the BCMCo. were slowing the pace of Africanization because they wanted to continue cheating the Bagisu of their fair share of coffee revenues. The opposing colonial point of view and its justification in terms of management efficiency and African incompetence are reflected in a report by a BCS board secretary, who described this period in the following terms: "Everything possible was done to make room for Bagishu in the salaried ranks of the Bugishu Coffee Marketing Company. . . . This replacement did not take place without a good deal of wastage of trainees, who would not or could not conform to the proper standards of efficiency and fair dealing which had to be insisted upon by the Management. Even so, the filling of key posts by Africans, particularly at drying centers, was not without trouble" (Haydon, 1953).

The BCS also resisted the devolution of greater responsibility to the cooperatives, but the Bagisu leaders had considerable support from the CCD. The CCD intervened several times to obtain concessions from the BCS. Correspondence and minutes of meetings between these agencies indicate that the CCD was working to hasten the takeover by a cooperative, while the BCS sought to delay it, arguing that the procedures of collection, payment, processing, bookkeeping, and transport were too complicated for the Bagisu to manage themselves. Even more significant than CCD support, however, were the leaders' increasing access to and influence over the district council. Through the district council and on the BCS advisory committee and in speeches and negotiations throughout the district, they pressured the BCS and the BCMCo. to give them greater powers and responsibility, to reduce the requirements for Bagisu control of the coffee collection in the various areas, and to allow the Bagisu to take over the functions of the BCS more rapidly. At the same time, they were campaigning among and organizing other Bagisu in GCSs to fulfill the requirements set by the board for their takeover. These men were faced with the task of transforming the principles of ethnic rights that they had used against the BCS into collectivist and cooperative principles that could be invoked to persuade Bagisu to join the new growers' societies.

Two cooperatives had been started in 1946; by 1947 nine were operating successfully; and in 1949 twenty-four GCSs collected a total of 500 tons of coffee, which was sold to the BCMCo. In 1950, under CCD pressure, the board ruled that when three-fourths of all the growers in an area had joined a GCS, that society could take over the Scheme's local property and equipment and collect all of the coffee there (Haydon, 1953:21-23).

The new Bagisu-controlled GCSs sought an enrollment sufficiently large that the board would allow them to replace the BCMCo.'s buyers and receive a one cent commission for every pound of coffee that they collected. Some societies were able to get loans from the Scheme funds to establish their operations. These societies opened up new jobs for the Bagisu in the villages, jobs that they could hold while they continued to cultivate their own land. The jobs were few, and the pay was little, but they created salaried employment where there had been none before and further strengthened support for the GCSs and for the Bagisu leaders of the cooperative movement.

Because of Bagisu distrust of and objections to the BCMCo., the Scheme did not renew its contract when it expired in 1950 but took over coffee sales through the board (Young, Sherman, and Rose, 1981:75-76). In 1950 the secretary-general and the county chief for north Bugisu were put on the board of the BCS, the first Bagisu members of that organization's executive body. The secretary-general was especially effective in this position. He was very active in promoting the cooperative campaign, and the Bagisu held him in very high regard. At the same time he maintained a position of trust in the BNA, and worked closely with the district commissioner (Lukhobo, 1949, 1950; BNA, 1950).

By 1952 the Bagisu had organized four cooperative unions of the GCSs in the regions around each of the Scheme's drying centers. These unions collected the coffee in their areas and sold it to the Scheme. Each union had a representative on the advisory and trustee committee, which became a standing committee under the board, and one of these men also became a member of the board. In 1954 the four unions were amalgamated into the Bugisu Cooperative Union (BCU), with Samson Kitutu as president. The Bugisu Coffee Ordinance, enacted in 1955, provided for the BCU to take over all marketing, as well as rights in land or buildings, from the BCS (Uganda Protectorate, 1955a). The BCU also assumed control of cotton marketing for the district (Figure 2).

The Bagisu leaders of the cooperative movement had fought a co-ordinated campaign on several fronts between 1945, when they started to organize, and 1954, when they finally took over from the Scheme. They had used their increased access to and influence in the district council and on the advisory committee, together with speeches and negotiations throughout the district, to pressure the BCS and the BCMCo. to hire more Bagisu and to give them greater powers and responsibility, to reduce the requirements for Bagisu control of coffee collection in the various areas, and to allow the Bagisu to take over the functions of the BCS more rapidly. At the same time they had been campaigning among and organizing other Bagisu to fulfill the requirements set by the board for their takeover.

The colonial government had transformed an increasingly threatening protest movement into formal local-level institutions subject to bureaucratic rules and regulations promulgated at the national level (Uganda Protectorate, 1946; BCU, bylaws). Though this formally constrained the popular leaders, it greatly increased the resource base from which they could attract more members to the cooperative movement and thus pressure the government for further concessions. In order to coopt opposition leaders, the government had assigned them formal positions whose functions were essential to the export economy. The state could now formally supervise and sanction these new office-holders, but the officeholders could use their formal control over key economic and administrative resources to bargain for greater autonomy and authority.

1933-38   Bugisu Native Administration (BNA)
↓

Advisory board to the Bugisu Coffee Scheme (BCS)
(included three Europeans and two Bagisu)
↓

Bugisu Coffee Scheme (BCS)
(collected, processed, and sold coffee)

1938-40   Bugisu Native Administration (BNA)
↓

Advisory board to the Bugisu Coffee Scheme (BCS)
(included three Europeans and two Bagisu)
↓

Bugisu Coffee Scheme (BCS)
↓

Bugisu Coffee Marketing Company (BCMCo.)
(collected, processed, and sold coffee under contract to and supervision by the BCS)

1940-50   Bugisu Native Administration (BNA)
↓

Advisory board to the Bugisu Coffee Scheme (BCS)
(included only Europeans)
↓

Bugisu Coffee Scheme (BCS)
↙   ↘

Bugisu Coffee   Advisory committee to the Bugisu Coffee Scheme (BCS)
Marketing   (included three Europeans and two [1940], three [1944],
Company   and four [1949] Bagisu)
(BCMCo.)

1950-54   Bugisu Native Administration   Commission for Cooperative
                    (BNA)   Development (CCD)
↓   ╱
Bugisu Coffee Scheme (BCS)   ╱
↘   ↙
Local cooperative unions
↓
Growers' cooperative societies (GCSs)

1954   Bugisu Cooperative Union (BCU) founded
(replaced local unions and took over BCS property)

Figure 2. The Changing Hierarchy of Coffee-Marketing Organization
in Bugisu, 1933-54

These same leaders stimulated and orchestrated mass demands for popular representation in the district council. As in the campaign for cooperative control, the advances of the late 1940s and early 1950s were realized at the local level with increasing proportions of elected representatives on the county and subcounty councils. These victories increased the local leaders' prestige by demonstrating their capacity to organize against the colonial administration and increased their power by creating formal political positions for them.

In 1951 a new local government ordinance allowed for the establishment of lower councils, which could elect one representative to the district council for every 1,000 taxpayers in the area. The first elections to the district council by the local councils occurred in 1953, one year before the establishment of the BCU, when organizing for cooperatives was at its height. The African Local Government Ordinance of 1955, which provided for direct elections, was put into effect in the district a year after the establishment of the BCU and greatly strengthened the position of the popularly elected BCU officers, who were by then agitating for more union autonomy from the protectorate-dominated Bugisu Coffee Board, which still controlled its finances.

The drive to establish the BCU and later to expand its power and autonomy had strong anti-official overtones and provided a core of popular figures well organized and allied through the cooperative movement. A large portion of both the BCU's staff and committee was elected to the district council; its coffee manager was the district council chair. These men were able to heighten their own prestige by using the BCU's considerable resources to dominate the council and by using their positions on the council to combat the colonial state on both cooperative and ethnic issues.

This group's importance grew rapidly at the expense of the previously ascendant chiefs and Bagisu civil servants. The chiefs saw their power erode as popularly elected officials took over many of their roles on the councils and as other government services, both at the district and national levels, took away many of their former functions. Civil servants, who had become increasingly important during the 1940s, saw their influence wane as the politicians became less dependent upon them for support and guidance. Affinities based on chiefly descent lost significance, and resentment of the civil servants' greater education and privileges grew. The chiefs' and civil servants' identification and involvement with the colonial administration became a political liability as the politicians increased their own demands for greater autonomy. The politicians increasingly included the chiefs and civil servants in their criticisms of the BNA, the BCS, and the BCMCo.

As the civil servants before them, these new political leaders were predominantly members of chiefly families. They tended, however, to be related to lower-level chiefs rather than to the county and subcounty chiefs whose sons had received the high levels of education necessary for civil service jobs. These politicians depended directly on popular support and so were constrained to push for higher crop prices, relaxation of onerous quality control regulations, tax reductions, and improved social services. They involved themselves in the programs for rural development as guardians of their constituents' interests, criticized failures in planning or execution, and presented demands for solutions to particular problems.

All of these demands threatened to reduce state revenues or increase state expenditures. This created a constant tension in the positions of these politicians. On the one hand, they had to challenge the state to maintain popular support, and on the other, the state could remove them from their positions if they were too successful in these challenges. The state, however, had learned to beware of the threat that the Bagisu would reduce crop production or withdraw from the market.

Actual destruction of coffee trees occurred infrequently in Bugisu, and provoked violence only during the struggles for power around independence in 1962 (see Chapter 5). Neglect of coffee trees and crop withholding were more immediate problems for the state, which took the threats seriously. The power of the Bagisu's popular leaders grew as they learned how to use this threat more effectively. Their success in demanding local control of administration and marketing had led to the creation of representative institutions that performed economic and political functions essential to the state. Their control over these institutions heightened the state's dependency on them and thus further enhanced their bargaining position.

In the rest of this chapter, and in those that follow, I will show how these new economic and political institutions affected the opportunities for wealth and power of all three ascendant groups—chiefs, civil servants, and politicians—that had emerged out of the struggle between the state and the peasantry from which it extracted its revenues. I will also show how these groups struggled against the state and against each other to increase their own power and privileges. At the same time, these chapters will show how the state contrived to use the new representative institutions to pursue its own fundamental goals, the maintenance of order and the extraction of revenues. The institutional features of Bugisu and the political economy of the Bagisu had changed dramatically by 1954, but the basic dynamic of the struggle between peasants and the state continued unaltered.

The Ideology of Cooperative Autonomy and the Reality of the State's Interests

The establishment of the BCU was a triumph for local leaders, but it was also an extension and continuation of the state's use of local organization to carry out its own economic programs as cheaply as possible. Bagisu demands to control coffee and cotton marketing had diminished the power of the central state and limited its ability to appropriate revenues from Bugisu's cash crops. The threat of crop reduction had made direct state control of marketing both costly and dangerous. The state directed the formation of cooperatives, however, in ways which allowed it to pursue its own goals of maintaining order and extracting revenues. It set up complex supervisory systems that allowed it to influence prices to farmers, to supervise crop grading and processing, and to regulate final sale abroad. It established norms for the internal management and fiscal accountability of the cooperatives that legitimized its intervention in their management. It promulgated an ideology of business efficiency and managerial responsibility that it could manipulate to undermine the cooperative leaders' power and authority.

By authorizing the establishment of the cooperatives, the state coopted leaders of peasant protest and thus reduced the threat of crop reduction. By supervising and regulating the cooperatives, the state attempted to assure that local authorities would run the cooperatives in ways that allowed the state to extract revenue from them. In these ways, the state was repeating its earlier strategies of coopting lineage heads as chiefs and of recruiting civil servants to work in their own ethnic areas. In all of these cases, the state attempted to turn local organization to its own advantage, using agents whose positions in local society heightened their ability to maintain order, and at the same time reduced the salaries or other benefits the state had to pay for their subsistence. The growing political awareness and organization of the Bagisu had enormously changed the environment which the colonists attempted to manipulate, and the growth of cash cropping had greatly raised the economic stakes for both central and local claimants to power, but the basic strategies of the colonial state remained the same.

As in its earlier strategies of cooptation, the state had to deal with the growing power and heightened demands of the groups it coopted. State supervision diminished these groups' power and autonomy and threatened their ability to satisfy the peasant demands and discontents they themselves had helped arouse and direct. Even after the BCU was established, therefore, the same issues which had motivated the

Bagisu leaders' campaign to establish the cooperative continued to drive their struggle to reduce state supervision and to increase their own autonomy.

The new cooperatives were all governed by the Cooperative Societies Ordinance of 1946, which gave the state extensive supervisory powers. The formal and legal establishment of cooperative societies in Bugisu thus subordinated the Bagisu leaders to statutory control by the state if and when they took office in the cooperative's representative committee or took employment on its management staff.

The cooperative ordinance incorporated the ideological principles and organizational guidelines of the Rochdale model, a product of the nineteenth-century British cooperative movement, which stipulates that:

1. A Cooperative Society must be run and managed by its own users.
2. A Cooperative Society must rely on its own capital, raised by its own members, and must not rely on outside sources of capital.
3. A Cooperative Society must have its own rules to which all members agree to adhere.
4. A Cooperative Society must promote education among all its members so that they fully understand the objects of the society and how it operates, and can thus, everyone of them, undertake its management if called upon to do so by their fellows. (Gates, 1966:2)

All three versions of Uganda cooperative legislation defined "cooperative society" as "a society which has for its objects the promotion of the economic interests of its members in accordance with co-operative principles" (Cooperative Societies Ordinance, 1946, Sec. 4; Cooperative Societies Act, 1963, Sec. 4; Cooperative Societies Act, 1970, Sec. 4).

In actual practice, however, the state's need to assure profitable crops created a dilemma for its cooperative policies. Although the Rochdale principles stressed membership determination and autonomy, Uganda's earliest cooperative ordinances and much of the official cooperative literature stressed that in the early phases of cooperative development a large degree of government supervision was essential: (1) because the cooperatives' members were in many cases illiterate; (2) because the idea of cooperative marketing was foreign to them; and (3) because the idea had in some areas been imposed by government decree. The cooperative ordinance of 1946 was largely based on the assumption that the cooperatives needed help in inculcating cooperative principles, that local farmers did not have the management skills or the resources to run the organizations themselves, and that therefore much more intense government supervision than was normally given to such an enterprise in a capitalist country was called for. It was stressed, however, that the cooperatives were gradually to take over the job of supervising themselves and that the government was to retire to an advisory and judiciary capacity.

The conflict between the principle of membership control and the aim of economic efficiency was resolved by declaring that government supervision was only temporary and was to be withdrawn as the members became qualified to handle their own affairs. In actual fact, successive cooperative ordinances and acts granted greater and more arbitrary power to the Commission, and later Department, of Cooperative Development. The department consistently opted for intervention in favor of economic efficiency rather than greater membership participation and control whenever the state's ability to appropriate revenues was seriously threatened. The principle of members' control and promotion of their economic interests was thus eroded by the principle that the cooperatives were to operate for the greatest national good, which usually meant to the state's benefit. The conflict between principles of member control and of government control, as well as direct differences in the interests of local actors and government agencies, led to major problems both for the cooperatives and for the Department of Cooperative Development.

The state needed the cooperatives to fulfill certain functions, but direct supervision was both prohibitively expensive and provoked popular resistance.

To the extent that the cooperatives were allowed to function independently, however, it was quite possible that they would follow policies that threatened the fiscal basis of the state. This dilemma occasioned numerous policy changes, a fair amount of polemic, and some scholarly debate. In one form or another the problem entered into most writing on the subject of cooperatives. As most of this literature focuses on the state's policy decisions, however, it does not directly take account of the power relations that this study addresses. It therefore ignores the significance these struggles have for either the peasantry's own self-protection or local leaders' political and economic strategies. It tends to accept uncritically the official ideology of the state and of its cooperative policies. Despite this shortcoming, this literature does reveal the form of these struggles, even though it overlooks their underlying dynamic. Within this literature the clearest handling of the problem comes from E. A. Brett (1970) on one side and John Saul (1969) on the other.

Brett argued that not only was full government supervision impossible but that it was also undesirable. He saw social advantages in cooperative autonomy because an independent cooperative could serve to stimulate its members to participate more and thus learn more, not only about the cooperative but also about politics, economics, and agriculture. He saw economic advantages in complete independence because then only economically viable cooperatives would survive, lessening the likelihood that badly run cooperatives would become a drain on the national economy.

Saul argued that economic and political development in East Africa would only be possible with a more highly centralized and integrated economy. Because the cooperatives were subject to strong local and particular interests, only through their direct submission to government would they ever be able to function properly.

Both Saul and Brett recognized that particular local interests might limit the economic efficiency of the cooperatives, and that this posed a special problem for government. Whether or not a particular cooperative's policies were directly integrated into national goals, the consideration of greatest importance for government was that the cooperative be economically viable. If it was not, it could benefit neither the government nor the member farmers.

The importance of the cooperatives in local economies greatly complicated the problem of economic viability. In many areas the cooperatives were virtually the only accessible sources of major power or wealth. Access to the positions within the cooperative was the only means of upward mobility available to most of the population. Struggles for power between members or factions tended therefore to preempt considerations of economic efficiency, and attempts by members who gained power within the cooperative to profit personally as much as possible could vastly increase operating costs (see also Hyden, 1970a, 1973). The relations between these same competing factions could change radically into a joint resistance against government intervention. The invocation of the ideologies of cooperative democracy or of business efficiency was as fluid, and opportunistic, as these alliances.

Because it was essentially oriented to questions of policy from the state's point of view, the earlier literature on cooperatives does not deal with the question of power struggles between the structurally opposed state and peasantry or between the different groups that may seek to achieve power by mediating between them. I have shown that the basic poles of power rested with the peasantry and with the state. The cooperative representatives could enrich themselves and gain more power by manipulating resources that their official positions made available to them, but they were finally subject to the conflicts between two poles, as they had to satisfy, at least partially, both the state and the peasants.

These conflicts emerged, were resolved, and set the stage for subsequent confrontations in an arena bounded by the formal structures, the internal organization, and the ideologies of the cooperatives and of the state agencies that were assigned to supervise them. The following sections describe this arena. They will show: first, how the Bagisu's lineage system affected the forms in which the exogenous cooperative institutions were actually established and functioned; second, the ways in which the colonial state used cooperative legislation to impose a Western-derived ideology of business management and popular participation; and third, the ways the state used special bureaucratic agencies to keep ultimate control of crop marketing. The Bagisu claimants to market control alternately exploited and fought against different features of cooperative legislation, ideology, and formal organization in their struggles against the state and in their competition with each other. As the legislation and formal organization changed little from 1954 to 1983,[1] I will present them in broad outline, indicating where and how change did occur, before returning to the chronology of specific events in the BCU in later chapters.

New Institutions and Lineage-Based Authority

The formal organization of the BCU and of the eighty Growers' Cooperative Societies (GCSs) it comprised, as well the provisions of the bylaws that governed both types of cooperatives, were mandated by the state's laws and rules. As was the case with all of the institutional structures imposed by the state, however, Bugisu's complex topography and its highly segmented social organization strongly influenced actual cooperative organization and process. The individual GCSs incorporated lineage organization within each *muluka* (parish). GCS representatives to the BCU annual meeting elected BCU committee members from among their own numbers, so BCU officeholders had to sustain a following within their own lineages as well as in other lineages. Their dependence on lineage support constrained them to fulfill lineage expectations of how influential and prosperous men should behave and meant that their strategies to enhance their own authority within formal district-wide cooperative organizations had to be strongly rooted in their kinsmen's and neighbors' belief that they were acting in both lineage and GCS interests.

As the BCU assumed control of the collection, processing, marketing, and price-setting functions essential to the state's ability to extract revenues from the coffee crop, the BCU officeholders' dependence on support within lineage-based organization increased the capacity of the Bagisu peasantry to challenge and bargain with the state. Committee struggles to increase BCU autonomy and state attempts to maintain central control revolved around these conflicting imperatives from 1954 until the Amin coup of 1971 ended all possibility of local challenge and effectively drove coffee growers to withdraw from officially controlled export markets.

Variations in lineage structure and size between ecological zones created considerable differences in GCS organization and administration. The ideal four-level, territorially exclusive lineage structure described by La Fontaine best fits the mountainous coffee-growing areas of the north. Even in the northern mountains, however, there were aberrant cases, especially where extensive migration had taken place. In the plains, the system was seldom as clearly articulated or as consistent as La Fontaine describes. Members of various minor lineages had often migrated to the plains from the mountains, usually as the result of conflicts over land. These migrant groups had settled in mixed and discontinuous fashion, so that there were usually only two levels of lineage, and in a few there was only one. However, the undifferentiated lineage tended to be larger in the south than in the north.

The rules of exogamy were not consistent either. In some places only the smallest lineage was exogamous, while in other cases the second level was. Kinship and territory were nowhere nearly as closely correlated in the south as they were in the north. Even though inheritance rules caused close relatives to live contiguously, residence patterns usually involved clusters of close kinsmen separated from other members of the same lineage by groups from different clans. Whereas in the north distance between residents tended to reflect distance of kin relationship, in the south one's neighbors might belong to a totally different clan.

This meant that in the south neighborhood and kinship did not provide the basis for solidarity that they did in the north, but rather might be the basis of cross-cutting ties (cf. Gluckman, 1964). This accounts for some of the differences in the reactions to new institutions such as cooperative societies and representative government in the two areas. The local GCSs in the north, for example, tended to be much more cohesive internally than those of the south. Competition for offices within them tended to be much less intense, as lineage relations were generally accepted as a suitable basis for the division and rotation of authority within each branch. The northern GCSs, however, tended to be much more suspicious of intervention by both the BCU and the DCD, and they also tended to be uneconomically small, as each major lineage was likely to insist on having its own society. Lineage cohesiveness tended to impede action against inefficient or dishonest management, as members were generally loathe to call for official sanctions against a kinsman. In the more heterogeneous southern areas, the location of GCSs tended to follow economic and geographic divisions rather than kinship boundaries, but each organization tended to show more internal tension. Competition for GCS office there occasionally led to violence between the various unrelated lineages. Significantly, all of the BCU's presidents through 1982 came from areas where extensive migration had broken the territorial exclusiveness of clans and had forced politicians to deal with a wider range of alliances than was common in the north. The southerners' political dominance created resentment and dissension in the BCU and led to several campaigns to split the union.

Lineage organization thus influenced both the organization of and political relations within the GCSs and the BCU. At the same time the new cooperative institutions also induced changes in political relations within the lineages. GCS officers were chosen in part for the same qualities as traditional leaders—wealth, generosity, and ability to mediate—but the GCS members tended also to choose men with more education, job experience, and contact with outside agencies. These men tended to be younger than traditional authorities. As the cooperative officers gained more experience and were able to solve more problems for their fellow members, they were often assigned to the traditional leadership roles in their lineages, thus reducing the influence of the older men.

The establishment of the cooperatives also reduced the already limited political participation of women. Membership in the GCSs required the sale of coffee grown on one's own land. As almost all of the land was owned by men, men were overwhelmingly the members and officers of the GCSs.[2] Women were often present at and participated in political decisions at the lineage level. They continued to play an essential role in political alliances based on affinity; and a man still needed to maintain good relations with his wife in order to secure support from his affines. Women had little chance, however, to learn about GCS politics or to influence the GCS decisions. As the GCSs became more important in local economic and political processes, women were correspondingly distanced from political and economic decisions.

They continued to be crucial in the cultivation and transport of crops, but had little control over their disposition.

Finally, the growing political importance of the GCSs increased the differentiation between the majority of landowners and the much smaller number of landless men (see Brock, 1969), because a man without land could not participate or vote in GCS decisions. As local politics increasingly revolved around cooperative control of crop markets, women and landless men had less opportunity for significant political participation.

Organization of the BCU

The BCU was established as a union of the GCSs, so these societies, rather than individual peasants, constituted the BCU's formal membership. The GCSs were responsible for buying coffee and cotton from their individual peasant members. GCS members elected a committee of from five to nine members who were responsible for running the GCS. The committee appointed a salaried secretary/manager, who collected the crops, disbursed money, kept books, arranged transport to Mbale, and provided the GCSs' main liaison with both the union and the DCD. The GCS committee could also hire other employees, depending on the size of the society and the volume of its business. The BCU gave each GCS a crop advance for buying coffee at the beginning of each season. This advance actually came out of the GCS's own reserves, which the union controlled. After the advance was depleted, the secretary/manager paid members for their coffee with the money he received for each load of coffee delivered to the mill.

The GCS committee chose two of its own members, or only one if the GCS had fewer than 500 members, to represent it at the Annual General Meeting (AGM) of the union. The AGM, as the expression of the GCSs' interests and rights, was formally the BCU's paramount authority. In addition to considering reports and the balance sheet for the year passed, it had the power to approve the accounts, decide how surplus funds were to be spent, approve the estimates for the following year, amend union bylaws, and set policy or special instructions. The AGM also elected the committee that set policy for the BCU; it was this power that, in principle, gave the GCSs representative control over the union and its policy. In actual fact, the BCU committee's activities were closely prescribed by the state's cooperative rules and by the BCU bylaws, and these bylaws were essentially the locally binding specification of the nationally legislated rules.

The BCU bylaws stated that "the committee shall direct the policy of the union subject to any directions of the general meeting and to those powers reserved for the general meeting. Its procedures, powers, and duties shall be prescribed in the rules." Among other powers and duties, these rules (Uganda Government, Cooperative Society Acts and Rules, 1963) stipulated that the committee "may bind the society in contract, borrow money on behalf of the society not exceeding the amount that may have been fixed in accordance with . . . these rules, and may institute, defend, and settle any legal proceedings on behalf of the society; shall scrutinize accounts, bankbooks and cash in hand, consider loans owing to the union and any action necessary in their respect, and conduct current business, and shall send an audited balance sheet to the registrar (of Cooperative Societies) annually as well as estimates of income and expenditure for the coming year if the latter are requested."

The rules explicitly stated the principles of business management that legitimated the state's intervention in the running of the union: "In the conduct of the affairs of a registered society the members of the committee and each of them shall exercise the prudence and diligence of ordinary men of business and shall be responsible for any loss sustained through any of their acts which are contrary to law, the bylaws of their society, or the direction of any general meeting" (Sec. 25). The BCU bylaws affirmed the committee's representative authority over management, and in the same paragraph stipulated the managerial powers of the state's representative. "The committee may appoint a secretary/manager who shall furnish such security as the committee may require. He shall manage the business of the union and carry out such duties as his contract may require. He shall submit to the committee such reports and in such forms as shall be agreed in consultation with the commissioner."

Neither the GCS rules nor the BCU bylaws explicitly outlined the division of powers and responsibilities between the secretary/manager and the committee. The generally agreed-upon formula was that the committee existed to set general policy and to serve as a guardian and representative of the growers' interests and that the secretary/manager was to run the day-to-day business of the union, but where policy stopped and daily business started was not altogether clear. In the BCU, as in many other East African cooperatives, this division shifted from time to time and was on several occasions the issue of particularly bitter and costly struggles within the union. The state, however, was able to invoke the ideological principles of business efficiency to intervene in these struggles when it saw fit. The union's committee, on the other hand, could invoke the principles of membership participation and representation incorporated in the state's own legislation. It used these principles both to maintain autonomy from the state and to assert its authority over the professional staff.

The professional staff's major claim to power rested on the assumption of technical knowledge, the division of responsibilities, and the routinization of management incorporated within the administrative ideology of efficiency invoked by the state, so the state was a natural ally for the staff in its contests with the committee. Like the civil servants from whose ranks they were drawn, however, the staff also had a vested interest in local autonomy and thus tended to ally themselves with the committee when the state threatened to restrict the BCU's power. The state would eventually act to restrict the rewards that staff members could derive from political activity, thus limiting the interests they shared with the popular representatives, but even then the staff was in the ambiguous position of deriving authority from criteria promulgated and defended by the state within an organization whose power was based in local interests opposed to those of the state. The staff's, and particularly the different secretary/managers', shifting strategies and alliances would crucially affect the outcome of the confrontations between the committee and the state at several critical moments of the BCU's history.

The secretary/manager directed a permanent staff that grew to sixty-three by 1970. Actual control over hiring shifted from the committee to the staff over time and was the subject of considerable controversy. After 1959, the mill manager, a senior staff member subordinate to the secretary/manager, ran a coffee mill and was responsible for the allocation of trucks and delivery permits to the GCSs.

The secretary/manager and the mill manager supervised the BCU's main business: the purchase, processing, and marketing of coffee. This involved numerous, fairly complex procedures of communication and coordination, as well as supervision of the GCSs. They were also responsible for accounts and correspondence with government and coffee agents and buyers. The union staff handled the BCU's considerable investments and properties, including extensive real estate in Mbale.

The Parallel Structures of State Supervision

The BCU, like all Uganda cooperatives, was so deeply affected by government regulation that its relation to government must be considered as a basic part of its structure. The cooperatives served the state as a means to accede to local growers' demands for greater control over the marketing of their crops, while the state was able to coopt local leaders into formal positions charged with ordering and disciplining the collection, processing, and sale of these crops in ways conducive to the state's requirements for revenue. The state maintained this control through enforcement of national legislation.

Bugisu's valuable coffee crop was so important that the state established an additional special body to assure continued control over its collection and sale. The same ordinance that created the BCU created a successor to the BCS, the Bugisu Coffee Board, "for the purpose of promoting and regulating the production, health, processing, marketing, and export of coffee in the scheduled area" (Bugisu Coffee Ordinance, Sec. 3). Under the ordinance, it was the "duty of the board to make arrangements for:

a) the purchase from growers of all coffee grown in the scheduled area;
b) the sale within the Protectorate, or the export and sale, of coffee grown in the scheduled area;
c) the promotion of the production of coffee in the scheduled area; and
d) the processing of coffee grown in the scheduled area." (Sec. 8)

The board was entitled to fix prices paid to farmers for their coffee, make all provisions for storage, sale, export, railage, transport, and shipping of the coffee, require any grower or processor of coffee to sell or dispose of his coffee to the board or anyone the board might designate, and to impose a tax on any coffee grown in the scheduled area: "So long as the union [was] efficiently managed," the board was to delegate all of these powers and duties except the right to set prices to the union, but the board retained complete control of the reserve fund and over any union expenditure. The board also had the power to regulate most of the union's activities, including the purchase, sale, storage, and export of coffee, and its planting, production, cultivation, and processing. The board, rather than the union, had the power to borrow money and to make contracts. All of the union's activities and assets were subject to regulation by the board according to the board's discretion.

Initially, the board members consisted of representatives chosen from the BCU committee, a representative from the district council, the secretary-general of the district (who was appointed by the state), and expatriate government officers, with the district commissioner serving as the board chair. The board soon became a focal point for center-local power struggles as BCU members regarded it as a heavy-handed arm of the state's Commission of Cooperative Development (CCD).

The BCU was also subject to supervision and audit by the CCD (which became the DCD after independence). The district office of the DCD was run by the senior cooperative officer for Bugisu, with whom the secretary/manager of the BCU maintained direct and frequent communication. He transmitted most of the messages between his department's head office in Kampala and the BCU, including most directives from the commissioner or the minister. By 1970 he directed a staff of thirty-eight, most of whom were assistant cooperative officers (ACOs) or cooperative assistants (CAs) working in the field overseeing the activities of the various GCSs.

An ACO in each of the four counties supervised the CAs there. Each CA was assigned to oversee specific GCSs, which ranged in number from four to nine, depending on their size and location. The ACO and the CA were responsible for auditing the GCS books and enforcing adherence to cooperative society rules, advising the GCS secretary/manager and committee on regulations and more efficient procedures, arbitrating disputes or referring them to a higher authority, informing their own office about any problems the GCS was having, supervising and reporting to the GCS Annual General Meetings, and chairing them from the time the old committee stepped down until the new committee took over. The CAs and ACOs had considerable power and discretion; but perhaps more important, many of them achieved considerable influence in their assigned areas, using their knowledge of the fine points of cooperative law and their ability to invoke the authority of the Cooperative Rules.

The GCS or any individual could appeal a CA's or ACO's decision or complain about his actions to the officer above him, and in some cases these complaints led to removal or transfer, but senior officers tended to uphold or defend the decisions of their subordinates except in cases of blatant malfeasance or misjudgment. In some cases the benefit of appeal was problematic at best, e.g., when a CA adjourned a GCS annual general meeting before it had completed its business because it was rejecting his directions, even though this rejection might be quite legal. In such a case the balance of power between competing factions might change by the time a new meeting was called, and there might be a tendency to follow the CA's dictates simply to get on with the business at hand. The power to chair the meeting during elections and to adjourn it at any time gave the CA considerable influence over the outcome of the elections.

The CCD's, and later the DCD's, organization in the district paralleled the union's structure from top to bottom, and its personnel had the power of supervision, intervention, arbitration, and the right to advise and report at all levels of the union's activities.

The CCD had been an important ally as the Bagisu leaders strove to fulfill the criteria set for the creation and registration of their own GCSs and eventually of the BCU. After 1954, however, the CCD became the primary instrument of the state's strategies to direct and control the BCU and to limit its leaders' autonomy. The anger and frustration that these leaders often felt in their campaign to broaden the BCU's powers were intensified by their perception that their former mentors had betrayed them.

The cooperative and other representative institutions in Bugisu emerged out of the struggle between the peasants and the state. Their actual forms and internal processes reflected the ways that the state had attempted to use local groups to achieve its own goals and the ways those groups had struggled with the state in order to expand their opportunities and privileges. They also reflected the speed with which the Bagisu had invented new responses—ideological and or-ganizational—to the exigencies of powerful alien forces. Successful struggle against central control required that Bagisu leaders learn the strengths and weaknesses of the state and then construct imaginative political actions and associations out of their understanding both of the state and of their own society. As the state adjusted its own strategies in response to the Bagisu's political gains, the Bagisu had to continue their own search for effective new organizational forms and actions. They became adept at using the resources and powers they had already gained from the state to mobilize the peasants behind their demands. The competition between the different ascendant groups as they al-ternately joined forces against the state or fought over the powers they had wrested from it intensified and complicated this search and the struggles that it fed into.

It should be noted, however, that even though the civil servants and the popular leaders were the primary innovators of new political strat-egies and forms, none of these would have been successful without the rest of the Bagisu learning to participate in them. The civil servants and popular leaders confronted the colonial state more intimately and directly and could more easily understand both its weaknesses and the organizational forms that they could usefully adopt from it. Nonethe-less, the rest of the peasants needed to understand the new political and organizational strategies to make them work. Also, they had to learn how to maintain the pressure necessary to make sure that their own demands and needs were satisfied by the leaders who mobilized them. Later dissident movements against the BCU would show that the peasants did indeed learn to discriminate between policies and to insist that they share in the resources over which the leaders gained control. They were never completely successful in this, but they did continue as a vital, dynamic force in the general configuration of the struggle to control crop marketing.

After the BCU was established, the supervisory powers of the Bugisu Coffee Board and the CCD presented immediate barriers to the Bagisu's political and economic aims. Bagisu leaders used the resources that their formal positions in the BCU and in the district council gave them to mobilize peasant protest against CCD and board policies. They also used these resources to reward the peasants for their support by pushing for higher prices and relaxed quality control, as well as by pressuring the state to improve social welfare programs, rural extension services, educational facilities, and infrastructure such as roads and bridges.

The leaders' drive to expand their own powers led to frequent confrontations with the state, and the state was at times willing to risk peasant protest in order to reduce the leaders' powers. It also attempted to invoke the principles of business efficiency and member participation in order to form alliances with the peasants against their own leaders. Subsequent chapters will show, however, that even though the peasants were concerned with their own rights and with the union's efficiency, their interests diverged from those of the state. The peasants could be mobilized against their leaders, but only by other Bagisu claimants to power. The state could not mobilize the peasants because its preferred model of modern business efficiency offered no satisfaction of the peasants' economic and political demands. The state consistently failed in its attempts to win the peasants to its own point of view.

In its simplest terms, the ideological struggle between the Bagisu leaders and the state and the failure of the state's attempts to make allies of the peasants in its campaigns for efficient management revolved around radically divergent concepts of authority's legitimate control over and disposition of wealth. For the British, .technical competence and efficiency legitimized authority, and the ultimate aim of efficiency was to accumulate, rather than to distribute, surplus. For the Bagisu, authority emerged from wealth and could only be properly exercised by generous, even if incomplete, redistribution. The British had not redistributed the surplus funds, as they had initially promised, and had thus violated expectations that authority would be both honest and generous. Rather, they had simply continued to accumulate these funds. The Bagisu quite correctly saw that the legal and organizational forms that the British imposed on the BCU would serve as devices to continue similar kinds of accumulation, however much the British insisted that the efficiency they demanded would serve the peasants' best interests.

The peasants themselves demanded efficiency. They wanted efficient collection of and payment for the crops their GCSs sold to the BCU; they wanted predictable and honest procedures when they delivered their own coffee to the GCSs; and they wanted reliable accounting and prompt payment of the money that the GCSs owed them. They opposed theft or embezzlement by GCSs' committees or management. All of these demands were consonant with the idea that the BCU was wealthy and powerful and constituted an acceptable authority that redistributed the wealth that flowed to it. They were, therefore, ready to support their leaders in political struggles to ensure that its resources were indeed redistributed, even though these struggles necessarily consumed some of the surplus that the British claimed should all have been accumulating to an efficient, routinized cooperative enterprise.

The British would justify their continued control over the cooperatives by arguing that the Bagisu and their leaders did not adequately understand proper business procedure. In fact, the Bagisu peasants would prove themselves quite competent in using cooperative principles against the state and against their own leaders when it served their purposes to do so. The peasants' support of their leaders was by no means unconditional, nor could it be. The various ascendant groups in Bugisu shared crucial interests with the rest of the Bagisu, but they were also very interested in increasing their own powers and privileges.

The strategies, processes, and outcomes of the struggles between leaders, peasants, and the state were determined in part by Uganda's changing relation to Britain and by competition between national parties before and after independence. They were also very much influenced by the evolving political organization and consciousness within Bugisu, and by struggles between various local groups. Before proceeding with the chronological narrative of how these groups and the state fought for control of the cooperative, however, it is necessary to show the extent to which the cooperatives and other representative institutions changed political and economic opportunities in Bugisu. In the following chapter, I will show how centrally important these institutions were in the Bagisu leaders' strategies for upward mobility and increased wealth. The primacy of political position in determining economic situation, in turn, will help to explain the tenacity and persistence of the leaders' struggle to increase their autonomous control of these institutions, which will be the subject of the subsequent chapters.

NOTES

1. Note, however, that various departments, e.g., the Department of Agriculture, became ministries after independence, and some new ministries were created, e.g., the Ministry of Cooperative and Marketing, after the republic was established in 1966.

2. A very few women, mostly daughters of men with no sons, inherited land. They kept this land when they married, but their sons, not their daughters, inherited it from them, usually at their maturity rather than when their mother died. Only one woman, the daughter of a Muganda chief who inherited considerable land, ever served on the BCU committee.

3

The Primacy of Politics

The expansion of cash cropping and the extension of the physical infrastructure and administrative organization necessary to maintain it had greatly changed both income and consumption for the Bagisu. Peasants used the money from crop sales to buy tin sheets for their house roofs, agricultural implements, clothing, lamps, and kerosene, as well as salt, dried fish, and alcohol. They also bought food such as ground nuts and maize, which are harvested at different times in different parts of Bugisu, and meat. Many of them spent a large proportion of their income to send their children through at least the first years of school. These new consumption patterns provided opportunities for business and trade in the rural areas. Bagisu opened small stores throughout the district, and other Bagisu provided the transport necessary to stock them. Rustic restaurants and bars appeared in the trading centers which grew up in the rural areas.

The collection, sale, and processing of crops provided jobs, and there were other jobs to be had in the wholesale agencies and a few small industries in Mbale. There was also employment for the better educated in the schools.

In relation to the total population of Bugisu, however, the number of jobs and trading opportunities was tiny, and for most of those Bagisu who did have jobs or a business, income was very low. The relatively high-paying jobs in civil service were reserved for the very few Bagisu with high levels of education. Education was expensive in Uganda, especially in relation to farm income. Competition for entry into high school and college was intense. High-paying jobs thus remained the nearly exclusive province of the already powerful chiefly families. Similarly, few Bagisu had sufficient capital to establish businesses capable of earning them much profit.

The formation of the BCU and of a popularly elected district council in 1954-55 opened avenues of upward mobility that allowed Bagisu with little formal education or wealth to compete for power, status, and income with the previously ascendant chiefs and civil servants. In this chapter, I will explain how positions in these new instititions could be and were combined with the other sources of income available to the Bagisu, and then I will analyze the career histories of the committee members of the BCU from 1954 until the Amin coup of 1971. This analysis will demonstrate the importance of political position in the upward mobility strategies of Bagisu leaders and thus provide some explanation of the intensity of their struggles to free the cooperative union from government control and supervision.

The Bagisu leaders' desire to use the union to increase their own wealth and power only partially explains their persistent campaign for local autonomy. Many of these leaders were also motivated by their feelings of ethnic pride. They resented the special rights and privileges of Europeans, Asians, and Baganda, and they wanted to help their own people, the Bagisu, to progress economically and politically. They believed that their people needed and deserved more money for their labor, more education, more health facilities, and better roads; and they thought the BCU should be used to provide this capital.

These feelings of ethnic identity strengthened their resolve to make the union more autonomous, but for some leaders, at least, they also involved personal conflict. George Waisi, who had been the BCU's most powerful president and had achieved its greatest autonomy, told me that he had had "two great desires, improving my people's condition and improving my own." As president, he was in a position to do both, but his desire to help himself got in the way of his desire to help his people.

Avenues of Upward Mobility in Bugisu, 1954-71

Between 1954 and 1971 there were four main sources of wealth and prestige, power and authority in Bugisu: (1) cash cropping, which I call farming; (2) employment for salary or wages; (3) private ownership in trade and business; and (4) political or cooperative positions. Upward mobility for most Bagisu involved dependence on several of these sources, but some jobs, mostly in civil service, were closed to simultaneous combination with other income sources.

Of these four sources, farming was the most important. The great majority of the approximately half million Bagisu relied exclusively on a combination of farming and subsistence agriculture.[1] Farming provided the basic cash and subsistence foundation for almost all of the upwardly mobile outside the higher grades of public or private employment, but almost no upwardly mobile Bagisu depended on farming alone, because large-scale agriculture was virtually impossible on an individual basis. It was difficult to buy large plots of land because land was scarce and because of the way Bagisu inherited and held land.

Lineage control of land and inheritance patterns significantly limited the potential for land accumulation. Ideally, lineages resided contiguously. Expropriations and land sales violated this ideal to some extent. The minor lineage (*kiguga*), however, still had formal control over the sale of any of the land within its borders to anyone from another lineage, and there was strong pressure against selling land to anyone outside the lineage (Gayer, 1957). This control was officially sanctioned by the courts as a part of customary law, but its enforcement varied from area to area. Within the minor lineage, land was owned by individuals.

Acquiring land outside the territory of one's own lineage area was difficult. The consolidation of large plots was further complicated by Bagisu inheritance customs. A man allotted each wife a portion of his land. This portion was eventually divided equally among his sons by that woman. Dividing land among all sons and at different periods of time led to increasing fragmentation.[2] Sale of land outside one's *kiguga* became more common as cash cropping expanded, and the traditional inheritance patterns were sometimes modified by the consideration that the land that a father sold to pay for a son's education should be subtracted from that son's portion. By far the greatest part of the land in Bugisu, however, was still controlled by the resident lineage and divided among all of a man's sons by each of his wives. Except for the local prison farms, there was almost no large-scale or plantation-type farming or ranching. Some men with large farms did hire porters to work in them, but in all but a few cases the owner's nuclear family did most of the work. Such porters as were hired generally worked only part-time or seasonally. The absence of a large labor force resulted from and reinforced the low level of land tenure concentration and lineage control of land alienation.

Second, few upwardly mobile Bagisu depended exclusively on farming as a source of wealth because other means of making money were both more remunerative and more prestigious. Even if a man could expand his land holdings sufficiently to allow plantation-type farming, his returns would start to diminish in proportion to his investment as his dependence on hired labor increased, especially if he was growing coffee.

Arabica coffee, the only type that could be grown legally in Bugisu, commanded a much higher price than the Robusta type, which was grown in most of the rest of Uganda; but it required intensive and careful cultivation. Not only did the trees have to be shaded, but they also had to be kept free of weeds and other plants, watched scrupulously for various bugs and diseases that could either kill the tree or spoil the coffee cherry, pruned to exact criteria annually, and fertilized. The cherry had to be picked at a precise stage in its maturation, and it had to be carefully passed through a number of steps in its curing. The rainy climate in Bugisu necessitated constant vigilance to make sure the coffee did not get wet while it was drying outside. It had to be cured at a certain pace to make sure that it did not rot. Finally, all of the bad beans had to be taken out so as not to lower the quality of the entire batch. The absence of well-trained farm laborers put a fairly effective limit on the profitable expansion of one man's holdings.[3]

Coffee prices, though high in relation to those of other crops, were low in relation to the labor required and fluctuated considerably. Cotton prices were even lower and were also unstable. If a man wanted to increase his wealth and his status, he could do so more efficiently by turning to other pursuits.

Despite these restrictions on agriculture as a means of upward mobility, however, cash cropping did heighten both social and economic differentiation among the Bagisu. Men controlled the sale of and income from cash crops, even though women assisted in their cultivation, processing, and transport. Subsistence cropping, over which women had more control, declined in importance. Men who inherited relatively large amounts of land—usually sons of wealthy fathers who had few or no brothers by the same mother—could use this land and the labor of their wives to accumulate more flexible forms of capital. Many of these men bought more land and married additional wives. This aggravated the land scarcity, which had always been a problem on the densely populated mountain.

Some farmers responded to the problem of land scarcity by paying the school fees for some of their sons and, in compensation, giving a greater share or all of their land to the sons who received less education or none at all. Many of the young men thus educated could not find land and so joined the ranks of those with little or no land who supplied occasional labor for the larger coffee growers.

Farming was a reliable source of income, and men who were successful in other more lucrative but less stable enterprises often invested at least part of their returns in agricultural expansion. The landless were only a small portion of the Bagisu, and even the largest of the landowners owned only a small portion of total cultivable land. Thus, despite significant differences in farming income and landownership, farming consititued a primary economic basis and a common political interest for the great majority of Bagisu.

Employment for salary or wages was the second most important source of income in Bugisu, but it provided a livelihood for only a small proportion of the over 100,000 households there. As late as 1969, total recorded employment in Bugisu provided only 10,314 jobs. Well over half of this number, however, were employed in Mbale[4] and so included a substantial proportion of non-Bagisu. There were over 70,000 tax-paying heads of households in the entire district.

Employment in industry was still quite low. The *1967 Survey of Industrial Production* showed twenty-eight industrial concerns in Bugisu, including grain milling, food and bakery production, furniture, clothing, printing, oil, chemical and metal products, and auto repair. Only one of these hired more than 100 (and still less than 200) employees in 1967; of the rest, two hired between fifty and ninety-nine employees, four hired between twenty and forty-nine, and the remainder between ten and nineteen. After 1967, a textile mill opened in Mbale hiring over 100 workers. But even with the addition of the mill, the maximum total possible jobs was 1,093. All but two or three of these industries were located in Mbale, and many of the positions in these industries as well as other town-connected jobs were held by non-Bagisu.

Jobs with the national ministries and departments, the district administration, the Ministry of Education, and the cooperatives, most of which were held by Bagisu, were more important in the district's economy and figured much more heavily in its social stratification.[5] The district administration in 1971 employed about 650 people, at salaries ranging from 1,560 shillings a year (7 sh. = US$1.00), starting salary for a deputy *muluka* (parish) chief, to 32,000 shillings a year earned by the secretary-general, the top-ranking officer in the district administration. There were about 875 teachers in primary schools administered by the district education committee, that is, inside Bugisu but outside Mbale, at salaries ranging from 2,520 to 9,290 shillings a year. Two cooperative unions together hired over 100 permanent staff members and took on several hundred temporary employees during the buying season.[6] The salaries for senior staff in the unions ranged from 18,000 to 48,000 shillings a year and for junior staff from 3,000 to 18,000 shillings a year. The two unions paid salaries totaling 874,600 shillings, excluding committee wages and staff bonuses, during the 1969-70 season. The ninety-seven individual GCSs, which made up the two unions, each hired from two to five employees, including a secretary/manager who could earn up to 4,800 shillings a year.

In addition to the district administration and the cooperative unions, a large number of district and regional offices for the various ministries were located in Mbale. The Uganda civil service tended to transfer its senior officers both frequently and widely, so that few of the senior civil servants in Mbale were Bagisu, although Bagisu filled many of the junior staff positions in these offices. The Department of Cooperative Development, the Department of Community Development, and the Department of Agriculture all hired Bagisu as field workers in the rural areas.

The great majority of the jobs available in Bugisu provided the minimum necessary for food and shelter. They were usually more a refuge from landlessness than a part of strategies for upward mobility. Most of these jobs, and especially the few which paid well, were held by men.

The number of employed with extra capital to manipulate was a very small proportion of the total. Those who did have extra capital, though, often used trade and business to increase their wealth and prestige. Over 600 wholesale and retail trading licenses were issued for the area outside the Mbale municipality in 1970; my impression from looking at the applications for these was that there may have been a substantial proportion of traders who had not registered their shops. Many of the shops in the district were clearly marginal, changing hands or going out of business fairly frequently. Individuals could open shops in their own buildings when they had capital and when there was money in the area, usually during the crop-selling season, but many had to close down again until they got more money from some other source. Except for selling staple goods in local and urban markets, women participated little in commerce.

For those who did have sufficient capital to stock a store properly, trade items like millet, ground nuts, maize, and paraffin allowed a substantial margin for profit, while items like sugar and cigarettes, though less profitable, could be stocked as a service or incentive for customers.

Opportunities for large-scale trade and commerce, however, were effectively bounded by the cooperative unions' state-granted monopoly on the purchase and processing of coffee and cotton, the primary sources of wealth in the district. Asian businessmen and members of other ethnic groups dominated commerce in Mbale. For all but two or three Bagisu, trade was limited to the unregulated staple crops and to petty commodities, and to illegal trading in coffee and cotton on a relatively small scale in the various rural localities. Business opportunities included transport for the unions and other trades, and construction, but occasions were limited, and the capital outlay required remained beyond the reach of all but a few.

Capitalizing trading or business operations usually required irregular or downright illegal activities or was possible only through other sources of income, either in the form of relationship to a rich or powerful man, such as a chief, or through high-level political connections. Many small-scale traders, for example, accumulated sufficient cash through illicit crop-trading to expand their businesses rapidly.

During the harvest season, crop-trading could net large profits. This was especially true during a season when a huge crop slowed down buying at the GCSs. Buying delays at the GCSs provided a strong incentive for growers to sell their crops to any buyer, even at a substantial reduction from the official price. Distance was also important. If the GCS was far away, growers were inclined to sell small amounts to traders for immediate needs. The profits for buying could be very high; traders told me of profits from 50 percent up to 200 percent (the latter figure for buying uncured coffee and drying it oneself). Turnover was relatively rapid, sometimes as little as a week. Only individuals with a source of income independent of the cash crop they were buying were able to buy others' crops, however. By law, only the cooperative unions and the GCSs were entitled to buy coffee and cotton and the scheduled minor crops. There was a heavy penalty for crop-trading, but neither I nor anyone else I talked to ever heard of any arrest, much less a conviction, for this offense.

There were various other opportunities in the rural areas for profitable investment of surplus income. Some traders bought sewing machines and hired seamstresses, combining the sale of material with the manufacture of clothing. Others dealt in cattle from neighboring districts. Both of these activities allowed a fair return on fairly small investments. One prosperous rural businessman and local politician told me that he started trading in coffee with a 180-shilling-a-year salary for teaching in a subgrade school[7] and had built that up to a 2,000-shilling-a-year trade in coffee alone within three years, in addition to capitalizing a shop and buying enough sewing machines and hiring enough seamstresses to bid successfully for school contracts totaling 1,500 uniforms in one year. Many traders used their shops for crop-trading, taking advantage of a central location and increasing their profits by paying for the crops in kind. Without crop-trading, shopkeeping alone was either too marginal or required too much capital outlay for anyone without other relatively substantial sources of income.

Transport and milling maize required a considerably greater investment and much more risk, but profits were high. Most people in these
businesses had multiple sources of income; many, for example, were
politicians. Some prosperous traders owned pickup trucks and station
wagons, which they used for their own business and in which they
transported people and goods to and from Mbale and to different rural
areas. This service was particularly flexible and was in great demand,
especially in areas with little bus service. Maize mill owners could
either grind maize for sale in their own stores or grind what peasant
farmers brought them for a fee.

In 1970 seven traders and businessmen also owned large lorries.
These trucks complemented rural wholesale operations particularly well.
They could be used for crop-hauling contracts with the unions, for
private crop dealing, for hauling one's own and other people's trade
goods, and for hauling building materials on private contracts for houses
and shops or on government or cooperative contracts for roads, schools,
and GCS stores. Contracts with the unions were advantageous to traders because the union paid for a round trip, so if a rural businessman
hauled from his own area he could carry goods home at little extra
cost. The cooperative unions paid well, but waiting in line to unload
could take as long as three days, so the lorry was tied up while the
driver continued to collect wages. A man who owned a shop, a maize
mill, and a lorry, however, could buy maize directly from growers, haul
and mill it himself, and then sell it in his store, thus taking all the
roles and profits of five potential middlemen. Some lorry owners also
did a substantial trade buying bananas in Bugisu for sale in other
districts or under contract to institutions. Few, however, were so fortunate.

To summarize, there were relatively few lucrative opportunities in
either employment or business. Most employment paid a bare subsistence wage, and most trade was only occasional. Employment in
occupations that paid a significant salary was only open to the few
Bagisu with high levels of formal Western education; trade or business
on a scale necessary to earn cumulative profits required more capital
than most Bagisu could earn from farming alone. The only means of
upward mobility available to most Bagisu, therefore, were the political
positions in representative institutions such as the cooperatives and the
legislative councils. The more autonomous these institutions were from
central state control, the greater their contribution to the upward mobility strategies of these officeholders could be. Bagisu leaders were
therefore strongly impelled to fight against direct state control and
supervision.

Political and cooperative leadership roles generated less direct income than any of the other three sources, but allowed the greatest flexibility and the most rapid accumulation of advantages. These positions provided the most direct access to the district's resources and assets, because most of the wealth in the district was controlled by government and the cooperatives. The cooperatives controlled crop sales; the district and national administrations controlled most of the salaried employment in the district. Various government agencies distributed a large proportion of the goods and services that individuals and communities required (i.e., medical attention, roads, opportunities for formal education, and the funds to pay for it).

As government and cooperatives controlled the major sources of money as well as the distribution of goods and services, political office was a crucial means of access to money and power. Political positions could provide both direct sources of money (i.e., salaries and allowances) and the chance to exchange support or services to others in return for various favors or benefits (e.g., reduced rates for goods or transport, rebates, facility in obtaining trading licenses, and contracts). They also allowed leaders to provide essential services to their constituents.

Direct cash payments for most political and cooperative leadership positions were quite small. In 1970-71, for instance, GCS committee members earned between 180 and 360 shillings a year, plus a small daily allowance for the time they spent at the GCS store as buying supervisors. At least one committee member had to accompany the GCS secretary/manager on his trips to deliver coffee to the mill and to bring money back, and they received an additional allowance for this travel. Lower-level political positions paid nothing at all, though party branch chairmen and their delegations were given travel and subsistence allowances when they went to certain official meetings. The forty-four ordinary members of the district council each received 2,880 shillings a year as an allowance, in addition to traveling expenses.

Advantages from even the lower levels of political and cooperative leadership could be quite substantial, however. These positions provided local leaders with power over jobs and votes that they could exchange for various considerations. Control of a GCS meant control over a number of jobs, the most important of which was the secretary/manager's. The secretary/manager not only received one of the largest salaries in the rural areas, but he also guarded and bought all produce and handled all the money. He was frequently a close relative of the GCS chairman. Collusion between committee members and the secretary/manager allowed considerable opportunities for theft or embezzlement.

Political and cooperative positions provided other advantages that regular employment would have restricted. The terms of service for certain types of work prohibited filling certain other types of roles simultaneously. The most obvious case in point was the law against civil servants joining a political party or holding political office or positions. Teachers were included in this injunction in 1967, although the law was less rigid in their regard; they could not hold government office but were allowed to belong to a political party and hold office in it. Chiefs, who were formally members of the civil service, were prohibited from engaging in trade or business. Cooperative staff could hold political positions only with the cooperative committees' approval. Because the combination of different roles was an important prerequisite for upward mobility in Bugisu, such restrictions limited the potential benefits of these jobs.[8] Political and cooperative representative positions did not entail such restrictions.

The location of work could also enhance or close off avenues of mobility. Working where one had land was much more economical than working where one did not have land. Having jobs in their home area allowed individuals to manage both subsistence and cash crops, and to save some portion or all of their salary for investment in land or trade. This strategy was open to teachers, agricultural and cooperative field staff, GCS secretary/managers, and *muluka* chiefs. However, they all were subject to transfer, and frequent transfer limited opportunities to engage in business or trade.

The leadership positions that entailed regular and frequent trips to Mbale offered much greater benefits than the strictly local ones. The paid trips into town allowed officeholders to establish important business and political ties and contacts. District council and cooperative committee meetings provided opportunities for local politicians to meet, talk, and stay informed about and involved in the political and business plans of more powerful politicians. Meetings and other official business also paid for many of the trips to town that individuals needed to make for their personal business.

The paid trips to town assisted the rural politician-businessman greatly. A rural trader with a large shop, especially a wholesaler, had to buy much of his stock in town. Having these trips paid for gave him a competitive advantage over other traders. He could afford more trips to town and could make connections to find cheaper sources of supply. As many of his fellow politicians or committeemen were also in business of different sorts, usually in areas where they posed no competitive threat, they often found that cooperation benefited everyone. Political alliances or simple friendships based on association in town were frequently the incentive for reduced rates or special services. Friends and allies who were not in competition could also provide useful information about trading opportunities and practices. Finally, those few politicians who accumulated enough capital to buy a lorry could use these political connections to guarantee that the cooperative hired them to transport crops.

The paid trips to town served to strengthen the leaders' political positions, as they helped them provide special service to their neighbors. A council or a cooperative union committee member could plead special cases or convey complaints or requests to various government agencies in Mbale. His official position, the fact that to be a formal leader at all meant he was wealthier and more articulate than the average rural peasant, and his greater acquaintance with the town, the offices, the officials, and administrative procedures all combined to make him effective in this role. The services that he performed for his constituents were necessary to maintain his position, but they also obligated the people for whom he performed them, strengthening his power at home and the alliances on which it was based. All of the attributes that allowed him to intercede for his constituents also enabled him to promote his own and his immediate family's interests.

The politician-businessman generally played a number of roles that complemented and strengthened each other by providing access to various networks of influence, power, and income, because few political positions in the district paid enough by themselves to be an important source of income. Involvement in politics was crucial in upward mobility, but alone it was not sufficient. Political position was a critical asset that could be exploited through exchange relations and alliances to gain economic advantage. Economic strength, once achieved, could also be an important factor in developing further political strength.

Office in the BCU and in the district council were thus decisive factors in the ability of their members to gain political and economic power. The BCU was especially important, as it controlled the crops that accounted for most of the district's income. State control of the BCU lessened the BCU leaders' ability to exploit these opportunities, so they were strongly impelled to resist any threat to their own autonomy.

In the following section, I will show how BCU committee officers figured in the systems of wealth and power I have just described. I will present a composite portrait of the career histories of all Bagisu who served on the BCU committee from 1954 to 1971, and a comparison of their incomes and status with those of chiefs, civil servants, and the rest of the Bagisu. I will also show how these political leaders continued to manipulate traditional systems of kin and affinally based alliances to complement the powers that they derived from the new representative institutions and the monetary economies. The career histories were completed in 1970-71, so the positions, income, and wealth reported refer to those years, but they reflect the history and accumulation of the previous seventeen years.

BCU Committee Office and Upward Mobility

Positions and roles within each of Bugisu's four systems of wealth and power — farming, employment, business, and politics — can be ranked in terms of relative status, power, or income. Within each employment and leadership system, roles were hierarchically structured. For example, the district administration, the district council, the cooperative unions, the political parties, and all government departments each contained chains of rank and command. Success in farming and business can be measured in terms of income or land owned. Ranking of roles across different sections of each system or between systems can be done by comparing the formal powers and responsibilities and the access to influence and wealth associated with each role.

Table 2 shows bureaucratic rank within the cooperative and district administrative staff and the estimated order of power and prestige in the Uganda People's Congress (UPC), cooperative committee positions, and the district council.[9] Only the list of political and cooperative committee positions is complete: the cooperative and district administration bureaucracies contained many more clerical and functionary posts than would be relevant to include. I have included all posts with executive authority, however. Comparisons in power and prestige across the three sections of the chart are approximate.

The succeeding tables show the income received directly from positions in the district council (Table 3), the district administration (Table 4), and the BCU staff (Table 5). All three tables show income actually earned by occupants of these positions in 1970. Discrepancies between relative status and actual income in Tables 4 and 5 reflect seniority.

Comparison of Table 3 with Tables 4 and 5 shows that BCU committee members received allowances that matched the income range of the subcounty (gombolola) chiefs, but were considerably lower than the salaries paid to BCU staff officers. BCU committee members did not enjoy the security of tenure that the civil servants and BCU staff did. They were, however, in a much better position to use both their time and their income to invest in trading and in other political activities.

Table 2. Estimated Rankings within and between Political and Cooperative Office, the BDA, and the BCU Staff in Descending Order of Power and Prestige

Political and Cooperative Office	BDA	BCU and GCS[a]
Member of Parliament		
UPC constituency chairman		
	Secretary-general	
	Assistant secretary-general	
	Administrative secretary	
	Treasurer	
	County chiefs	
BCU committee chairman		BCU secretary/manager
MCU committee chairman		MCU secretary/manager
District council chairman		
District council committee chairman		
BCU committee officers	Subcounty chiefs	
		BCU mill manager
MCU committee officers		BCU accountant
District council members		
UPC constituency officers		
	Subcounty magistrates	
UPC constituency committee members		
UPC branch chairman	Parish chiefs	
County council member[b]		
	Deputy parish chiefs	
		GCS secretary/manager
GCS chairman		
Subcounty council member[b]		
UPC branch officers		
GCS officers		
UPC branch committee members		
GCS committee members		

NOTE: BCU = Bugisu Cooperative Union; BDA = Bugisu District Administration; GCS = Growers' Cooperative Society; MCU = Masaaba Cooperative Union; UPC = Uganda People's Congress.
[a] Both the BDA and the BCU hierarchies include field staff and clerical staff. The members of these staffs are scaled in terms of qualifications required and responsibility, but have no executive authority. Relative status can be assessed only in terms of salary. See Tables 3 and 4.
[b] Disbanded in 1967.

Table 3. Income Received Directly from District Political Positions

Position	Annual Remuneration (sh), 1970
District Council	
Chairman	8,400 plus travel expenses
Deputy chairman	3,600 plus travel expenses
Members	2,880 plus travel expenses
BCU committees	
Union chairman	7,700 plus travel expenses
Union vice-chairman	6,700 plus travel expenses
Union treasurer	6,700 plus travel expenses
Union committee member	5,700 plus travel expenses
GCS chairman	180 to 360 and occasional travel expenses
GCS officers (vice-chairman or treasurer)	120 to 240
GCS committee member	120 to 240
UPC	
Constituency chairman	Travel expenses
Other constituency officers	Travel expenses
Constituency committee members	Travel expenses
Muluka branch chairmen	Occasional travel expenses
Branch officers	Occasional travel expenses
Branch committee members	Occasional travel expenses

NOTE: BCU = Bugisu Cooperative Union; GCS = Growers' Cooperative Society; UPC = Uganda People's Congress.

Almost all of the men who served on the BCU committee had also held a number of other political positions, before, during, and after their tenure (Table 6).

Fifty-seven Bagisu[10] had been members of the BCU committee between its establishment in 1954 and the Amin coup of 1971. Over half of them entered some political position before they were first elected to the committee. Entry into the subcounty, county, and the district councils preceded much more often than followed BCU committee membership, while UPC and Democratic party (DP) office tended more to follow BCU committee membership. This difference occurred in part because the UPC was founded eight years after the first direct elections to the district council and the establishment of the BCU. The BCU committee was recruited largely from established local politicians; it then served these men as a springboard to high positions in the national

Table 4. Income Received Directly from Positions in the District Administration

District Administration Position	Remunerations (sh), 1970
Secretary-general	32,000 plus travel expenses
Assistant secretary-general	29,000 plus travel expenses
Administrative secretary	31,020 plus travel expenses
Treasurer	28,800 plus travel expenses
County chiefs	15,660 to 18,780 plus travel expenses
Assistant administrative secretary	15,660 plus travel expenses
Assistant treasurer	13,740 plus travel expenses
Clerk of council	16,640 plus travel expenses
Subcounty chiefs	4,788 to 11,940 plus travel expenses
Parish chiefs	1,902 to 3,864
Deputy parish chiefs	1,560 to 2,160
Clerical scales	2,244 to 26,440
Primary school teachers	2,520 to 9,300
Bugisu land committee chairman[a]	14,400 plus travel expenses
Bugisu land committee member[a]	7,320 plus travel expenses
Public service committee chairman[a]	14,400 plus travel expenses
Public service committee member[a]	7,320 plus travel expenses

[a] These were actually defined as national civil service posts, but they were constituted entirely of local influentials. None of the standard civil service qualifications was required, nor were members excluded from political activity. The demands of these posts were sufficiently limited that they interfered very little with members' other activities. Appointment to these positions was used as a reward for political service, especially to the national parties.

Table 5. Income Received Directly from Positions on the BCU Staff

BCU Position	Remunerations (sh), 1970
Secretary/manager, BCU	46,800
Mill manager, BCU	49,200
Accountant, BCU	42,000
Assistant secretary/manager, BCU	21,600
Assistant mill manager, BCU	23,400
Bookkeepers, BCU	7,860 to 16,490
Field officers, BCU	18,000
Secretary/managers, GCS	2,400 to 4,800
Clerks, BCU	4,600 to 16,300
Porters and messengers, BCU	1,800 to 3,600
Weighmen, GCS	800 to 1,200
Guards, GCS	600 to 800

NOTE: BCU = Bugisu Cooperative Union; GCS = Growers' Cooperative Society.

Table 6. Number of Men Holding Political Posts before and after Their First
Election to the BCU Committee

Political Posts	Before	After
Subcounty Council	30	6
County Council	29	9
District Council	24	11
District Council chairman	0	2
Uganda Legislative Council (pre-independence pre-		
decessor to Parliament)	1	0
Uganda Constitutional Conference	0	1
Uganda Parliament	1	1
UPC		
Constituency chairman	1	8
Constituency vice-chairman	0	1
Constituency treasurer	0	1
Constituency secretary	2	1
Constituency committee members	0	4
(Parish) branch chairman	4	12
Branch vice-chairman	0	2
Branch treasurer	0	3
Branch committee member	0	8
DP		
Constituency chairman	2	2
Constituency treasurer	0	4
Branch chairman	1	1
Branch vice-chairman	0	1
UNC		
District chairman	1	1
District secretary	2	0
District committee member	1	0
Subcounty chairman	1	1
Subcounty vice-chairman	1	0
Subcounty committee member	0	1
Uganda Cooperative apex organizations	0	7
Bugisu Land Committee[a]	0	6
Bugisu Public Service Committee[a]	0	5
Total posts held	101	99

NOTE: BCU = Bugisu Cooperative Union. The DP (Democratic party) was the opposition party from 1962 to 1969, when it was banned. UNC (Uganda National Congress) was the pre-independence parent party of the UPC. UPC = Uganda People's Congress.
[a] See Table 4 for salaries and official status of these positions.

parties and in Parliament. The political parties drew many of their highest officers in Bugisu from men who had served on the BCU committee. Eight of the eleven men who became UPC constituency chairmen and one of the three men who became members of Parliament had served earlier on the BCU committee. BCU committee membership played a significant part in a high proportion of successful political careers in the district. BCU committee members' local prestige helped them gain further political support, as it enabled them to perform vital organizing services for the politicians at higher levels. They thus could become crucial in maintaining the political apparatus of much stronger men and could use these men to secure favors for themselves and for their local constituents.

Such considerations were especially important in moves to higher-level or particularly lucrative posts. After independence in 1962, for example, the members of Parliament (MP) had considerable influence in the appointments to the public service and the Bugisu land committees. They could use these extremely lucrative posts either to reward allies or to buy off threatening opponents. The campaigns for constituency chairmanships were in some cases so closely contested that influentials who had only recently joined the UPC were coopted to high positions within the district party organization because their local support was essential for one of the candidates. Thus district-level position could enhance purely local support, which in turn could serve as a lever to gain higher office. Alternately, faithful service within the UPC or a notable political career could be rewarded by granting the individual a high post. This was especially apparent in the large number of committee members who were appointed to the land and public service committees. Over half of the men who had held these lucrative positions (note a, Table 4) had already served on the BCU committee.

Committee membership was not particularly useful in gaining high-status employment. In fact, employment tended to precede rather than follow BCU office: ninety-seven of 132 employment positions (73.5 percent) held by men who served on the BCU committee were entered before election to the committee (Table 7). For the most part, however, these were relatively low-paying jobs. Interestingly, the only two job categories entered by more men after than before committee service were the two highest ranking jobs on the list, subcounty chief and senior civil service officer. In a few individual cases, committee membership did contribute to upward mobility in employment; the senior civil servant, for example, gained his position on the basis of training that the BCU financed after he joined the committee.

Table 7. Number of Men Entering Different Types of Employment before and after Their First Election to the BCU Committee

Types of Employment	Before	After
Church layman	3	0
Bus conductor	1	0
School carpenter	2	0
Primary school teacher	23	2
Clerical work in private enterprise	23	11
British army	7	0
BCS or BCU clerical	7	5
GCS secretary/manager	8	3
BCS, BCU, or MCU field supervisors	3	2
Deputy parish chief	3	1
Parish chief	5	4
Court clerks of subcounty magistrates	4	4
Department of Agriculture field staff	2	0
DCD field staff	2	0
Large farm manager	2	0
Qualified surveyor	1	0
Subcounty chief	1	2
Senior civil service officer	0	1
Total	97	35

NOTE: BCS = Bugisu Coffee Scheme; BCU = Bugisu Cooperative Union; DCD = Department of Cooperative Development; MCU = Masaaba Cooperative Union.

A smaller number of BCU members were engaged in business or trade, and BCU membership significantly improved the capacity of those who did so to invest relatively large amounts of capital (Table 8). Shopkeeping and cattle trading required relatively little capital investment. Only three committee men were engaged in any of the types of business that required major investments prior to their election to the BCU committee, while men who had already been on the committee started eleven highly capitalized businesses.

In relation to their number, the fifty-seven Bagisu who had been elected to the BCU committee occupied a remarkably high proportion of the political, employment, and business positions available in the district. These men had achieved their positions by exploiting a number of channels to economic and political resources that the new representative institutions had opened for men without professional qualifications or high education. BCU committee membership was a major factor in their access to a higher political position and major capital investment. Most of the committee members started their careers with

Table 8. Number of Men Entering Trade or Business before
and after Their First Election to the BCU Committee

Trade/Business	Before	After
Low Capital		
Shopkeepers	16	12
Cattle traders	2	2
Subtotal	18	14
High Capital		
Bar owners	0	2
Coffee nursery	0	1
Maize milling	0	2
Taxi owner	1	2
Pickup owner	1	2
Lorry owner	2	2
Subtotal	4	11
Total	22	25

NOTE: BCU = Bugisu Cooperative Union.

considerable advantages, however, and they manipulated traditional
alliance strategies to increase them. Cooperative positions were open
to all Bagisu, but a remarkably high proportion—75 percent—of the
BCU committee members were the sons of men of higher status than
that of cultivator (Table 9). Unlike the fathers of the most highly
educated civil servants, most BCU committee members' fathers did not
occupy high-level chiefships or other administrative positions. Thus,
they did not start their careers with major financial or affinal advantages,
but they were nonetheless somewhat wealthier, more educated, and
more favorably connected than most Bagisu.

In addition to the advantages of relatively greater wealth and family
prestige than most of their rural neighbors, these men often were able
to use the consanguineal and affinal relations they had with other
influential Bagisu through their fathers' kin network. This tendency
toward higher-status kin patterns among the BCU committee members
also applied to their selection of wives, which reflected both their
privileged parentage and their later prominence. The number of wives
a man had was an indication of wealth among the Bagisu. Affinal
connections to strong or influential families formed an important basis
of political power and prestige, because affinity, which was basically

Table 9. Number of BCU Committee Members Whose Fathers Occupied Higher Status than that of Cultivator

Status Position	Number of Committee Members	Percentage of All Committee Members
Saza chief	1	1.8
Gombolola chief	5	8.8
Muluka chief	6	10.5
Mutongole chief	4	7.0
Mutala chief	4	7.0
Mugasya	14	24.6
Trader	5	8.8
Teacher or cleric	4	7.0
Total	43	75.5

NOTE: BCU = Bugisu Cooperative Union.

Table 10. Numbers of Wives of BCU Committee Members

Number of Committee Members	Number of Wives
11	1
14	2
18	3
5	4
2	5
4	6

NOTE: BCU = Bugisu Cooperative Union.

an exchange relation, implied strong obligations of mutual aid and support (see Chapter 1). Most BCU committee members used traditional strategies of marriage alliance to strengthen their political and economic positions, both by marrying more than once and by marrying the daughters of wealthy or powerful men. The fifty-four BCU committee members for whom these data are available had a total of 148 wives, with the distribution shown in Table 10.

Among these 148 wives, the fathers of fifty-two had been chiefs, clan leaders, traders, clergymen, teachers, or other government employees. Thirty-six of the fifty-four committeemen for whom these data are available were married to women in this group (Table 11).

Table 11. Number of Wives of BCU Committee Members
Who Are Daughters of High-Status Fathers and Number of
Committee Members with Wives from Each Status

Position of Father	Number of Women	Number of Committee Members
Saza chief	1	1
Gombolola chief	9	8
Muluka chief	9	9
Mutongole chief	8	8
Mutala chief	4	4
Mugasya	5	5
Clergyman	3	3
Teacher	2	2
Other government worker	5	5
Trader	6	6

NOTE: BCU = Bugisu Cooperative Union.

Of the thirty-six men whose wives were the daughters of high-status men, twelve had two or more wives from this group, with the following combinations of wives' fathers:

two *gombolola* chiefs and a *muluka* chief;
a *gombolola* chief and a government employee;
a *gombolola* chief, a *mugasya,* and a trader;
a *gombolola* chief and a teacher;
a *muluka* chief, a *mutongole* chief, and a *mutala* chief;
a *gombolola* chief and a trader;
a *muluka* chief and a clergyman (two cases);
a *mutongole* chief and a government employee;
a *mutongole* chief, a *mutala* chief, and a clergyman;
a government employee and a teacher;
a government employee and a trader.

The largest group of committee members' wives' fathers was made up of *gombolola, muluka,* and *mutongole* chiefs. That is, among the committee members who took wives from high-status fathers, the tendency was to take wives from fathers with power at the local to the subcounty level. The men who took these wives were also most frequently those who took wives from more than one high-status father.

In addition to the high-status wives' fathers in Table 11, the husbands of ten other women said that those women's fathers had been rich. Four committee members married other committee members' sisters.

Thus the committee members as a group tended to follow the Bagisu pattern of marriages between powerful or influential families.

BCU committee members tended to expand their landholdings (Table 12), sometimes past their ability to cultivate them. Landownership and successful farming did confer prestige, however. More important, land accumulation was useful, as it allowed for the division of land between more wives and was thus part of strategies to extend affinal ties. Land could also be lent, thus reinforcing political and economic alliances.

Of the fifty-seven men who served on the committee, all but five had bought land. The landholdings of the committee members tended to be considerably larger than the average landholdings of the rest of the Bagisu.

These comparisons are only rough. Both the Census of Agriculture figures and my own are based on landowners' statements. Very little of the land in Bugisu had been surveyed, so exact figures were not

Table 12. Size Distribution of Landholdings of Bugisu/Sebei Compared with Those Claimed by BCU Committee Members (CM)

Acres	Bugisu/ Sebei: Number of Owners	Percent	Acres	BCU CM Number of Owners	Percent
1-1.24	10,000	14.3	0-2	3	5.45
1.24-2.48	12,000	17.1			
2.48-4.96	16,000	22.9	3-5	4	7.25
4.96-7.44	8,000	11.4			
7.44-9.92	5,000	7.1	6-12	16	29.09
9.92-12.40	4,000	5.7			
12.40-24.80	6,000	8.6	13-25	12	21.82
24.80+	9,000	12.9	26-35	5	9.09
			36-50	3	5.45
			51-60	3	5.45
			100	4	7.27
			300-500	3	5.45
			no response[a]	2	3.64
Total	70,000			55	

SOURCE: *Uganda Census of Agriculture* (1966), 3:18, Tables IV.4 and IV.6.
NOTE: This table allows for rough comparisons only, as acreage classes are not coterminous.
[a] The two committee members who gave no response to questions about the size of their landholdings were known to have large acreages, most of which they acquired during their work as *gombolola* chiefs. One said he could not reply because he had so much land he really did not know how much he had.

available. Land ownership has been a delicate subject in Bugisu since a plan of the protectorate government to declare all of Bugisu crown lands was interpreted by many Bagisu as a conspiracy to take their land away from them, and there is a fair chance that some of these figures are distorted. Unfortunately, the Census of Agriculture figures do not distinguish between landholdings in the plains and in the coffee-growing area, where they are much smaller. As all committee members of the BCU after 1964 were coffee growers, the comparisons between their landholdings and those of the agriculture survey would be more dramatic if the difference between plains and mountain holdings were controlled. Also, the inclusion of Sebei in the agriculture figures tends to skew these figures toward larger holdings, as Sebei was considerably less densely populated than Bugisu.

The great majority of BCU committee members with six or more acres of land bought, rather than inherited, most of it. Table 13 shows the relative proportions of land bought or inherited by BCU committee members according to each landholding size category used in the previous table.

Table 13. Number of BCU Committee Members' Land Bought or Inherited, according to Size of Holding

| Size in Acres | Number of BCU Committee Members[a] | | | | |
	Inherited All	Inherited Most	About Equal	Bought Most	Bought All
1-2	1	1			
3-5	1		2		1
6-12	2	1	3	5	5
13-25		2	2	6	2
26-35			2	2	1
36-50		1		2	
51-60			1		2
100		1		2	1
300-500				3	
Total	4	6	10	20	12

NOTE: BCU = Bugisu Cooperative Union.
[a] One man interviewed is excluded, as he neither bought nor inherited land.

Access to Wealth and the Exchange Bases of Support

The BCU committee occupied a pivotal position in the political structure that determined who among the Bagisu had access to economic benefits.

Political position or power was the most important key to wealth in colonial and postcolonial Bugisu. The union was crucial in the careers of a number of its committee members not only because it gave them direct access to political power and the economic resources necessary to increase it, but also because committee membership tended to provide resources that could be exchanged for access or recruitment to other positions of political power. Thus not only were political and economic positions integrally related, but also economic and political power tended to accrue to a fairly small group of men.

While there was relatively little difference between the absolute numbers of those political and business positions entered before and after men were elected to the BCU committee, there was a definite tendency for men to enter the higher-ranking political offices and the more highly capitalized businesses after rather than before their election. BCU committee membership by no means guaranteed further success in business or in politics. Success in business required both skill and luck, and there were relatively few higher political offices available. Committee membership, however, greatly assisted the political and business careers of some Bagisu. Four of the six who served as BCU president worked their way up through the cooperative to positions of considerable wealth and prestige in the district. None of these four had more than six years of formal education before they joined the committee. (The union sent two of them overseas for further education while they were committee officers.) Of the remaining two, one was already an established businessman before his election, the other served only briefly before being removed for misuse of authority and union funds.

Committee membership had less impact on upward mobility in employment than in trade or politics. In comparison to the total level of employment in Bugisu (total number employed in Bugisu in 1969 was 10,314, with over half this number in Mbale; total number of tax-paying heads of households in Bugisu in 1969 was over 70,000), a high proportion of committee members held salaried jobs, but most of these jobs were entered before committee membership. The average years of formal education completed by committee members was only 7.9. This was quite high in relation to the rest of the Bagisu, but it was well below requirements for the higher ranks of the civil service, so most committee members could not expect to achieve high status through employment. For this reason it was more advantageous for them to abandon employment altogether and concentrate on business and politics or to combine employment with business and politics.

Some education and early employment served many committee members as the first steps in upwardly mobile careers by introducing them to modern bureaucratic and political institutions and by providing them with cash and prestige in their local area. The men who successfully transferred their activities into politics and trade frequently achieved incomes much beyond what they could have earned in employment. The income of the men who served on the BCU committee in 1970 is reported in Table 14.

Table 14. Income Range of BCU Committee Members, 1970

Number of Men	Income (in thousands of shillings)
12	1-3.99
10	4-7.99
13	8-11.99
5	12-15.99
3	16-19.99
3	20+

NOTE: BCU = Bugisu Cooperative Union.

The income of the nine men on the committee in 1970 averaged 13,600 shillings for that year, with a range from 8,000 to 23,500 shillings. The average years of education completed by these nine men was 7.9, with a range from three to thirteen years. All but one started their careers in employment, but only the two with the greatest amount of formal education, both teachers, were still employed in 1970. Their range of income, however, paralleled the range of district administration salaries from subcounty chiefs and senior clerks to county chiefs or of cooperative salaries from bookkeepers to senior staff (Tables 4 and 5). Obviously some district administration and cooperative staff had other sources of income as well; at the least, many owned land in rural Bugisu, and a few had small businesses in town. They were, on the other hand, tied down by the requirements of a full-time job and the necessity to stay wherever their work demanded.

The BCU committee members were necessarily rural dwellers; they were eligible for their BCU position only by being a member of the GCS committee. Living on and farming their own land, they needed to spend much less of their income on housing and food than town workers did. This saving and the fact that they were not bound by the time limitations of regular jobs allowed committee members to exploit the allowances they received through investment in other sources of income. All of the committee members in 1970 had multiple sources of funds; all but two occupied more than two political or cooperative positions.

The BCU committee members who achieved high status and wealth did so by combining multiple positions and occupations in the recently established marketing and political systems with kin and affinal alliances based on the more traditional system of lineage organization. Political positions alone did not generate much income, but they provided a key element in these men's ability to accrue the several sources of income and power that enabled them to compete with civil servants and chiefs who enjoyed considerably higher levels of family privilege and formal education. The new channels of political participation thus diluted the effects of highly unequal education on income differentiation, rather than enhancing them, as Kelley (1971) and Kelley and Klein (1981) predicted. Only a few Bagisu held these positions, but their dependence on the rest of the Bagisu prevented them or the other ascendant groups from forming a separate class. I explain how the ascendancy of the politicians blocked class formation in the following section.

Status Group Competition and Constraints on Class Formation

The establishment of representative positions in the BCU and in the district council gave officeholders in these institutions formal ascendancy over the chiefs and civil servants who were subordinate to the council and over the trained staff who were subordinate to the BCU committee. Political office also provided access to incomes that rivaled those of the two previously ascendant groups. Like the chiefs and civil servants, the politicians enjoyed powers and privileges that markedly distinguished them from the rest of the Bagisu. Their desire to maintain and expand their own powers motivated their struggles with each other and with the state over control of the union. Different factions in Bugisu would continue to mobilize and manipulate peasant protest in their pursuit of these goals.

Like the chiefs and civil servants before them, the politicians performed functions essential to the state's goals of maintaining order and appropriating revenues. In the increasingly complex political economy of the district, the three groups played complementary roles, but they also competed with each other. The specialized civil service jobs undercut the power of the chiefs in their own areas, and both chiefs and civil servants were threatened by politicians' claims of popular sovereignty. The politicians themselves were threatened by the possibility that their rivals would win their positions in subsequent elections or that the state would reduce their authority.

All three groups were distinguished from the rest of the Bagisu by their wealth and by the essential functions they performed for the state. They were partially united by various common interests, but their dependence on peasant support, the differences in their own power bases, the opposition between them, and their susceptibility to state intervention in the organizations where they held office or employment kept their ascendancy over and differentiation from other Bagisu within tight bounds and prevented their forming a separate class. Thus, the same forces that these groups manipulated to achieve more wealth, land, and power than the rest of the Bagisu also limited the degree and forms of social differentiation between these groups and the rest of the Bagisu.

The local groups that competed against the state and each other derived power from positions created and sanctioned by the state, but they also depended on the Bagisu peasantry for their tenure and effective use of power in their positions. They mediated in a constant struggle between the peasantry and the state over crop prices, crop quality, and the conditions of exchange involved in selling the crop. They were simultaneously accountable to the state and to the peasantry and occupied different structural positions in their separate relations to each of these.

Cash cropping, administrative and bureaucratic employment, commerce, and political position all increased social and economic differentiation in Bugisu, but the three groups that benefited most from these activities — chiefly families, civil servants, and local politicians — cannot be defined as a class except in a limited sense and in a specific context. They cannot be consistently distinguished from the rest of the Bagisu by their relation to the means of production; though some of their members acquired considerably more land than most Bagisu had, others did not. In any event, most of them depended on agriculture as their economic base, and most of them continued to exploit their own labor. As Domar (1970) has suggested in an article that systematizes some of Marx's and others' ideas about rural precapitalist classes, any two, but never all three of the elements — free land, free peasants, and nonworking landowners — can exist simultaneously. Free land and free labor make a centralization of capital and production based on control of labor impossible. The members of these three ascendant Bagisu groups emerged as a class only in a limited political sense, through their mediating position in administration and in the organization of marketing and the appropriation of surplus by the state. Even though the politicians enjoyed a considerable advantage in rural commerce and consistently acted to maintain and strengthen this advantage, their success in commerce depended directly on their political and agricultural activities. Thus, although their commercial activities and income differentiated them from the rest of the peasants, they did not make them a separate class. All three groups enjoyed special powers and privileges and were aware of their common interests in defending them. Their utility to the colonial and national states, however, depended on their capacity to organize and mobilize the Bagisu masses. Their *class* identity was therefore with these masses.

Their capacity to organize the masses gave them a resource with which to bargain, in their own interests, against the state, and against each other. They could maintain this resource only by satisfying both the autochthonously defined, lineage-based requirements of high status and the newer expectations of a fair return for labor in cash crops. Their ascendance or dominance was strictly local, yet their functions fulfilled national demands. They were a class only in the sense of mediating specific political and commercial processes, and were only able to maintain their intermediary position by responding to two structurally opposed constituencies—the state and the peasants. The maintenance of their position, necessarily, served to represent the interests of their local constituents to the national government; at the same time it assured the national state's ability to appropriate surplus production. Their class position in the national structures that mediate the state's appropriation of value, moreover, depended on their functioning as local status groups with rights that had been defined in the struggle between the lineages and the BNA but that individual members could only maintain by conforming to lineage-based criteria for achieving high status. They could not form a separate class because their economic base and their political power remained embedded in the same relations to land and to production that defined the peasants as a class. At the local level they were thus members of the class of peasants.

The positions from which each group derived its special status created opposition between them—especially between the politicians, who were directly elected, and the chiefs, who worked in the same areas and had to satisfy local administration as well as Bagisu constituents. Because of opposed bases of power and divergent needs for mass mobilization, the three groups could not constitute a "class for itself" in either the local or the national context. Their specific situation as a mediating class essential to the state for the organizing of production, exchange, and surplus appropriation placed them in a position from which they could make important demands for the peasants as a commodity-producing and -exchanging class in and for itself. As separate status groups, each was constrained to make these demands to maintain the local power base necessary to its own functions as well as to promote and defend its particular privileges.

Finally, both the chiefs and the politicians, and in many cases civil servants, derived a considerable share of their income from agricultural activities. Their class position within crop production and commercialization systems was that of the Bagisu peasantry. Their own interests as peasant farmers usually were best served by mediating the interests of the Bagisu to the central government.

The economic centrality of peasant farmers in Bugisu restricted the development of class opposition. Even though the three ascendant status groups in Bugisu benefited greatly from the opportunities of their positions, their dependence on the Bagisu peasants for legitimation and support, together with their positions as producers in the same agricultural and commercial systems, led them to identify most of their interests with those of all of the Bagisu and forced them to balance these interests against those peculiar to their own status group. Thus the ascendant local groups generally allied themselves with the peasants and served as their intermediaries to the larger society and economy. The subordination of these status groups to the central state and the groups' dependence on the Bagisu masses prevented crystallization of a dominant class. Even in the limited political sense of serving specific mediating functions within national systems of administration and marketing, they formed only a fragmented intermediate class inseparably bound to the common interests of all the Bagisu.

Thus, their relations to the means of production and their dependence on political support from the peasants combined to locate all of these groups within the peasant class, and their opposition to each other restricted their ability to pursue common interests that might have eventually established them as a class separate from the peasants. Even their mediating functions within the national structures of state control and appropriation that defined the limited sense in which they could be called a class ultimately depended on their participation in the social and economic relations that identified the Bagisu peasantry as a class. Thus, the political sense in which these groups can be said to form a separate class is not only limited to their mediating functions, but it also applies only to a part of any individual member's social relations and activities. Nevertheless, the emergence and actions of these groups simultaneously differentiated them from the rest of the peasants and critically influenced the forms and outcomes of the peasants' struggles against the state. Any analysis of the class nature of these struggles must incorporate the ambiguities of these groups' class identity into its account of how these struggles evolve.

The Bagisu peasants controlled the primary means of production, and their lineage organization provided the basis for both administration and crop production. It was this control over both revenues and administration that made the peasantry strong enough to give local leaders a bargaining lever against the state. The leaders' dependence on the peasants created strong social constraints that effectively prevented the separation of interests and the oppositions necessary for class formation. These groups, and especially the politicians, were constrained to oppose those demands of the central state that would prejudice the economic position of the district's direct producers. Because the state ultimately controlled the only apparatus capable of direct appropriation and accumulation, these groups' obligation to oppose the state and to limit its powers effectively limited their own ability to accumulate means of production or exchange at rates that could have led to their formation as a separate class.

It is precisely because the possibilities for significant independent accumulation of wealth or capital were limited and because representation of the peasantry against the state provided the major avenue for individuals and groups to improve their own status that the groups considered here consistently challenged the state to achieve local autonomy and competed among themselves for local power bases. Economic predominance was effectively impossible; competition thus focused on the political means to power. These political means were ultimately rooted in an economic base, controlled in Bugisu by cohesive peasant communities. It is for this reason that individual and group strategies to gain power and status were only viable to the extent that they strengthened the political power of these communities against the state (see also Bunker, 1983a). The political power that resided in these peasant communities provided the essential basis for the ascendant groups' demands for local control against the state. These groups' fundamental dependence on the peasantry's political power, however, also limited their ability to form a separate class at the local level.

Their dependence on local support and their interest in and aspirations to local preeminence also limited their possibilities for uniting in political action with similarly placed ascendant groups in different districts across Uganda. This, in turn, impeded the potential for the Bagisu peasants to participate in a national class capable of developing its own political consciousness and political action. While it is impossible to extrapolate from the Bugisu experience to Uganda as a whole, it does seem that the peasant movements and opposition to the state that others have described are similarly local (see, e.g., Vincent, 1982; Brett, 1973; Kasfir, 1970), even when they occurred simultaneously in different parts of Uganda (see Mamdani, 1976). However similar the conflict between the state and the peasants was in various districts, the power bases for opposition to the state remained rooted in locally defined issues, strategies, and organizations. The political isolation of the different Uganda peasantries was exacerbated by organizational, cultural, and linguistic differences between them. In the absence of political unity and coordination between the ascendant groups of different districts, there was no way these differences could be overcome, and no possibility of class action by a national peasantry against the state or for the peasantry to take power over the state.

The following chapters will show how the local status groups competed with each other and with the state for peasant support, and how this competition, by limiting the power of all competitors, contributed to the maintenance of the peasants' economic and political centrality. They will also show that although the peasants maintained their power to veto the state's political and economic projects, and were therefore able to win concessions to their own economic demands at the local level, they could not develop or implement a political project of sufficient scope to affect contests for power at the national level.

NOTES

1. I have no idea how many men in Bugisu owned no land. Land shortage has been one of the major incentives, direct or indirect, for migration for at least the last 100 years. Relatives and friends did lend land to the landless in different situations and for various considerations, so that some technically landless men did in fact earn at least a partial living from their crops. See Brock (1969:17, 18) for a fuller discussion of landlessness.

2. The division of land usually started at the sons' maturity and was completed when the father died. Each son was supposed to receive some land when he was circumcised, which generally occurred between the ages of twelve to sixteen in the central and southern areas and between sixteen to twenty-one in the north (La Fontaine, 1960; Heald, 1968).

Status and wealth were always highly correlated in Bugisu. Many fathers therefore delayed circumcision or gave little or no land to a circumcised son. Sons were usually as eager to have land as their fathers were eager to keep it. The timing and the amount of land-giving were frequently causes of violent conflict between fathers and sons and between brothers. Dividing land among all sons and at different periods of time led to increasing fragmentation. Because wealth was associated with both land and number of wives, the fragmentation of land between sons affected the large landholdings the most and increased its leveling effects.

3. The largest privately owned coffee plantation in Bugisu, with 5,000 trees, was chosen as an experimental and demonstration site by the Ministry of Agriculture, which worked it intensively with trained cultivators for five years.

All of the coffee grown remained the property of the owner of the land. The consensus about his case was that without such luck and assistance there would have been no profitable way to develop anywhere near that large a coffee plantation.

4. Six thousand seven hundred fifty-eight (6,758) were employed in Mbale municipality (Uganda Protectorate, *Uganda Statistical Abstracts*, 1970). These would include employees in the national, provincial, and district civil service.

5. In Mbale (population 23,539, provisional results, 1969 census), total cash wages paid in private industry were 8,694,000 shillings; in public services, 13,232,000 shillings. In Bugisu District but outside of Mbale, private industry paid 5,788,000 shillings in wages, and the public services paid 5,705,000. The private industry figures include BCU, Masaaba Cooperative Union (MCU), and GCS salaries.

6. These were the BCU and MCU, which handled all of Bugisu's cotton crop after separating from the BCU in 1963.

7. Subgrade schools were community controlled and supported. Standards and wages tended to be much lower than in regular government schools, but fees were much less.

8. Mobility within the civil service or cooperative staffs was much slower than it was in either politics or business, but the rewards for high-level civil service or cooperative staff positions were relatively high. Rank within these jobs reflected objective qualifications like education and experience much more than political or trade positions did. If a man were sufficiently qualified to enter the civil service at a professional level, his chances of advancement within a bureaucratic system were much greater than they would have been in the much less stable spheres of leadership and business. Civil servants in the upper levels tended to have consistent career histories; most rose through the civil service. The most usual exceptions to this rule were men who were made chiefs because of political service, but chiefs tended to have less education than other civil service employees at similar rates of pay. Highly educated men were clearly not dependent on multiple roles to achieve high status, although many upper-level civil servants invested part of their wages in business.

9. Political and cooperative positions are ranked according to size of constituency, type of authority, and the extent to which they open access to other sources of power. See Bunker (1975:67-9, 169-73) for a fuller discussion of how ranking was done.

10. Four Sebei served on the committee at different times during the years before the Sebei founded their own union. These four men are not considered in any of the following tabulations.

4

The Struggles for BCU Autonomy, 1955-58

By 1954 the Bagisu leaders had first mobilized and then formalized a power base that allowed them to present progressively stronger demands to the British. The colonial government during this period had been moving to accommodate African demands for more autonomy and political participation throughout Uganda, and the creation of the BCU coincided with more general sentiments of nationalism and the beginning of independence movements. Although stated colonial policy was to prepare the way for African self-determination, the British continued to control all of the higher levels of power and even local organization was subject to close supervision. Many, though not all, of the divisions that were to emerge later between Bagisu competitors for power remained latent during this period, as most Bagisu leaders made common cause against British control. The colonial government's main concern—and the focus of its own exercise of power—was that the transition to cooperative control not diminish the efficiency or the profitability of coffee collection and processing. The Bagisu leaders, for their part, were anxious to continue expanding their powers.

The union was still very susceptible to direct state intervention through the actions of the BNA, the CCD, and the Bugisu Coffee Board. The new leaders responded by forming strong alliances, based on their overlapping memberships in marketing and administrative institutions (i.e., the cooperatives and the district and county councils). The tensions between the state's statutory power over the cooperative and the power that the Bagisu leaders could generate through political alliances and popular mobilization caused major administrative problems both in the BCU and in the district government. The state could impose its own legislation and its agencies' supervision on the union, but the conflicts of the early years show clearly that alliances built on common interests at the local level could limit the effectiveness and thwart the objectives of state control.

The personal characteristics, beliefs, and goals of the men who occupied the newly created representative positions had been molded by their long fight against the state. These personalities influenced the forms and outcomes of their continuing struggle to secure and amplify the powers that they had now won. Preeminent among the new officeholders was Samson Kitutu, co-founder of the eventually outlawed Bugisu Welfare Association in 1923, an ardent champion of ethnic rights and political power, a strong voice in the district council, and the BCU's first president. Alone among the men who eventually served as BCU president, Kitutu spoke no English and claimed, many believed falsely, to understand none. He was also the only BCU president who had not been employed in a civil service or cooperative bureaucracy in some job requiring Western-defined technical or managerial skills. He usually wore a *kanzu*, the long gown adopted from the Arabs, but thought of as the traditional men's garment, rather than Western clothes. Immensely popular among the Bagisu, particularly for his "fearless" willingness to confront and debate even the governor, his actions and statements indicate that he saw himself as an elder, a father of a whole new pan-Bagisu unity in which the common interests, loyalties, mutual obligations, and authority patterns of the lineages were broadened to encompass the entire ethnic group. True to this vision of himself and his relation to the Bagisu, he saw himself as dominant but also as bound to support and be supported by the other prominent men in the new social unit, men who had fought with him to establish the cooperatives and to widen the representative base of the district council. Notions of a formal separation between private and public goods and authority were alien to him; both were at his disposal, and he should use both as needed to lead and assist his people; but clearly his ability to do so well depended upon his having the requisite wealth, dignity, and power. He was owner of a substantial store in his home area by the time his presidency ended, but the stories I heard about him stressed his courage, loyalty, and dedication to the Bagisu rather than the personal benefits he derived from his position. His son, however, who followed him into politics and became an MP, was widely feared and distrusted for personal use of public goods. Not only did this son not behave like a lineage elder in redistributing much of what he took but the Bagisu's expectations of public servants had also changed in the intervening decade.

The other political notables with whom Kitutu worked also defined themselves and their positions in terms of the long struggle for ethnic identity and rights against the British, the Asians, and the Baganda. Together with Kitutu, they took their new positions in the euphoria and with the hopes and expectations of having just won a major political victory. They responded with deep anger, indignation, and growing frustration to the barriers the state's agencies placed in the way of what they felt were their proper rights and obligations.

The Continued Decline of the Chiefs and the Ascendancy of Elected Representatives

The fervor of these popularly elected representatives' struggle against central state supervision of the BCU and the district council exacerbated the representatives' conflicts with the civil servants and the chiefs. The position of the civil servants as a group was weakened, as many went to work for the BCU or were elected as members of the district council, where they made common cause with BCU leaders.

Implementation of the 1955 Local Government Ordinance had brought about significant changes in the distribution of power. In 1956, forty-three of the seventy-seven seats were filled by representatives directly elected from the subcounties. The seven senior officers of the district administration remained on the council, as did various influential men appointed or coopted in various ways, but the district commissioner could now only attend meetings by invitation. Not only was the majority of the council now elected by popular vote, but also the council itself had greatly increased powers. It was in charge of running the district administration, including the preparation of its estimates and the raising of revenue through taxation. This responsibility gave council members supervisory powers over the chiefs and over the departments of police and prisons, health, agriculture, roads, and primary education, all of which were part of the local civil service.

The faction that had gained control of the newly constituted council was dominated by officials of the BCU. These men were particularly eager to expand the control of the Bagisu over their own affairs. The chiefs and their families, both because they constituted a small and exclusive group which had hitherto controlled almost all the power accessible to the Bagisu and because they were the direct agents of colonial domination, continued to be a natural target of this faction.

The movement against the state defined the council as representative of Bagisu popular power. The councillors thus tended to see themselves rather than the chiefs as legitimate authorities in their areas. In fact, the individual councillor had no formal power, for the chief continued to be the official executive power. The councillor, however, belonged to the group that ultimately controlled the chiefs. Between 1956 and 1959 the council as a body could recommend both appointments and promotions for the chiefs. Although the public service committee assumed this function in 1959, the council elected this committee until 1966, when it became a central body appointed by the government. Thus, though the chiefs were technically independent of the councillors in the execution of their local duties, the threat of opposition, recrimination or accusation, and dismissal gave the councillors considerable power over them.

The district commissioner attempted to protect and encourage the chiefs, but he himself had lost considerable power. The council could reject his advice, and it was the provincial commissioner, rather than he, who had the power to approve or disapprove the council's decisions. As the dominant faction of the council saw itself in opposition to the state, the district commissioner's intervention frequently only served to intensify disputes.

The district commissioner himself felt beleaguered and incapacitated by the new powers of the district council. In the *Bugisu District Annual Report* for 1956, he reported attempts by district councillors

> to lord it over the Chiefs by announcing their own personal powers of appointment and discipline. . . . Powers of appointment and discipline of Chiefs of Gombolola status and above are now vested in a political body. This situation, which appears to be contrary to all accepted practice, caused the Chiefs distress, and much regret was felt that the District Commissioner's influence and powers seem to have been weakened. Every attempt was made to keep up morale, particularly of senior chiefs who still sit on the council, but unfortunately they have not learned . . . to stand together as an official group, in the face of possible unpopularity. Fortunately, a salutary lesson was taught to unofficials when a proposed appointment for Gombolola chieftainship was not confirmed by Government. (BNA, 1956:6)

The same report went on to describe a

> struggle for political power in the Council. In past years . . . this has of course been concentrated in the office and person of the Secretary-General, who has also been the Chairman of the Council, a post not highly regarded. Government's declared policy of building up this post was opposed by a small group of unofficials who were making . . . a determined attempt to achieve power. The "pressure group" was made up young men of some education,

not much experience, and with leanings toward an extremist or tribal attitude . . . circumstances gave them an entirely exaggerated power and influence. The majority of its members happen to be employees of the Bugisu Cooperative Union, Ltd. (perhaps not unnaturally, as the Union is itself somewhat an expression of tribal nationalism). The committee of the Union . . . went to the extreme in failing to impose any restrictions on their participation at all, but allowed these men to employ as much of the Union's time and also transport and office machinery as they wished on political ends. By the time the new Council had settled down, it was clear that the group largely controlled the voting in the Council, with its unofficial majority. (BNA, 1956:7)

The plaintive note struck by the district commissioner when he wrote about a situation "contrary to all accepted practice" and the "regret that his influence and powers seem to have been weakened," together with statements in the rest of his report for that year that the chiefs were not performing well because of their fear of the councillors, can be read as both an appeal and an excuse to the higher authority from which he derived his own power. The colonial state had granted ample new powers to a previously disenfranchised group, which was now competing directly for the power that his office had previously controlled. With this new grant of power had gone control over some of his former responsibilities. He implicitly reported that without his former powers he was unable to perform his duties, and that the new power-holders were not fulfilling theirs properly. The contradiction on the next page of his report between his calling the militant faction a "small group" in one line and his admission that that group actually controlled a majority of the council in another can be seen as an attempt to discredit his opposition while complaining—or advising—of their strength. He repeated the same theme more explicitly the next year, when he wrote: "The morale of the chiefs could not be considered high as it suffered considerably from the irresponsible politicians, and the ever present knowledge that appointments were to a large extent in the hands of the Councillors. This constituted a serious threat to the maintenance of law and order" (BNA, 1957:4).

It is fairly clear from the *District Annual Reports* and from the minutes of council meetings that while the BCU and the district council were both assuming strong antigovernment attitudes, they were directing them at the district-level agencies of the state. Both the BCU and the district council had been empowered by the colonial state, and any increase in their power would have to come from the same source. Thus, they did not directly challenge the central government. They were far more concerned to gain control over local marketing and administration and to assert their ascendancy over the chiefs and civil servants who had until then implemented BNA policies and decisions. Their struggle against the state, their competition against the other status groups, their strategies to expand their own power and wealth, and their need to mobilize peasant protest against the BNA, the CCD, and the board were inextricably intertwined.

BCU Relations with the State's Agencies

After the BCU was formally founded in 1954, its officers moved into the building that had been constructed with BCS reserve funds. Sir Andrew Cohen, then governor of Uganda, had been instrumental in promoting the idea of cooperation in the district. He personally had intervened to help the Bagisu leaders on several occasions and had met with them in the district. He dedicated the new building in a ceremony attended by many Bagisu and government officials. The tone of his address and of the Bagisu leaders' replies stressed cooperation and congratulations between the colonial state and the Bagisu; their major theme was the coming of the age of the Bagisu as part of a modern society and economy.

The cordial sentiments expressed at this ceremony masked numerous unresolved conflicts between the extent of the BCU's autonomy and the strength of the state's control in marketing the district's crops. Europeans still controlled both collection and sales as well as many of the union's activities. Europeans and Asians still occupied key staff positions.

The interweaving of politics and cooperation that had arisen during the drive for greater Bagisu participation in the district's affairs and the populist approach of the union's leaders often looked more like demagogic corruption than business management to the colonial officers responsible for various aspects of the union's affairs. Competition for control between BCU officers and colonial agents made the union seem turbulent, contentious, and inefficient. Conflicts between clans and between different regions of Bugisu spilled over into fights within the new organization. The political activities and concerns of many of the BCU's organizers, especially those of the full-time staff members, contributed to both the tensions and the inefficiencies that the union suffered. Bitter sectarian disputes between coffee and cotton growers, which eventually led to a schism in the union, started during these early years.

Much of the union's early years were taken up by its leaders' struggle to establish an independent power base from which to oppose the powers of the state. To do this, these leaders had to expand their own powers and their control over resources that they could use to reward support, compliance, and organization among the Bagisu. Control over prices and the disposition of surplus funds was crucial to their plans. The establishment of the union was probably the most important single step in the Bagisu's struggle to control the sale of their own coffee, but the local power it granted was strictly qualified by the state's formal controls, through both the Bugisu Coffee Board and the CCD.

The relation between the BCU committee and the board was the first major issue discussed within the union. All of the committee members objected to the bylaws of the board, believing that they gave the board far too much power. The union's approval of the bylaws was a necessary condition for their adoption, so the committee started a campaign against them with fairly high confidence. The 1955 Bugisu *District Annual Report* gives one version of the struggle:

A major political argument started with the BCU Ltd. over the Bugisu Coffee Bill. The Bill had been modelled on the Ordinance governing the relationship of the Kilimanjaro Native Cooperative Union and the Tanganyika Coffee Board; as specifically requested by a report of Bagisu who had visited Moshi, and as confirmed by the BCS Board including Union representatives. Unfortunately, as so frequently happens, the publication of a new Bill drew attention to various legal forms which were happily accepted in previous practice, and in particular to the fact that the Board was to have overall legal powers, a situation which had always existed, but had been of course obscured by the forward administrative policy of devolving power to the Union. Some of the BCU leaders clearly let power go to their heads and used strong words at times; and one extremely impertinent memorandum was addressed to the governor.

Finally the BCU appealed to the District Council for support, and a sub-committee of the latter produced some relatively moderate recommendations for further concessions to the Union. In discussions, Government went a long way toward pacifying the violent extremists, but when finally the Bill went to a Select Committee of Legislative Council, some most sweeping changes were made conferring on the Union by law duties and responsibilities which it had always been felt would have been better conferred by administrative practice in the past. The Bill eventually became law in November, and although an extremist party in the Union led by the President had always threatened that they would accept no bill at all, it was clear that this did not command general support;

and particularly in view of the concessions that had been won, all indications were that the matter was happily settled. (BNA, 1955:8)

In fact, the matter had not been happily settled at all; eight years of intense conflict between the BCU committee and the board followed. The committee's discontent with the board's bylaws was exacerbated by the manner in which they were finally forced to accept them. The BCU had been founded in 1954, but it was still not officially registered a year later. At the BCU general meeting, the commissioner of cooperative development informed the members that if they did not accept the board bylaws as a part of the Coffee bill, the BCU would not be registered (speech of E. M. Kerr, CCD, entered into BCU Annual General Meeting Minutes, 1954). All indications are that the general membership, and not simply the "extremist" faction described in the report, adamantly opposed the bylaws, but this threat settled the matter in the state's favor. The state could still exact compliance from the Bagisu leaders by the threat of depriving them entirely of the formal organizational power base that they sought. The *District Annual Report* does not mention the CCD's blatant and heavy-handed use of its powers in the supposedly happy settlement of this matter.

The union's leaders strongly objected to the board's control over the coffee reserve funds. The BCU committee members found this European control of funds, which they considered their own, particularly galling. For most purposes, the committee had access to these funds only in the form of loans, which the board decided whether or not to make. The union could also borrow from banks, but, again, only with the board's approval. The committee frequently and bitterly complained that the union had to pay interest to the board and the banks instead of being free to use money from the fund.

From 1955 until 1958, there were more Bagisu on the board than Europeans. There were five expatriate government officers, five representatives from the union, a representative from the district council, and the secretary-general of the district. The balance of votes, however, was very delicate.

The district commissioner was the board's chairman, and as such had both a deliberative and a tie-breaking vote. The secretary-general, though a Mugisu, was appointed to his office by the commissioner. He had a seat in the district council and served as liaison between the district council and the commissioner. Although he had strongly supported the establishment of the BCU, he was clearly identified as the colonial state's representative rather than the union's. Because of the secretary-general's ambiguous position and the extra, tie-breaking vote of the district commissioner, neither the colonial administration nor the Bagisu felt they had a clear majority on the board. There was considerable friction, and committee members and other Bagisu spoke out harshly against the board and the BNA.

The position of the secretary-general frustrated everyone. The Bagisu charged that there was no way that the secretary-general could oppose the wishes of the state that empowered and paid him, and that for all intents and purposes he represented colonial interests. The Europeans, on the other hand, saw him as an eloquent and effective champion of Bagisu interests, and they used his place on the board to counter union criticism of the board's composition. They claimed that the board contained a majority of Bagisu and therefore adequately incorporated the idea of Bagisu control.

Probably the most frustrated person on the board was the secretary-general himself. He was continually attacked in the meetings of both the board and the district council and was widely criticized throughout the district. The antagonism generated toward him over his membership on the board affected his position with the council, making his job much more difficult. The appointment of a new secretary-general in 1957 only exacerbated the problem. The former secretary-general at least had the advantage of his early association with the cooperative movement, and despite the criticism, he was widely respected among the Bagisu. His successor was less prominent, and he took over at a time when the conflicts between the board and the union were intensifying. He was frequently rebuked in the district council for his failure to support Bagisu aspirations, and there were numerous requests for his dismissal. This unfortunate man eventually withdrew from public life, bought land outside his own lineage area, and became a recluse. When I went to his home to request an interview, he claimed he was someone else.[1]

The secretary-general's and the board's task had been complicated by the actions of the newly appointed district commissioner. In his first meeting with the members of the BCU's committee in 1954, he had replied to the committee's objections to the proposed bylaws by scolding them rather severely and calling them, among other things, stupid. The committee had responded with a strained and dignified protest against such intemperate language and adjourned the meeting. The members later sent a formal protest to the provincial commissioner, the district commissioner's immediate superior, and thereafter strongly protested his position on the board. The district commissioner may not have been initially popular, or might never have become so, but his heated outburst remained a sore point throughout his tenure and colored many of the contacts between the BCU and the official administration. The secretary-general, as his representative, shared in the opprobrium against him, thus raising personal as well as political issues to considerable importance on the board and certainly contributing to the difficult times encountered in its meetings.

Conflicts of Interest: Issues and Priorities

I can only speculate about the basic reasons or ideas underlying the conflict between the colonials and the Bagisu, as my interviews were surely influenced by the passing of time and events. I did have access to a wealth of correspondence between the contending parties and between them and the higher-level state agencies, as well as to minutes of the BCU committee and the Annual General Meeting. These are all highly biased statements, but they do recount key events and show the reasons and motives that the various groups alleged. These sources allow some tentative inferences about the motives that fueled the struggle for power.

For example, it was impossible to inquire directly about the attitudes of the European district officers who strove to maintain their power on the board, but it is worth noting that the Bagisu, or at least some of the committee members or leaders, imputed their motives to personal benefit and prejudice against the Bagisu. The success of the coffee crop continued to be important for the success of the district and the protectorate economy, and in this sense the welfare of each colonial officer depended on the success of the crop. This in itself certainly explains part of their reluctance to hand power over to the Bagisu. The colonial officers had certain ideas about how a business or a cooperative should be run. Some of these were based on whatever degree of information they had about the world coffee market, the economics of coffee growing and processing in the district, and the sales relation between the two. Others were based on a not totally relevant set of norms derived from British culture about how an organization should be run and what the appropriate conduct of its officeholders should be.

The primary concern of the British colonials was that the union should be run honestly and efficiently, that coffee production should be regulated in such a way as to ensure the good quality of the crop, and that there should be a profit. It is also possible that they had an idea as a group that they did not really wish to see their own jobs Africanized too fast. All were there by choice, and it is perhaps significant that few of the members of the board returned to England at independence; most stayed on in East Africa, often with considerably reduced authority and in some cases in private or self-employment.

Speculation about the concerns and priorities of the Bagisu leaders is considerably easier. While records of the deliberations of the colonial officers among themselves are very difficult to find, the BCU had kept complete records of all its general and committee meetings since some months before its official founding. Also, the colonial officers had far greater access to the meetings and records of the Bagisu's meetings than the Bagisu had to theirs, and official reports and correspondence, which are still available, carry considerable information about the European interpretation of what the Africans wanted.

Bagisu were limited in their struggle for autonomy by having to appeal to the colonial state, which delegated authority to their positions. The issues that they raised as justification for their attacks on the board were directed to both their own members and the state. They were in the difficult position of having to use the power they derived from the state to mobilize the Bagisu and to oppose the state at the same time. Since they did not have a sufficient power base in Bugisu to oppose the state directly, the tactics they could use against the state were limited and almost entirely subject to the state's continued acquiescence to local pressure.

The leaders had stressed in their campaign to found the BCU that the Bagisu could receive much more money for their crops if the trade were cooperatively controlled. Not only would the middlemen be eliminated, they said, but the British theft of large portions of what should belong to the Bagisu would end. The leaders had achieved power through these claims, and in order to maintain their power they had to provide at least some of what they had promised. When these leaders took over the union, immediate and visible evidence that they were fulfilling their promises would be high prices for coffee to the peasants. They were therefore less concerned to continue the accumulation of a solid financial base for the union. The Bagisu viewed the union as already tremendously wealthy and hardly in need of solicitous attention. The leaders of the BCU were much more interested in questioning the cooperative officers about the disposition of the reserve funds than they were in listening to arguments that the coffee prices they were demanding for the peasants would produce a loss for the union.

The union was also seen as a means to equalize the highly unbalanced relationship between the Bagisu and the other ethnic groups. This goal was especially important for the leaders, who had had more contact with Europeans and Asians and were in a position to experience directly the Bagisu's subordination to these groups. Europeans and Asians dominated government, trade, industry, and employment. They were obviously better off than the Africans, and their legally sanctioned privileges maintained the Africans in a disadvantageous position. Control of the union and its considerable resources was seen by the BCU as a means to compete with these two groups and to affirm that Africans deserved equal treatment and were equally competent.

The British and Asian dominance of commerce clearly symbolized ethnic inequality. The absence of African trading firms in Mbale and the paucity of African trade in the rural areas of Bugisu were recurring themes throughout the meetings of the first committee under President Samson Kitutu. While there was little suggestion that the union could or should do anything for individual Bagisu businessmen, committee statements frequently invoked the lack of Bagisu-controlled business to justify the union's drive to expand its activities to credit and savings, to starting a cooperative consumer goods department, to control of more cotton ginneries, to the establishment of a Ghee factory, a leather-processing plant, a restaurant and maize mills, and to office rentals. The board and the CCD opposed all of these proposed activities, and only a few of them ever materialized.

The same issues of ethnic rights, competence, and privileges came to a bitter head over the future "ownership" or control of the coffee-processing mill being constructed with coffee reserve funds. The Bagisu leaders maintained that as the coffee mill was being constructed with profits withheld from the sale of the Bagisu's coffee, and as they were the Bagisu farmers' legitimate representatives, the BCU should own the mill and its committee should control its operation. The BNA and the European members of the board maintained that the Bagisu were not competent to run the mill and that it should therefore remain under the ownership and control of the board.

The Bagisu leaders effectively linked their demands for autonomy with the notion that their union should serve to establish the Bagisu as equal to Europeans and Indians in rights, abilities, and resources in their campaign to stimulate and direct popular resentment against the board. They used the board as a symbol of Bagisu subordination to greater European skill, knowledge, and power. They encouraged the Bagisu to see the BCU as a base for ethnic rights and resistance to the British rather than as an exclusively economic institution. By presenting themselves as champions of the Bagisu against colonial power, the BCU leaders were able to gain more power, suggesting as they did that the more control they had the greater rewards they could offer to the Bagisu (Bunker, 1984b).

The issue of employment continued to be highly important as well. The Bagisu were very eager to take over the responsible and high-paying jobs in the industry then held by Europeans and Asians. Control over employment was strategically crucial to the BCU committee, as it could use appointments of politically powerful and well-connected civil servants to build stronger alliances against the board. Technically, the committee had the right to select these employees, or at least to argue very strongly to the board that they be appointed. Once again, the CCD was able to use its powers to hint very directly that if the union did not accept and retain the "expert and experienced professionals" who, in the CCD's view, were essential to the industry's smooth and profitable running, the union would not be registered. Once again, the committee officers acquiesced, but, as with their acceptance of the board, they did so with bad will, and their resentment against the European staff created considerable friction and numerous problems. The committee, and especially Kitutu, came to feel that the only acceptable management was one highly amenable to frequent and direct intervention by the committee.

The role of the CCD in this situation was difficult for the Bagisu to accept, since the CCD had been the champion of Bagisu control of the union and had worked with its leaders to fulfill the requirement of having viable local societies in order to take over the union. Now it was in the position of communicating, justifying, and enforcing the board's and the state's regulations and orders.

In actual practice, the threat that the Bagisu leaders could direct popular resentment against the CCD and against the board moderated these agencies' use of their formal powers. Ironically, the state insisted on maintaining its own power, but its agents often restricted themselves to reprimanding the union for not taking their advice. Two incidents show most clearly their reluctance to use their powers, one a clear case of fraud by committee members, the second a highly questionable consideration of a building bid.

In 1955 Kitutu was hospitalized for some time because of a nervous collapse allegedly precipitated by his conflicts with the board. He was replaced as president during his illness by S. M. Masika. In January 1956 the commissioner for cooperative development convened a special general meeting in which he produced evidence that Masika and J. N. K. Wakholi, the committee secretary, had made a contract with C. H. Patel, an Indian who owned a supply house in Mbale, to buy all of the building materials that were to be sold to members of the GCSs. The president and the secretary had ordered two large shipments of iron sheet from Patel at highly inflated prices without informing the rest of the committee about either the contract or the purchase of the sheets. There was a clear implication they had received kickbacks from Patel. When the committee learned about this purchase, it ordered the two members to return the iron sheets. Patel refused to accept them back and threatened to sue.

The commissioner for cooperative development urged the union to hire a lawyer and defend its case, saying that it would be dangerous for the union to acquire a reputation as an easy mark for unscrupulous businessmen. He said that since the president and the secretary had acted illegally, the Indian had no defensible claim in court. The meeting, led by Kitutu, refused this advice. Kitutu said that Masika and Wakholi were their sons and brothers, that they therefore should not send the matter outside the union for settlement, and that furthermore they should pay the Indian the amount necessary to avoid a lawsuit. The commissioner expressed his strong disapproval, but did not persist in his urgings; nor did the board take any action to change the meeting's decision. When the commissioner finished his final speech, one of the committee members moved that Wakholi and Masika be dismissed from the committee. The meeting passed this motion, but in the next minute appointed the two men as members of the Bugisu Coffee Board. Note that the board, by virtue of the fact that it controlled union expenditures, had the power to stop payment and to fight the case in court. Similarly the CCD had the power to prosecute the two committee members. Neither agency used these powers.

The second case involved considerably more money, and the motives of different agencies are harder to untangle. The board invited bids for the construction of the new coffee mill. Instead of accepting the lowest and quickest bid, they accepted a higher and longer one. The commissioner again appealed to the general meeting, explaining that there was no justification for accepting this bid and that it was a waste of money. He said that he was ashamed that five of the seven Bagisu on the board had voted to accept this bid, and urged the meeting to direct their representatives on the board to reconsider their vote. The meeting refused and instead resolved that its representatives had been right. When the CCD appealed to the governor, the latter decided that the people should choose whomever they wanted as their builders.

As I did not have access to the discussions of the board, and as the answers I got from people on the board at that time were ambiguous, contradictory, or both, I can only speculate on the reasons for the CCD's lack of success and the choice of the more expensive bidder against all expert advice. Five out of seven of the African members would not have been sufficient by themselves to constitute a majority of the board. They would have been able to put through such a motion only if some of the Europeans voted with them. There is no reason to conclude that the Europeans would have been united in their choice of the bid. Nor is there any reason to dismiss the possibility that European officers may have been bribed. Bugisu has been full of rumors of official corruption, colonial and independent, since well before 1956.

These two incidents of state agents' disapproving but refraining from intervention suggest several interpretations. The first of these is fairly obvious: the state was in no way presenting a monolithic front to the Bagisu, and different departments and different officers were frequently acting at cross purposes, occasionally with such curious results that the possibility of corruption is the first explanation to occur to the imagination. The second is that different branches of government were willing to countenance some fairly irregular procedures to reduce conflict on the board over specific decisions in the union, even though the union was still de jure subject to much stricter control by the board than was in fact exercised. The third is that the CCD approach of rational appeal to the general meetings to overrule some decision of the committee almost never worked, because it usually evoked a response from the meeting in defense of their own committee members, but the CCD felt that the risk of directly overruling the committee and further alienating the Bagisu was too great.

As I was not able to obtain records of board meetings, all of this interpretation is based on records of union meetings in which board meetings were reported. I found that interviews with people who had been in the board meetings simply did not correspond with the documentary evidence. It seems that the relationship between the board and the union was so complicated that many of the actors then were now confusing what each body was doing or was responsible for. It is fairly clear from various pieces of correspondence and interviews that many of the board meetings were very tempestuous.

Kitutu remarked in an address prior to the selection of BCU representatives to the board that he thought the meeting should consider very carefully whom it elected, as the Europeans were very clever, could convince the Africans of things that were not correct, and often hurried the meetings and the discussion in order to confuse the Bagisu. One of the European board members told me that Kitutu frequently became very agitated during the meetings, and at one had to be taken to the hospital because he had lost control of himself. Whether the tensions of his fights on the board also caused his longer hospitalization shortly afterward, or whether for other reasons Kitutu was moving toward emotional problems that would temporarily incapacitate him, his feelings and their expression in board meetings certainly contributed to the high degree of animosity on and toward the board. At any rate, difficult as it is with only partial records to disentangle what happened on the board, it is clear that the Bagisu were unhappy about not having more control of the union. Nevertheless, they left the board staff in charge of maintaining accounts and handling almost all activities related to crop improvement.

The BCU committee's relation with the CCD was equally cloudy. The CCD during all of this time was left in charge of reviewing the BCU books and controlling advances to societies—a function that should have been done by BCU staff. While the CCD frequently expressed disapproval over the policies and activity of the committee, it intervened much less often than it had the power to do. The district cooperative officer did on several occasions appeal to the government to invalidate a board or committee decision, but even then, as in the case of the building bids, the government tended to allow the Bagisu to go their own way.

The union's and especially the committee's prime interest in power during this time seems to have been centered on direct access to controlling wealth, in the form of management of surplus funds, the letting of contracts and purchases, appointments to jobs, and the fixing of coffee prices and bonuses. Control over these decisions would give the BCU committee more resources to exchange in the district for more support both from the membership in general and with other power-holders. Some of them would also provide the means for personal enrichment.

These same powers demanded by the committee were among the most crucial for the maintenance of efficiency and low costs. For this reason the state insisted on maintaining final control. Its agents' reluctance to exercise their own powers did not extend to the crucial issues of crop prices or staff appointments, nor were there any concessions on the issue of who would control the mill.

The Management Staff: In-House Conflict

Much of the competition for power between the committee and the board was replayed in the committee's relations with the professional staff, and especially with its European manager, Roland G. Woods. Woods was hired at CCD insistence and against the committee's wishes. For both the committee and high-placed Bagisu members of the staff, he represented an obstacle in their own use of the BCU.

Woods had been working in Bugisu since 1929, when he was hired to manage the BCS. He had been in charge of training most of the Bagisu who were accepted for upper-level employment. He was generally thought of as totally honest, very exacting, and severe in the case of any malfeasance or omission by those who worked under him. Some cooperative leaders claimed he was prejudiced against the Bagisu. Men who worked successfully under his tutelage, almost all of whom went on to fairly high positions in various fields, described him as extraordinarily hardworking and dedicated and an exceptional teacher. Bagisu whose work he did not find satisfactory portrayed him in considerably less favorable terms.

There is little doubt that Woods did his work efficiently and well. There is also little doubt that he was the most prominent reminder that the Bagisu did not yet fully control their own union but had to bow to European desires about high-level appointments. He was an accessible and vulnerable symbol. He encountered a high degree of criticism and obstruction in his work, especially from the committee, which officially set his policy for him. The committee complained that he was arrogant and short with them and took little interest in their ideas. The records do show that he attended very few of their meetings. He complained to me that the committee never asked him to, and very seldom even consulted him (interview, Nairobi, 1970).

The committee was especially eager to expand the popular base of its own support. For this reason it was more interested in paying high prices to the peasants and was directly opposed to any plans for improving efficiency or coffee quality that might alienate its followers. It was also anxious to maintain the strong support of other powerful Bagisu. The Bagisu whom committee members wished to see in the manager's role had strong political and family connections in the district. These men technically were working under the European manager, but the community of interest between them and the committee made them natural allies against Woods.

The CCD had insisted that the basic staff arrangements be taken over fairly directly from the BCS. This entailed a continuation of the BCMCo. staffing arrangements, as many of the key personnel working for that company had been seconded civil servants employed by the BCS. A number of Bagisu had been appointed to various staff positions before the union itself was established, and it was from the Bagisu who had stayed successfully in those positions that the African members of the staff were chosen. The major exception to this was Paulo Mugoya, who the committee insisted be appointed assistant coffee manager. He had worked for a while for the BCS but had been returned to the CCD because of problems in his work. British supervisors in both the CCD and the BCS saw him as a contentious, arrogant, and incompetent manipulator who had exploited his kinship and political ties to rise in the civil service and who continued to use these ties to thwart their attempts to discipline and direct his work. There was direct and open hostility between him and Woods, who had been BCS manager when Mugoya worked for that agency.

This enmity complicated Woods's position and work. Woods had opposed Mugoya's appointment as assistant coffee manager, but there was little he could do about it. Mugoya came from a powerful, well-educated, chiefly family. Because of his education and well-placed family connections, he had held a series of government jobs. Most of these, including his BCS work, were agricultural and cooperative-related jobs; he had also worked closely with the organizers of the union. He was a strong force in the district council and thus in an important position in relation to the committee, most of whose members were also on the district council. Mugoya obviously had much greater access to and influence over the committee than would be normal in conventional staff-committee relations in a cooperative, and his privileged position enabled him to circumvent many of Woods's directives and any sanctions Woods might have wished to apply to him.

Woods got on considerably better with the next African in the union hierarchy, V. P. Mungoma, from central Bugisu; he was the Bugisu representative in the legislative council and highly influential in the campaign for the union. Mungoma was in charge of one of the coffee-drying centers under the supervision of one of the three Europeans who ran the rest of them. Because he did not work in the central office, however, Mungoma was rather removed from the daily struggles there, and so was of little direct help to Woods in his political problems. It is possible that he was able to maintain good relations with Woods precisely because he was not working in the central office.

The situation in the central office was further complicated by clan and personal hostilities between Mugoya and two of the other high-ranking Bagisu on the staff, A. G. Gimugu, the chief bookkeeper and later chief accountant, and C. M. Wakiro, the staff secretary. All three came from the same clan, the Bawalasi, but from different lineages. Mugoya was from the Bamuddu lineage, while Gimugu and Wakiro were both Babeza. Long-standing boundary disputes between the Bamuddu and the Babeza had resulted in numerous fights and deaths. Relations between the two lineages had also been complicated by the Babeza's claims that the Bamuddu had seized the chieftaincy by complicity and that the Bamuddu chiefs ever since had discriminated against them politically.

Gimugu and Wakiro supported Woods. Mugoya and Gimugu became involved in a long and bitter competition, aggravated according to some by the fact that Mugoya had married Gimugu's sister and then treated her badly. The enmity between these high-ranking members set off considerable friction within the organization. Whether the sources of these conflicts had more to do with clan rivalry and ethnic resentment, or with nationalist feelings against the continued employment of Europeans, they effectively obstructed any efforts to apply discipline or sanctions throughout the union staff. Woods's attempts to impose unpopular quality controls aggravated his conflicts with the committee and his difficulties in maintaining discipline. Neither peasant-farmers nor buyers in the local societies were willing to follow his instructions on quality control in buying or his insistence that the fermented cherry from the central pulperies be taken back to the farms for use as fertilizer.

Woods wanted to have the peasants trained to pulp and dry their own parchment. This would have kept the husks, an important source of fertilizer, on the farms. The committee, however, opposed his plans for a training program and resisted his attempt to establish a bonus for high quality coffee because it was causing resentment from the peasants who had lower quality coffee. Woods had no power to control the buyers in the local societies, and the committee's opposition to him reduced whatever influence he might have had in convincing the GCSs that it was in their own interests to control their buyers more carefully.

Lack of committee support also impeded Woods's control of pruning teams. Arabica trees need proper pruning to give a decent yield. While pruning itself is fairly simple, few farmers were interested in pruning or knew how to do it. The BCS had therefore instituted pruning gangs who were paid for each tree that they pruned. After the BCU was founded, pruning gangs started claiming to have pruned trees on farms they had not even visited. Woods was unable to end this problem, as the committee was using employment on the pruning teams to reward support. His failure contributed to a serious decline in coffee quality after 1956.

Woods resigned in 1957 because "I was sick of the dishonesty and inefficiency and I thought the whole thing was going to collapse. Besides, I wasn't allowed to do anything. I was just a figurehead. They wanted an African, not a European" (interview, Nairobi, 1970). As soon as Woods left, Mugoya was appointed coffee manager, and Mungoma became coffee supervisor shortly afterward. It is a little difficult to understand why both posts were necessary since the job descriptions were virtually indistinguishable. Both Mugoya and Mungoma were deeply involved in politics at the time. Mugoya had been elected to the chair of the district council in 1956, which kept him quite busy and left him little time for union work. Mungoma was still a member of the legislative council and also served as an ex-officio member of the district council. The creation of two staff posts when one should have sufficed was probably an accommodation to their political activities.

Several other members of the BCU staff were also involved in politics. The chief accountant, the cashier, and the assistant manager all served on the district council. While these men probably spent less time on council business than Mugoya did, there were reports and official complaints about staff members not being present during working hours because of council duties. The committee passed a resolution against staff participation in politics, but it was never implemented. Because mutual support between committee and staff members was so crucial, and because their common interests outside of the union made their alliances, especially against the government, very useful, neither side was eager to exercise its function of controlling the other. The union served both committee and staff as a resource they could exploit in exchange relations to expand their own powers.

Committee Business: The Betterment of the Bagisu

Political alliances against the BNA, the CCD, and the board tended to blur the already hazy lines between the powers and responsibilities of the popularly elected committee and those of the professional management. The committee could use managerial resources in its political struggle, and management joined the committee in its opposition to the board. The committee under Kitutu included many older and well-respected campaigners in the cooperative movement as well as a number of young men with more than average education. Many were also closely related to chiefs of different grades. The BCU committee used both its resources and connections to rally popular support.

The committee used Annual General Meetings—which were called up to five times a year and often lasted four or five days, and on some occasions over a week—to air its complaints against the board's restrictions of their powers. Since attendance at these meetings ranged from 80 to 139 GCS representatives, the meetings were fertile grounds for marshalling support. GCS representatives themselves performed a diffuse set of services, which included pressuring the BNA to maintain roads and bridges in their areas, resolving questions of school fees or taxes, requesting visits from the Department of Agriculture personnel to advise on pest control, communicating complaints against local chiefs, and demanding that the BCU send trucks to collect coffee from their GCSs. They could also take care of their own business on these paid trips to town. The GCS representatives were increasingly inclined to use the local influence that the services they performed gave them in their area to encourage popular support of the committee against the board.

In addition, Kitutu and other committee members frequently used BCU vehicles to travel around the district to address meetings, settle disputes, and encourage enrollment in the GCSs. The long, frequent meetings and extensive travel were expensive and to some extent disrupted the routine business of the union, but the support they achieved for Kitutu made the board very reluctant to use its own powers (Uganda Protectorate, 1958a; Haydon, interview, 1970). In committee meetings, the CCD officers spoke out against Kitutu's frequent use of BCU vehicles and drivers, and the committee agreed that it was a bad use of money. Nothing was done about it, however, so the practice continued despite persistent rumors that Kitutu was using the union trucks for his own personal business.

The committee created other management problems as well. It continually interfered with what should have been routine staff decisions. Committee intervention in hiring and firing of lower staff resulted in extensive kin, political, and regional favoritism. Its meddling in the scheduling of trucks to pick up crops from the GCSs led to serious inefficiencies and delays. The union already had ninety member societies. It did not have adequate transport or storage facilities. The bad condition of many of the roads during much of the harvest season necessitated efficient scheduling of trucks and storage plants in order to process the entire crop with minimum waste or spoilage. Committee members, especially Kitutu, tended to interfere with this schedule, sending trucks to their own areas or to the areas of political allies whenever there was a load ready to deliver, and in some cases before there was a full load there. These unscheduled shipments, in addition to discriminating against other societies, occasionally created bottlenecks at the plants, tying up a truck for some time because there was nowhere to off-load it, and at other times caused stoppages at the plants because insufficient amounts of coffee were coming in.

The committee's role as the main focus of opposition to the colonial state, to the board, and to the European management diminished and overshadowed concern with the inefficiencies and expense its actions caused. A large proportion of actual meeting time was taken up with objections to taxes on Bugisu coffee, criticisms of the board's disposition and investment of the surplus funds, resolutions against the board's continuing power, and demands for African appointments to new jobs. The committee also served as a forum on the district's problems. This was in part because it received numerous requests for aid to special projects, such as medical dispensaries, maternity homes, associations for the blind, road building, and the construction of new schools. Arguments for the establishment of various businesses with BCU funds also absorbed the members' time and attention.

The committee was also very much concerned with its own privileges and those of the staff. A common topic of discussion in its meetings was the purchase of cars, or loans for the purchase of cars, for various staff members. Committee members also urged the board to raise the wages of union employees and to provide some of them with free housing in Mbale. There were also debates about how members should be transported to meetings. While statements that they should use buses, as these were cheaper, were generally well received, the notion that it was beneath the dignity of the new leaders of the Bagisu to ride in public conveyance together with "matoke (bananas), goats, and chickens" generally carried the floor. Most resolutions to limit expenses on private transport for the members were defeated. The committee was as deeply concerned about maintaining and augmenting its own dignity as it was about establishing itself as a powerful source of services and favors to the rest of the Bagisu.

The committee members abused some of their privileges, such as the use of vehicles, but there is no question that Kitutu and at least some of the members devoted great amounts of time and energy to encouraging the new societies, exhorting the members to work hard and honestly, settling disputes and problems, and agitating among the Bagisu against the state and particularly the board. Their relation to the Bagisu staff was equally intense. The line between staff and committee was obscured, and their collaboration was enhanced, by important connections based on politics and friendship between individual committee members and individual staff members. In its relations with the staff and the rest of the Bagisu, the committee continually propagated the idea of autonomy and the use of the BCU as a force that could assure Bagisu rights and make them a strong and respected people.

It was perhaps this thrust more than any other factor that gave Kitutu especially, and the rest of the committee by extension, the popular support with which to resist official pressures concerning the running of the union. As a district councillor, Kitutu was noted and lionized for his ardent ethnic nationalism. He repeatedly insisted that the Bagisu assert their collective strength in order to achieve their full potential. He was the major force in the campaign for the union of the Bagisu with the Babukusu, with the incorporation of both groups into Kenya. Kitutu gained a popular reputation as a clever and extremely brave and difficult opponent for the British, and as a strong political power among the Bagisu. This not only gave him great support from the majority of the Bagisu but also made direct criticism of him in the committee politically dangerous and extremely rare. In all of the records I read, the committee opposition to some of his actions, including the frequent use of BCU vehicles, is so cautious as to be hardly noticeable.

The State Strikes Back

The ambiguities and problems that had plagued the BCU intensified during 1957 and finally provoked a definitive intervention from higher levels of the state. Relations with the board continued to deteriorate as the BCU increased its attacks on the secretary-general and as it articulated increasingly strong feelings over the question of whether the board or the union would control the coffee mill.

Relations on the staff itself also deteriorated during this period. European domination of the staff was no longer an issue after Woods left, but increasing hostilities between Mugoya and his two Babeza rivals, Gimugu and Wakiro, impeded efficient management. As the highest ranking staff officer after Woods's departure, Mugoya took every opportunity to criticize Gimugu and to display his anger at receiving committee instructions from Wakiro, who as secretary was responsible for transmitting decisions to the staff. The managerial problems in the union did not incline the government to make any concessions to the union in their demands against the board. On the contrary, the government gave every indication that the board would continue indefinitely. The abusiveness of the Bagisu toward the board increased with their frustrations at not being able to abolish it.[2]

The ambiguities of the BCU's being perceived and used simultaneously as a vehicle of ethnic nationalism and as a business operation created constant tension between the political preoccupations of both the staff and the committee and their need to continue conducting daily business. Increasingly, it was the latter that was neglected.

The ambivalence of the state and its reluctance to exert its power over the BCU heightened the tensions. From 1946 onward, the state had encouraged the development of a strong cooperative union. At the same time, the state clearly intended to ensure that the BCU made a profit and maintained the viability of the crop, that certain laws and principles of business were followed by the committee, and that generally the crop continue as a source of income for the protectorate. Direct opposition to or intervention in the elected committee, however, posed the danger of provoking disruption of coffee deliveries. The agencies at both the district and national levels were still quite sensitive to the danger of violence or withdrawal into subsistence. Thus, even though government agents were empowered and encouraged to supervise the crop, they were generally reluctant to oppose Bagisu wishes even when they were in disagreement with them.

The delicate balance between the state's tolerance of partial BCU autonomy and its concern for the viability of the crops finally collapsed over board actions concerning the coffee prices paid to the peasants. Officially the board controlled prices and was responsible for setting them realistically. BCU influence on the board, however, was strengthened in 1957 by the threat of a dissident separatist movement to establish a rival to the BCU. BCU committee members were able to attribute this movement to low coffee prices, and eventually they convinced the board to authorize the higher prices they were demanding.

B. B. N. Mafabi, a former subcounty chief who had provided important support to the campaign to establish the BCU and who had served a term on the committee, started this movement. He claimed that if the committee were not so extravagant it could pay its members higher prices. He founded a separate marketing organization and applied for a license to buy and export coffee. Two visiting MPs from England recommended that the group be granted a license. This reinforced Mafabi's claims and strengthened the determination of his followers. At Mafabi's urging, they withheld their coffee in order to sell it through the new organization. Mafabi was not granted a license, however, even though he continued his appeals for over a year. This coffee was thus temporarily lost, and in danger of spoiling.

Mafabi's movement was based on many of the ideological principles that the state's agents had attempted to inculcate. Mafabi invoked ideals of business efficiency, equality among cooperative members, and popular representation and control. All of these principles were incorporated into the cooperative rules to reduce the powers and possible abuses of power of the elected committee. Ultimately, however, Mafabi's invocation of these principles strengthened the committee's position. It also worked, though, to the peasants' immediate advantage. The BCU leaders were able to use this movement's clear manifestation of peasant discontent as a demonstration that they should be allowed to raise coffee prices. Under the threat that peasants would withhold more coffee, the committee convinced the board to authorize 2/30 shillings a pound instead of 1/50, which the Europeans argued was appropriate for the 1957-58 crop. Moreover, the board permitted the committee to abolish central pulperies and unpopular quality controls. Both of these measures directly threatened to reduce state revenues.

The state responded by having the governor appoint two more Europeans to the board, including the provincial commissioner, who became the chair. The Bagisu objected, plausibly enough, that the governor had acted to guarantee a clear European majority, and resolved to boycott all future meetings, which meant in effect that there was to be no further communication between the governing or controlling body and the implementing one. This was clearly an impossible situation. Shortly thereafter, the governor appointed a board of inquiry headed by a European, R. H. Gretton, to consider the condition of the BCU and to make recommendations for its improvement.

The three-member commission conducted interviews and received evidence in Bugisu for a month in April and May, 1958. In their report, they were critical of much of the board's handling of relations with the Bagisu, claiming that not nearly enough effort had gone into informing the Bagisu of its functions, thereby allowing a situation in which the union could use the board to cover its own weaknesses. They also considered a number of suggestions, including some from members of the board, that the board should be terminated and its functions carried on in some other way. The committee concluded, however, that the union itself was not nearly well enough run to take on the board's functions in quality control and handling of the reserve funds.

The commission directed most of its criticism at the union itself, primarily for bad business management. It reported a lack of staff control, very badly kept accounts and records, waste, and extravagance. According to the commission, books were not up-to-date and figures of income and expenditure were often not available for any time during the previous eight months. They attributed this in part to a highly inefficient accounting system but also to the fact that so many of the staff were involved in politics.

The commission's report (Uganda Protectorate, 1958a) claimed that there were no means of providing the committee with financial information other than the annual audit, which was performed by an outside firm. The commission also cited several instances where the committee's decisions were simply not implemented. It was very critical of the large amounts of money spent on transportation for committee and general meetings and said that Kitutu was far too dominant in the union, both on the staff and on the committee. It attempted to document disaffection among the peasants and reported its impression that the peasants felt very much in the union's power, rather than feeling that the union was their organization and could be controlled by them.

The commission backed its assertion of "the growers' feeling of helplessness," however, with only a single quotation; "one of them actually said, 'we feel like prisoners, unable to make any choice'" and with a reference to "a few members" who wished to return to individual bargaining with private traders (Uganda Protectorate, 1958a:18). The paucity of documentation for this claim contrasts strongly with the detailed evidence it presented of mismanagement and inefficiencies. The claim that the growers felt helpless in their relations with the BCU also appears incongruent with the commission's own statement that all of the GCSs and their members supported the BCU's campaign against the board and its boycott of board meetings. Indeed, the commission's claims that the members were dissatisfied with the BCU appears to be an attempt by the state's agents to forge an alliance with the peasants by invoking principles of management efficiency and democratic control. Subsequent events, however, showed that peasants' resentment of the leaders was outweighed by the peasants' distrust of the state. The state needed to exploit the peasants, so an effective alliance with them was highly unlikely.

The report also included a warning about the rapid deterioration in the quality of Bugisu coffee during the preceding year and a half. It claimed that the union had lost many of its international buyers and recommended reinstating some form of quality distinctions with bonus incentives. Because of the inflated prices paid for coffee and because of the general extravagance in the union, the commission predicted a deficit for that season of over two million shillings, pointing out that the loss would be greater if the union made the second payments anticipated by the peasants.

Finally, the commission recommended that the Uganda Cooperative Laws be revised to allow the commissioner of the CCD, if he was convinced that a society was not being run satisfactorily, to appoint a suitable person to run it with full control over its liabilities and assets and with "the powers, rights, and privileges of the duly constituted committee" (Uganda Protectorate, 1958a:30). It was this recommendation that had the greatest effect on the union. The law was enacted as proposed, and the commissioner of the CCD appointed W. E. Neal, a British cooperative officer and a trained accountant, as supervising manager of the union. Kitutu and most of his committee were replaced at the next general meeting, and the supervising manager ruled that Kitutu could not be elected again as a committee member.

The BCU thus lost much of the power it had gained, and one of its most powerful leaders was barred from office. The long campaigns to create the BCU and then to increase its autonomy, however, had deeply changed political and economic organization in the district. They had also changed the Bagisu's understanding of the colonial system and of their own place in it. Before continuing the narrative of how the Bagisu struggled to regain and then expand the powers they lost in 1958, I will review some of the ways these early campaigns exemplify the general processes and relationships, described in the introduction, through which the peasants and their leaders actively and creatively participated in shaping the social and economic bases of their evolving struggle with the state and of their own position in the world economy.

A Political Assessment of the BCU's Early Years

Kitutu and his colleagues instilled cooperative trust, ethnic pride, and collective identity necessary for the BCU to exist. Their own rights and powers depended on the organized strength of the Bagisu as a unified and mobilized group. Kitutu and his committee had had to persuade, educate, mediate, and arbitrate. They had had to arouse, heighten, and marshal suspicion of and hostility against the Bugisu Coffee Scheme, the Coffee Marketing Company, and the board and to create enthusiasm for the union. They had had to allay the Bagisu's fears of entrusting their coffee to the GCSs without immediate payment, to convince them that by allowing the societies to earn money by selling their coffee they themselves would be earning more money, to show them how to run their own societies, and to instill in managers some respect for accurate figures and balanced books. In all of this they had had the assistance of a remarkably shrewd and energetic European cooperative officer, Colin Campbell. The main burden, though, of organizing the whole of a large ethnic group spread over a large and extremely mountainous territory into an institution that incorporated numerous exogenous ideas rested on a small group of men who themselves had come to understand those ideas only relatively recently.

The new ideas did not arrive entirely intact, but rather were adapted to traditional and well-understood modes of organization. Lineage and district divisions and unities were incorporated into the new structure and were built upon; they became both a source of strength and a cause of dissension within the union. The political divisions that arose after the establishment of the union deeply affected its operation. The early leaders themselves did not entirely comprehend the principles of modern business organization that the CCD kept urging on them, but often understood that the CCD was invoking these principles against what they saw as their own rights, obligations, and best interests.

The CCD defined its own mandate as assuring that the societies and unions were run well and that the membership was not exploited by its leaders. The leaders, however, had started and were still working toward enormous institutional change; and they tended to maximize communication and influence with the membership. They had a fair amount to talk about—questions to answer, points to make, problems and disputes and doubts to resolve, enthusiasm to raise. Their success in these activities increased their own power and the menace they presented to colonial goals of administrative control and increased revenues, but they were also essential to stabilizing the BCU as a cooperative organization. The CCD had encouraged and assisted in this communication during the movement's inception and initial growth; after the union became a legal corporation set to specific economic tasks, it aimed at the very different goal of rationalizing and routinizing its operation.

The conflict between the CCD and the BCU was both economic and cultural. The CCD represented a state that required a steady, predictable source of revenue. CCD staff members, in implementing these goals, rationalized their decisions in terms of their own ideals of proper business and organizational management. The CCD's orientation was appropriate for and typical of an agency committed to "modernism," but it appears to have assumed that modernism can be legislated. The CCD was committed to the principle of member education, but it insisted that committee members hold quick, efficient meetings in which business decisions were made in a businesslike way (see especially Cooperative Rule No. 25) and that trained cooperative officers specifically assigned to the task of education and supervision would educate and supervise. This modernist bias was also congruent with the state's goals of control over a predictably commercialized crop. The culturally based insistence on "modern" procedures served to rationalize and mask the state's strategies to keep control.

The committee members and the delegates to meetings, chosen by the membership as leaders, were in fact more effective socializing and mobilizing agents than were the trained cooperative officers. The CCD, subject to the structural and cultural imperatives set forth in the Cooperative Societies Ordinance (Uganda Protectorate, 1946) and to the economic and political imperatives of state market control, had to restrain this potential and so moved to restrict committee expenditure, time, and activity that were not compatible with its professed orientation toward bureaucratic efficiency and rational management. Its insistence on routinizing the committee's job and on the assignment of specialists to instill cooperative principles in the union's members served the state's goals of keeping ultimate control over marketing and thus ensuring its own revenues.

CCD agents, however, continued to express frustration, indignation, and surprise that neither the BCU leaders nor the peasant members of the GCSs had accepted the ideals and principles of cooperative organization. These agents, especially the European ones, saw their own modernist ideology as natural, right, and logical, and as therefore being in the peasants' best interests rather than a means to increase the state's rate of appropriation from them (interviews with Haydon in Mbale and with Woods in Nairobi; CCD correspondence in DCD files in Mbale). Their view of themselves as working for the Bagisu's benefit accounts in part for their impatience with BCU demands and for the tensions in their meetings with local leaders.

The hostility that the committee expressed toward the European manager undoubtedly hurt the smooth running of the organization, but this same distrust of Europeans had hastened the process of establishing a Bagisu-controlled union. The laxity of the staff certainly should have been avoided, and probably could have been, if the union had been seen primarily as an economic organization. As a vehicle of political and economic self-assertion for the Bagisu, however, the use of time had to be apportioned politically as well as economically.

On the other hand, the enthusiasm that the BCU and its leaders generated among the Bagisu had potentially positive results for the state. Neither the Gretton report nor any of the CCD's assessments of the union mention it, but coffee production increased markedly after the Bagisu took control of coffee sales in 1954 (Table 15). Declining quality and higher prices to farmers reduced the state's benefit from

Table 15. Arabica Coffee Production in Bugisu/Sebei, 1947-59

Season	Tons	Season	Tons
1947-48	2,561	1953-54	3,021
1948-49	2,857	1954-55	6,170
1949-50	2,852	1955-56	4,098
1950-51	3,896	1956-57	5,175
1951-52	2,200	1957-58	4,805
1952-53	2,307	1958-59	4,912

NOTE: See Appendix 1 for coffee production, 1915-82.

this increase. The state's agents chose to ignore the positive effects of Bagisu enthusiasm and refused to work with it. Instead, they used the indications that the BCU would not make a profit to justify their intervention, turning enthusiasm into bitter indignation and opposition.

Kitutu had been attempting to expand the committee's power, and he had exploited the union's assets to do so. When he became too successful and when it appeared that his use of the union might reduce its economic utility to the state, the state from which he derived his own formal power cut him out completely and seriously limited the powers of his successors. After successfully establishing and expanding the range of the union's autonomy and control, he so threatened the state that he lost a great deal of what he had gained.

His successes in establishing the Bagisu as a unified power base were more enduring. The campaign for the union and a representative council had been the first expression of Bagisu unity. The coincidence of the union's establishment with the first open elections to and popular control of the district council and the dominance within the district council of BCU committee and staff members provided a strong focus of opposition to colonial rule. The campaign for the union had been largely based on anti-British sentiment. This sentiment was carried over into the district council, which started to act as a strong threat to the dominance of the district commissioner and the appointed chiefs.

The council and the union together established much broader possibilities for gaining power and allowed a direct challenge to the previous dominance of the chiefs and their educated sons. They opened the way for continued agitation against the British, as the councillors and the committee members were far less subject than the chiefs were to government disapproval, sanctions, or removal.

Their power to combat the board and in many cases have their way over it came as much from the state's perception of these representatives' standing among the Bagisu as from any other factor. Within much broader limits than the chiefs, the new representatives could claim the rights and desires of the Bagisu to oppose colonial programs. The sacking of Kitutu and his committee showed fairly clearly what these limits were, but within these limits the representatives could claim that they acted on behalf of the Bagisu without having to accommodate other masters. They would later use similar organizing tactics, strengthened by their access to formal position, to push these limits further. Their struggle against the state, however, would continue to reflect the lineage organization from which they had first drawn power. Kitutu and others established the basis of opposition to the state by manipulating exchange-based alliances. Both before and after the creation of the union, whatever power these leaders could muster, other than that which was derived from the state, depended on the goods and services they could offer the Bagisu, both as a peasantry and as separate power or status groups.

Kitutu and others like him had stimulated the development of the Bagisu peasantry as a district-level power base. They defined a particular social situation to their fellow Bagisu as harmful and unjust and then proposed a series of group actions that they claimed would solve the problems they had defined. They started from bases of clan and local influence and proceeded by coordinating their separate powers there, often through the medium of chiefs and civil servants who had wider influence. The movement proceeded from a series of local accords to groups integrated at the county level before it could be united in a district-wide power base. Each major lineage, clan, parish, subcounty, and county had to be persuaded and organized in turn. Only by using the powers, influence, and success granted to them at each level could the leaders attempt to function at the next higher level. Until the establishment of formal cooperative groups, first at the parish, the subcounty, and the county levels, the leaders themselves had no power other than the influence they derived from their prestige and their ability to persuade.

The formalization of their power started when the BCS ruled that any GCS that counted three-fourths of the peasants in its area as members had the right to handle the entire crop for that area. For the first time, the GCSs gained legal rather than moral or influential powers. This legal power grew as the level of unification expanded, first to the county and later to the district level. With the establishment of the union the cooperative leaders, who initially wielded power solely on the basis of personal influence, became position holders with certain powers that were independent of their Bagisu followers but were derived from and guaranteed by the colonial state.

As I showed in Chapter 3, the growing power of the BCU leaders and of other politicians opened up new avenues of upward mobility for a small number of Bagisu. Both in power and wealth, their positions rivaled those of the chiefs and civil servants. Much more than either of these previously ascendant groups, however, they depended on and were constrained by support from the autochthonously defined social units in which the peasants were organized. The electoral constituencies for the district council positions were sufficiently small that members were directly bound by lineage demands; BCU committee members could only be elected from among GCS officeholders. Thus, both major avenues for upward mobility required that officeholders closely attend to lineage-based demands and expectations in order to stay in power in their own local areas. At the same time, their struggle to expand the authority and autonomy of their official positions required them to mobilize the Bagisu as a unified mass. This they could only achieve by attempting to satisfy popular demands for high prices and accommodate popular resistance to labor-absorbing quality controls.

These constraints made political tenure unstable and ultimately limited the extent to which the politicians were differentiated from the rest of the Bagisu. Leaders achieved political position by mobilizing and channeling popular resistance against the state's attempts to increase its appropriation of peasant surplus. Bagisu leaders assumed formal positions within the apparatus that the state used to appropriate value and received in return a portion of the surplus appropriated. The leaders' dependence on popular support constrained them to support policies that reduced the amount of surplus that the state could appropriate. This clearly limited the values that the state could accumulate and invest in productive or commercial infrastructure or in social welfare programs. Price rises made more money available to peasant consumers, and the reduction of quality controls on coffee freed peasant labor for other tasks, including subsistence farming. Subsistence farming, in turn, sustained the exit option from cash cropping. It was this option that gave the peasants and their leaders a strong bargaining position against the state. The leaders' dependence on peasant support assured that they would use this bargaining position to reduce the state's rate of exploitation by pushing to raise prices and relax quality controls, even at the risk that the state might remove them from office.

The Bagisu's freehold tenure and the state's dependence on their coffee thus allowed the Bagisu to reduce the rate at which their labor was exploited. It also reduced the developmental potential of the state. The tensions between these two results and between the political groups, national and local, whose power they affected became more acute as the approach of independence raised the stakes for both national and local actors. If the leaders threatened too seriously to reduce state revenues, the state could reduce or eliminate their formal powers.

The leaders' positions, however, were increasingly strengthened by their essential functions in crop marketing. Leaders were able to expand this control by exploiting their positions and powers in the district administrative structure. They could enhance their autonomy by bringing pressure to bear on the BNA from the district council. BCU staff members, also interested in increased union autonomy and the heightened control over resources that this would give them, joined with BCU committee members on the council to work toward these ends.

The alliance between the BCU and the district council effectively increased the power of each institution and enhanced the popular support each could claim. The individuals who managed this alliance, especially through positions in both institutions, expanded their power rapidly. These leaders' ascendancy reduced the local authority of the district administrators and of previous ascendant groups—the chiefs and local civil servants. The popular representatives were by now directly mediating the struggle between the state and the peasantry, and their power rose and fell in their own confrontations with the state.

NOTES

1. He was not, finally, unwilling to talk, however. We had a long, interesting, and informative discussion about district council politics, in which we both referred to him and his role as secretary-general in the third person.

2. The assets at issue were quite significant. By June 1957 the board controlled assets valued at £11,550,000.

5

National Independence, Politics, and Conflict within the BCU, 1958-63

The imposition of direct colonial control over the BCU under a supervising manager coincided with the first stages of the constitutional conventions and parliamentary elections leading to internal rule and final national independence in 1962. The increased emphasis on African nationalism prior to independence enhanced local resistance to the state, while the opening of new political opportunities intensified the struggles between African parties and politicians. The state could not have chosen a worse moment to reduce BCU autonomy. The close nexus between peasant protest and the struggles for power between individuals and groups at the national, district, and county levels and the ways in which these struggles were reflected in attempts to gain and exploit power within the union are most dramatically seen in the BCU's struggle to remove the state-appointed supervising manager and in the competition to take control of the union after he was withdrawn in 1961.

The Widening Political Arena

The opening up of new political avenues through an increasingly representative district council, which had changed the power relations and opportunities of different groups of Bagisu just before and during the union's first years, proceeded even more rapidly as national parties were built up from local bases on the promise of eventual control of both national and local institutions and resources. The district council increased its autonomy from the BNA, further undermined the chiefs' power, and continued to mobilize popular opposition against the BNA and the other local agencies of the state. Although the imposition of a supervising manager greatly reduced the BCU committee members' formal power, many of the committee members, including S. K. M. Mutenio, the committee president, X. M. M. Gunigina, the vice-president, and J. N. K. Wakholi, the committee treasurer,[1] were on the district council. Their positions permitted the BCU to continue its influence on the council, broadened its base of opposition to the supervising manager, and allowed certain individual members to increase their personal power.

The conflict between the BNA and the district council was played out in large part by competing demands on the secretary-general and on the chiefs, who were responsible to both agencies. Both the secretary-general and the chiefs were frequently accused in the district council of being too loyal to the European administration. This conflict reached a peak in 1960, when there was serious rioting in Bugisu and Bukedi over the question of taxation. Much of the violence was directed against the chiefs. Mutenio, Gunigina, and Wakholi were the main leaders of an antigovernment faction in the district council that wanted to reduce the tax base radically. The district commissioner strongly objected, maintaining that a reduction could cause a huge budget deficit. The district council, in a direct challenge to the state, overrode his objections and cut the number of chiefs and local government services to eliminate the resulting deficit (Uganda Protectorate, 1960a, 1960b; Young, 1978).

This crisis precipitated the appointment of a commission of inquiry by the colonial government to look into the poor relations between the BNA and the district council. Little was done about the problem, however, other than removing the chiefs from the council altogether, along with other administration and lower council nominees. In 1963, the year after independence, the entire council for the first time was chosen by popular election, an action that further weakened the BNA and the chiefs. In addition to the increasing number of seats on the district council, powerful new roles, such as member of Parliament and district- or county-level party chairships, became available during the pre-independence period. Committee members often either occupied or competed for these positions. Mutenio was selected as one of Bugisu's two representatives to Uganda's constitutional conventions in London, and on several occasions he used resolutions passed there about the future policies of the independent country to combat resolutions of the board and the Commission for Cooperative Development (CCD). Neither the disturbances over taxes nor the London conferences had a direct relationship with union business, but they all contributed to the atmosphere of distrust, belligerence, and violence toward the colonial state that was growing during these years in Bugisu.

Very evident during this period were the ways in which organizational changes in the colonial state and economy affected both the structure of the Bagisu's sociopolitical environment and the opportunities for exploiting it. Intense fights to control the new political roles and the rich rewards they promised led to the development of powerful factions both outside and inside the union. Internal disputes on the BCU committee and staff were temporarily submerged, however, in their resistance to the continuance of the board and the supervising manager. The Bagisu had expected the board's functions to end when the supervising manager was appointed. When that did not happen, there was a concerted effort to eliminate the board. Colonial legislation was drafted to that effect as early as mid-1959, but the board continued to function for three more years, notwithstanding the committee's sustained protest and boycott.

Power Struggles in the BCU: The Committee versus the Supervising Manager

The new committee elected in September 1958 was different in several respects from the Kitutu committee that preceded it. It was smaller, with seven members rather than twelve, and more stable in membership. The members were all young men; the oldest of them was thirty-four. All had had at least six years of school, and all but two of them held teaching or other professional diplomas.

S. K. M. Mutenio, the new president, had completed more than twelve years of education and had been trained in Nairobi as a technician in the British army. He also had worked there in hotel management and as a law clerk. In 1955 he had returned to Mbale and had founded a successful business college there. That same year he became a member of the district council. Although he had never before held a cooperative post, he was elected to serve specifically because the BCU Annual General Meeting delegates felt that his business experience would enable him to moderate the conflicting forces that had led the union into trouble.

In many ways Mutenio was the personal antithesis of Kitutu, and by electing him the Bagisu were indicating a willingness to adjust to many of the business principles the CCD espoused. Where Kitutu rejected Western ideas of organization and management, emphasizing instead Bagisu norms of rights and obligation, Mutenio had actively studied and embraced Western managerial skills and legal forms. He believed that the BCU should follow the organizational principles he had learned from his long association with British institutions. He was particularly keen on keeping the union out of politics and reducing nepotism and other forms of committee interference with the staff. Instead of working with Mutenio and his committee, however, the CCD and the supervising manager insisted on using their powers fully and thus drove the entire committee into intransigent resistance. Instead of being able to implement the management reforms he believed in, and was perhaps uniquely suited to institutionalize, Mutenio had to moderate the turbulent and disruptive forces that the state's attempt to impose total control had engendered.

Relations between W. E. Neal, the newly appointed supervising manager, and the committee were difficult from the beginning. The new manager directly and frankly took away almost all of the committee's powers except its right to hold meetings, and he, or at least the government, did not even acknowledge the meetings. The *District Annual Report* for 1959 claimed that the Bagisu had refused to hold a meeting or to elect a committee since the appointment of the supervising manager, even though the BCU records show minutes of both meetings and elections. Members of that committee told me that the supervising manager was rude and arrogant with them, refusing to consult them or listen to their advice,[2] a strange omission for a man whom the Gretton report had urged should be particularly "sensitive to African aspirations."

The totality of the supervising manager's powers and his decision to consider the committee and staff only as he chose effectively precluded much of the internal maneuvering for power and bickering that had characterized the last years of Kitutu's presidency. His refusal to negotiate with the union's popularly elected leaders, however, limited his ability to implement programs that required coordination of the GCSs and the cooperation of the general membership.

Neal bluntly stated in his first address to a general meeting in 1959 that he intended to exercise his powers fully. He spoke against various forms of dishonesty and violation of cooperative regulations, and then instructed the meeting: "Elect a good committee. It is no good electing people who are going to waste your time and money opposing government and refusing to cooperate with the General Meeting. Any committee member who does this will be removed from office" (BCU Annual General Meeting Minutes, 1959).

He urged the members to accept directions from the union management: "It is no use for GCSs to pass resolutions opposed to a union ruling." The cooperative officer, Bugisu, the CCD's highest local official, who spoke after him, said that dishonesty, mismanagement, excessive expenditure and waste, illegal loans, and bad debts were rife and that some societies would have to be closed because they were in such bad condition.

The societies were indeed in bad financial shape. Eighty of the 114 GCSs in the union on January 14, 1959, were running in the red, with a collective deficit of 900,000 shillings. Amounts of up to 40,000 shillings had been stolen, embezzled, or simply lost in individual societies, with the committees of most of them unwilling to take legal action against those responsible. A number of societies had taken out loans against the guarantee of their second payment, which they were not going to receive that year.

Neal's response to this situation was to put GCSs in economic or management difficulties directly under his own supervision, suspending their committees and appointing secretary/managers who reported directly to him. As a result, opposition to Neal extended to the local influentials who were debarred from positions they had formerly controlled.

The content of communications between the committee and BCU members changed drastically during Neal's tenure. Antigovernment suspicions and hostilities, which had been aroused against the BCS and later against the board, were now turned against the supervising manager and the CCD for which he worked. The enthusiasm and pride that control of the union had generated in the Bagisu were doubly affronted by the loss of power and by what they saw as the humiliating and contemptuous attitude of the supervising manager toward them.

The Nairobi coffee mill burned down shortly after Neal was appointed, and he had to rush the BCU mill into partial operation earlier than had been planned. The urgency and extra work of this period may have been an important factor in his giving the impression of riding roughshod over the committee and of ignoring his assignment to train the committee and staff. He appointed a European as coffee grader, a sensitive job. He also changed the Bagisu hierarchy on the staff, raising the secretary, Wakiro, to be his most direct assistant and having as little as possible to do with Paulo Mugoya. Though he later praised V. P. Mungoma as an able administrator, he was at first highly critical of him because he was absent so much on political business. Many staff members reacted by using their influence on the committee to undermine Neal's authority, and some, particularly Mugoya, approached the committee several times to complain about Neal's favoritism and his refusal to implement certain pay raises demanded by the committee.

The committee of inquiry had warned in 1958: "The union has become a symbol of Bagisu unity. Any proposals to reorganize it are liable to be opposed on emotional grounds, and the authors of such proposals may find themselves accused of 'divide and rule' motives" (Uganda Protectorate, 1958a, Sec. 25). This prediction was quite accurate; the committee no longer urged cooperation on the members: it urged them to oppose and obstruct the union while it was run by the supervising manager. *District Annual Reports* from 1959 and 1960 indicate that the committee was widely supported in its campaign against the supervising manager and that many GCSs complained against the union's operating procedures.

The committee's struggle to regain its autonomy limited the supervising manager's capacity to implement his own programs. Neal was especially concerned about the quality of coffee, but he was unable to overcome the committee's support of popular resistance to his proposals. The BCU initially had cured all coffee in central pulperies, which had been highly unpopular with the peasants, who were forced to carry heavy, wet (uncured) cherry to these centralized locations. Because of expense and economies of scale, these pulperies were situated at considerable distance from each other. If peasants were allowed to cure their own cherry, they could carry parchment, which was about one-fourth the weight per unit price of the wet cherry. They would not have to carry it as far either, as buying stations for parchment required only a set of scales and storage space and could therefore be established at much closer intervals. The BCU committee had discontinued the central pulpery program in 1957.

Since then, despite various programs and resolutions to train the farmers to cure their own coffee, very little had been done to protect coffee quality. As a result, home-cured coffee tended to be lower and irregular in quality. Every discussion about improving quality centered on arguments for and against central pulperies and about the establishment of price incentives for higher quality coffee. Neal was not in a position to establish central pulperies again because of the high cost and long-range planning required. To institute them without the full support of the committee and the GCSs would have been a foolish waste.

Neal and even some members of the committee were in favor of more stringent grading procedures and of paying different prices to the peasants in the form of bonuses for quality coffee in the second payment. Mugoya consistently opposed this idea and was increasingly successful in turning the committee's attention to other possibilities. In 1960 he claimed that in fact Bugisu coffee had not declined in quality, but that the BCU was being discriminated against at the Nairobi auctions by their own broker in complicity with Neal.

The debate between Mugoya and Neal over declining prices for Bugisu coffee was aggravated by the committee members' general distrust of Neal and their desire to defend themselves and not alienate the peasants. Mutenio had brought back reports from London buyers about the problems with the Bagisu coffee, and the committee had talked a great deal about improving quality. Price differentials, however, had never been popular among the peasants, as only a few would receive the bonuses. Although several of the GCSs strongly supported quality differentials, the Annual General Meeting as a whole was in favor of sharing the bonus equally. It was thus in the short-term interests of committee members to look outside the union for the reasons for the falling prices and to agree with Mugoya's interpretation of the problem and his proposed solution.

At Mugoya's urging, they decided to review the new brokerage contract signed by Neal and demanded that the broker come to talk to a general meeting. The meeting itself was cordial, as all of the accusations of cheating were made while the broker was out of the room. The meeting decided that the contract should be renegotiated and instructed the secretary to write a letter to the broker explaining what new provisions they wanted in the contract to guarantee their prices. The secretary, however, sent a transcript of the minutes of the entire meeting, including the consideration that the broker was cheating them. The broker threatened to sue the union for defamation and refused to attend any more meetings. He subsequently dealt with the committee entirely through Neal by telephone, but the committee refused on two occasions to consider Neal's notes of their conversations, saying that they were unsigned and in Neal's rather than the broker's hand. The situation demanded resolution as the coffee season had almost started, and any delay in sales would hurt the union badly. Neal was apparently unwilling to use his authority to write the new contract himself, since it would have left him open to committee charges that he was assisting another European in cheating them. The new contract was finally worked out after intervention from the commissioner for cooperative development, but the delay ran the agreement perilously close to the beginning of the buying season. The union did get an agreement on its prices, but the committee's refusal to accept Neal's word hindered the proceedings considerably. The consideration of ways to improve coffee quality was completely lost in the fight with the broker.

It may be that Mugoya and the committee were right to trust neither the broker nor Neal, but that is impossible to judge on the basis of the highly partisan statements from all sides of the conflict. The issue consumed a vast amount of both general and committee meeting and staff time. Not incidentally, it further strengthened Mugoya's position in the BCU. The issue of the broker's contract arose both as a means of avoiding BCU responsibility for the low quality of coffee and as an attempt to discredit Neal and gain support among the peasants. By supporting Mugoya's claim, the committee could bring another complaint against Neal without weakening its own position by proposing burdensome and unpopular solutions.

The BCMA: An Outside Challenge to the BCU

A second separatist movement, which began soon after the imposition of the supervising manager, intensified local protest against the state, but it also threatened the BCU's monopoly. This movement, led by a northern politician and later member of Parliament, Stephen Muduku, tried to establish a rival to the BCU, the Bugisu Coffee Marketing Association (BCMA). Like the earlier separatist group, the BCMA was organized around the promise of higher coffee prices, the relaxation of quality controls, and the provision of marketing arrangements more convenient to the growers. It openly and directly threatened crop reduction. The BCMA strategy was to urge peasants to withhold their coffee for sale in the BCU-affiliated GCSs and to work toward withdrawing the GCSs from the BCU. The cooperative officer for Bugisu had relayed word from the CCD that any GCS with a 75 percent vote in favor could withdraw from the BCU. The BCMA had not yet been granted a buying license, but the CCD did not appear likely to prevent BCMA sales. Members of at least twenty GCSs eventually joined the BCMA. Three of these GCSs ultimately left the BCU altogether after a majority of their members voted to join the BCMA.

Although Muduku himself was from a lineage farther up the northern valley, BCMA strength was centered in Buwalasi and neighboring *gombololas*, where political and lineage tensions had always been high. The BCMA was strongest in Buwalasi, where Mugoya's lineage predominated. As a BCU staff member, Mugoya steadfastly denied being a member of the BCMA, but it is clear he often encouraged and manipulated it in his own campaign for power within the BCU, first against Neal and, after Neal was withdrawn, against the committee.

The campaign to urge peasants to withhold coffee and to vote to leave the BCU became violent in the Buwalasi area quite early. Growers who favored the BCMA started to slash the coffee trees of growers who continued to sell their coffee to the BCU and who refused to vote for withdrawal from the BCU. The BCU supporters retaliated in kind.

There were violent confrontations between the opposing sides, and several murders were attributed to revenge for coffee slashing. I was unable to find any estimate of the number of trees destroyed, but the 1961 *District Annual Report* referred to "widespread intimidation and tree-slashing" in Buwalasi and Buyobo. Interviews in 1970 also indicated that there had been extensive damage there and some farther up the valley. There was also some disruption of coffee collection due to threats on the truckdrivers' lives.

Even though the BCMA ultimately failed, its campaign exerted intense and sustained pressure on both the state and the BCU to accede to popular demands on issues of prices, quality controls, and marketing arrangements. The BCMA bought coffee from 1960 to 1963 and was appealing for a license during all of that time. The state vacillated on its position about giving the BCMA a marketing license, so the BCMA was of continuing concern to the BCU, which was very eager to maintain its monopoly. Though committee members were concerned about the threat which the BCMA posed to the BCU monopoly, they also used it to fortify their campaign for the BCU's autonomy.

The BCMA provided the BCU leaders with a platform from which to attack Neal and the CCD. They invoked peasant discontent, which the BCMA represented, to underscore their claims that Neal and his appointees did not respect and in fact discriminated against the Bagisu. They were able to blame Neal directly as well. The BCMA's officers claimed that they had founded the organization when one of them, a GCS representative, had been beaten by one of Neal's mill employees, a European. When the GCS committee complained to Neal, he dismissed them, telling them to try to sell their coffee somewhere else. They decided to follow his suggestion. This episode heightened the general notion that Neal was abrupt and insensitive to Bagisu dignity. Thus, even though the BCU committee was deeply opposed to the BCMA, its existence was convenient to them in their fight against Neal.

The conflict between the BCU and the BCMA was intense. It heightened enmities between factions at the district level and between lineages at the subcounty level. Within some GCSs the fights between adherents of the BCU and followers of the BCMA led to killings, beatings, and houseburnings. Yonosani Mudebo, the BCMA secretary, was Mugoya's brother, and there were persistent reports that Mugoya was encouraging the BCMA and giving it confidential information and advice. This intensified the BCU's internal conflicts. To the extent that the union's leaders could impute these problems to Neal, they could further justify resistance to him.

Neal's Withdrawal

Neal did manage during his first two years to improve dramatically the financial conditions of the BCU (Table 16). The 1961 *District Annual Report* claimed that the improved payments for coffee and larger bonuses had led to greater cooperation between the GCSs and the supervising manager. Bagisu leaders pointed out, however, that Neal's direct control over the BCU and the GCSs precluded the training that he was supposed to give their committees and staff. They continued to petition the government for his removal and the committee started looking for other ways to get rid of him.

Table 16. BCU Coffee Trade Balance (in pounds)

Year	Surplus	Deficit
1958	—	(118,209)
1959	354,286	—
1960	409,482	—
1961	328,430	—
1962	1,226	—

NOTE: BCU = Bugisu Cooperative Union.

The most serious of these attempts was a proposal to hire a European-owned firm, the Uganda Company, as managing agent, apparently on the rationale that the Uganda Company would be working for the committee rather than for the CCD. The committee claimed it did not object to having a supervisor, but it did object to Neal. There was little protest over the fact that the Uganda Company would hire more Europeans than were currently employed by the union, as the committee was quite enthusiastic about the idea that one of the company's main responsibilities would be to train Bagisu in both staff and committee affairs, which Neal had failed to do. The commissioner for cooperative development was in favor of the idea. Negotiations between the committee and the Uganda Company lasted for two months, but finally broke down over the company's insistence on a seven-year contract as the minimum needed to get the entire coffee operation running properly.

Thereafter, the committee's and the general meeting's main initiatives against Neal took the form of obstructing and objecting to his decisions and actions, numerous resolutions to various branches of government to have him removed, and occasional delegations, usually led by Kitutu, to petition the government and the commissioner for cooperative development for his dismissal. The CCD finally acceded to the Bagisu's repeated petitions and removed Neal from his position in late 1961.

The committee recognized in its meetings that Neal had vastly improved the union's financial situation and that all of the GCSs were once again financially solid, but committee proposals for various gestures of appreciation were all voted down by large majorities.

Despite the problems of mistrust, the campaign to get rid of Neal, and its inability to deal with the problem of quality, the committee under Mutenio showed much more direct concern with the actual running of the union than the Kitutu committee did. Even though it lacked executive authority until Neal left, the committee sought appropriations or acted as liaison with the state for acquiring new roads, new buildings, and insecticides for the GCSs; it passed on loans and decisions for training and appointing staff and considered a much more detailed kind of financial reporting than the earlier committee had done. It kept a much tighter rein on staff activity, whose efficiency it regularly reviewed. The maintenance of standards in the GCSs, however, was still considered to be the responsibility of the CCD and the Department of Agriculture.

In March 1962 the Bugisu Coffee Board was finally dissolved. The committee protested that the supervising manager had turned down a board offer to turn £121,000 over to the union, saying that the union did not need it. The union claimed that money. It was also given power over a loan of £50,000 the board had made to the District Administration. This the BCU waived payment on, saying that the equivalent amounts of the payments were to be given to the Masaaba Senior Secondary School in north Bugisu. The rest of the coffee reserve fund was turned over to the Ministry (formerly Department) of Agriculture to be administered as a trust fund for the improvement of the Bugisu coffee crop with a board of trustees to include one member appointed by the BCU. The committee was forced to acquiesce to this transfer as a condition for dissolving the board. I do not believe that the committee fully realized that national level or ministerial control of the fund would put the fund and its disposition completely beyond the reach of the Bagisu. Once it had been so transferred, however, the reserve fund, about which there had been so much contention between government and the Bagisu, was transformed into something that Bagisu could no longer hope to control and thus removed as a cause of further dispute at the district level.

The initial ineffectiveness of the committee's opposition to the board and Neal indicates fairly clearly the extent to which the members' power was dependent on the state-imposed structure, but the problems and obstacles they created for Neal in particular show the limitations of structural power without consensus. Neal had trained Wakiro to take over from him, but once again Mugoya was appointed to the highest staff office as general manager, with Wakiro as secretary. Once Neal had been removed as supervising manager, the various personal and group interests represented on both the committee and the staff involved the entire union in costly competitions for power both inside and outside the union.

Political Struggles in the BCU

After Neal was removed, the growing politicization of relations in Bugisu became an important source of dissension and one of the major issues with which the committee had to deal. The BCMA was no longer a convenient issue for criticizing Neal, but it remained a threat to the BCU's power and the center of political struggle in the district.

While Neal remained as supervising manager, he posed a common threat that tended to submerge dissensions and opposition within the union. After Neal left, these dissensions emerged and were aggravated by competition for the newly available political opportunities and for control over the district's expanded fiscal capacities. Increasingly this competition for power within the union was played out through appeals to the Bagisu peasants for support. As in local struggles against the state, these appeals once again centered on questions of coffee prices, collection and grading procedures, and bonus payments. As these were exactly the same issues that the leaders of the BCMA were using to mobilize support, there was inevitably common cause between the BCMA leaders and dissident factions within the union. At the same time, pressure from within the union for higher prices, and especially statements to the farmers promising higher prices, were seen as "treacherous" support for the BCMA (BCU committee minutes, 1961). Mugoya, however, used the BCMA and gave it some support in seeking to increase his own power in the union and in the district.

While the DCD (formerly CCD) was not particularly interested in supporting the BCU monopoly, it was concerned about maintaining coffee production. Worries about the BCMA were clearly an important factor in Neal's early withdrawal and in the DCD's accession to changes in the staff arrangements that Neal had instituted. Neither Neal's withdrawal nor the reappointment of Mugoya as head of the BCU staff, however, ended the BCU's problems with the BCMA and Mugoya's apparent support of it. Nor did they silence Muduku's accusations or make him willing to negotiate with the BCU. Mugoya effectively refused to subordinate himself to the committee and continued to use the BCMA and its demands as a platform to speak against the committee and to expand his own power within the union. Once Neal had left, the BCU committee was the object of the BCMA's criticisms, with Mugoya on the one hand maintaining that prices were too low and that quality had not deteriorated, and Muduku on the other maintaining that he could negotiate more favorable brokerage arrangements in Nairobi.

Mutenio tried hard and consistently to keep politics out of union considerations, but the struggle between the two national parties, the Democratic Party (DP) under Benedicto Kiwanuka, a Muganda, and the Uganda People's Congress (UPC) under Milton Obote, a Lango, was becoming increasingly intense in the district. Mutenio and Gunigina were both founding members of the DP in Bugisu and held high positions in it. Most of the rest of the committee were UPC members. Mugoya had stood for the Legislative Council in 1959 as an independent, but had lost to Muduku, the DP candidate. It soon became evident that Mugoya planned to run again. Muduku was working to identify the BCMA as a DP organization. Yonosani Mudebo, the BCMA secretary who was Mugoya's brother, told me that Mugoya gave him a great deal of advice on how to run the BCMA, though he was never a member. Mugoya himself, though he denied in a 1961 general meeting that he was helping the BCMA, did admit that he had told some of the peasants at a public meeting in the north that the BCU was not paying them fair prices. Mutenio consistently disallowed any political discussion during meetings, but several times it was claimed that the DP was going to ruin the union. The BCMA, Mugoya's activities, and the attacks on Mutenio all served to exacerbate the divisions in the committee along party lines.

Mugoya's personal influence, his technical knowledge of coffee markets, and his powerful political connections had made him a useful ally in the committee's campaign against Neal. The committee had followed his initiatives and his advice in ways that gave him far more political power than his staff position as secretary/manager could ever have provided. After Neal was withdrawn, however, it became quite clear that Mugoya's ambitions extended beyond getting rid of Neal and that he was quite willing to use his position in the BCU to achieve political office, even to the detriment of the committee and the union. His personal hostility to the Babeza members of his staff and his kinship with officers and members of the BCMA enhanced the disruptive effects of his drive for personal power. The complex amalgam of lineage loyalty and personal ambition led to the curious result that Mugoya sometimes worked against the institution that provided his central base of power — the BCU. It is quite possible that he himself vacillated between different strategies according to his own perception of opportunity. He had become so powerful, though, that even his tactical errors reverberated through the union and the district.[3]

At the beginning of the 1962-63 season, Mugoya promised the growers that they would receive two shillings (2/=) a pound for their coffee; the BCU committee estimated it could pay only 1/45, given that year's coffee market. The committee felt itself in a tight situation; the BCMA seemed to have a very good chance of getting its license under Kiwanuka's DP government, which had just won the national elections. The BCU would risk another state intervention if it raised prices so high that it faced a loss. The committee had heard that a Nairobi company had offered Muduku a price that would enable him to pay 2/= a pound in order to get the BCMA established. There was great concern on the committee that the BCU would lose large numbers of its members to the BCMA if it could not give them the price Mugoya had promised. Mutenio, however, threatened to resign if the higher price was paid, arguing that it would hurt the union badly and that it went against all of the principles of cooperation and education of the members. He did accede, however, to a resolution petitioning the Bugisu Coffee Trust Fund for the amount necessary to make up the difference in price to the peasants.

Mugoya was obviously becoming a political and financial liability to the union. He consistently opted for actions and policies that would enhance his popularity with the peasants. He became careless with confidential committee and official information and claimed authority beyond the powers of his own position. The committee had twice reprimanded him, Gimugu, and Wakiro for the problems their conflict was causing within the staff. There were also complaints against him by the staff for neglecting parts of his work and for spending large periods of time away from his office. The most serious accusation against him was complicity with the BCMA. His opponents claimed that he was actively supporting the BCMA and that he had told the growers that Muduku was correct in his claims that the BCU could pay higher prices to the farmers. Finally, the committee appointed a subcommittee of three of its own members, headed by George Waisi, a young and energetic northerner who had worked for the Bugisu Coffee Board and the BCU before being elected to the committee, to investigate and submit a report on staff problems.

Problems were also starting to develop between the cotton and the coffee departments of the BCU, complicated by the distrust between the north and the south. Each side was jealous of its representation on the committee, of the number of jobs it had in the union, and of the possibility that its crop was cheated to the profit of the other's.

There was talk of splitting the union between the two crops. Mutenio and Kitutu both opposed this, but Waisi, who was becoming better known and more popular throughout the north and was admired for his tough and imaginative ideas about improving the cooperative, was working for the split, as well as maneuvering to increase his own power on the committee. While there was neither then nor later any direct competition with Mutenio, Waisi and Gunigina were in clear competition for the second spot in the union. In a cooperative totally controlled by coffee growers, no one was strong enough to compete with Waisi.

Before the committee election in 1962, Mutenio announced that he would not accept the presidency or any other committee position. He said later, and it was generally accepted, that he refused to serve on the committee because it had been impossible for him to keep politics out of the union and that his own position in the DP had made the union vulnerable. He was also clearly worried at his own failure to control the committee and the staff sufficiently to normalize their relations. If he had a major competitor on the committee, it was Mugoya, who theoretically should have been taking orders from the committee, limiting his influence there to providing technical information. Mugoya still had direct access to a large majority of the committee and was instrumental in having Gimugu, his old foe, fired shortly after Mutenio quit.

Gunigina was elected president, and Waisi was elected vice-president. Both men received scholarships for six-month study tours to the United States during Gunigina's year and a half in office, and so one or the other was away during a good part of the time. The basic concerns and functioning of the committee remained much as they had been during Mutenio's term. The short-lived Kiwanuka government did recognize the BCMA and gave it a marketing license. A second national election brought a coalition of the UPC and the Kabaka Yekka, the Buganda royalist party, to power; the BCMA's trading license was revoked soon after, in January 1963. This ended its threat to the BCU's formal monopoly, but its political activities continued.

The Waisi Report and the Partition of the Union

Shortly before the BCMA license was revoked in January 1963, Waisi and four other committee members submitted the report of the investigations that they had been commissioned to make. They had spent a full month hearing evidence and complaints from peasants in GCSs throughout the coffee-growing areas. They reported that they had met attempted obstruction by politicians and some union employees thought to be connected with the BCMA.

Their report was couched in terms of what they were told by the peasants, but it had strong overtones of the conflicts within the union itself. Waisi was particularly keen on having the union broken up into separate organizations for coffee and cotton, and he was in direct competition for power in the coffee branch with Mugoya. Whether or not the report he submitted depicted exactly what he heard in the GCSs, it reflected heavily the same political directions that he was taking; it ultimately worked very much to his advantage. Just as the Gretton report used claims of peasant discontent to challenge the authority of BCU leaders, the Waisi report used claims of peasant discontent to attack the legitimacy of other Bagisu who held political positions that Waisi and his allies hoped to control. Waisi, however, was much more successful than the state had been, because he presented the peasants with a credible option.

No doubt there was real discontent among the coffee growers. Waisi's report emphasized the number of times coffee growers said that both prices and procedures had been much better under both Woods and Neal. According to the report, the peasants were also very unhappy with what seemed to be inordinate staff privileges and compensation. They complained about excessive pay scales, excessive and unbalanced pay raises, and the number of employees who were allowed to use union vehicles and other equipment, often for their own purposes.

The distribution of employment between the various regions was also strongly criticized. The report mentioned the various problems caused by the feud between the Bamuddu and the Babeza on the staff, but said that the membership resented the fact that so many of the top staff positions were dominated by the Bawalasi, the clan that included the two feuding lineages. Other complaints about the staff included charges of "clanism" and favoritism in hiring generally, redundant posts, and staff favoritism to their own areas and kin.

Waisi also reported criticisms of Mutenio, especially for supporting the Uganda Company. By and large the report was favorable to Neal. It accused the former committee and the staff of causing administrative problems and widespread disruption and confusion among the peasants in their campaign against him and criticized them for changing Neal's staff arrangements. The report also accused Gunigina of introducing political conflict into the committee.

By far the greatest part of the report, however, and the sharpest of its criticisms were directed against Mugoya. The report claimed that Mugoya had been directly involved in establishing the BCMA, that he had repeatedly given it financial and organizational advice, and that he had made the brokerage arrangements for it in Nairobi. It accused him of being most responsible for the disenchantment of the peasants with the union, for having promised them impossibly high prices, and for alienating many of the GCS members by bad management. It also took Mugoya to task for being the most responsible for perpetuating the feud with the Babeza staff members, Wakiro and Gimugu.

The report made a strong case for the separation of the cotton and coffee branches. According to Waisi, the coffee growers were unhappy with what they saw as domination by the cotton farmers. All three of the presidents up to that time had come from the south, and although Mutenio and Kitutu both grew some coffee, they, as well as Gunigina, were seen as cotton men. The report thus reaffirmed earlier statements in the BCU committee that the BCMA had been, in part, a reaction by northern coffee growers against dominance within the BCU by southern cotton growers. Thus, the report's criticisms of former committee action and Gunigina's behavior included some sectarian resentment against cotton.

Waisi used his tour effectively to increase his own prestige with the peasant farmers and to promote the idea of having a separate coffee union. Within the committee and in the district at large, he spoke much more openly about the wisdom of splitting up the union.

Mugoya had mustered enough support on the committee to fire Gimugu while Waisi was making his report. He managed this, however, just as his own power was collapsing. The union had received enough money from the Bugisu Coffee Fund to make up a part of the difference between their estimate and Mugoya's promised prices to the peasants, but the committee was angry at having to use this resort, and the peasants were disillusioned with Mugoya because they had received less than he had promised them. The growing evidence of Mugoya's political use of the union and of the trouble he had caused cost him the rest of the support he had had on the committee. Finally, the end of the BCMA as an effective threat left the union much less susceptible to the kind of pressure that Mugoya had been exerting. The next Annual General Meeting, which met in March 1963, was highly indignant at Gimugu's firing. The meeting dismissed Mugoya, thus eliminating what had been one of the major influences in the union and ending whatever chances Mugoya might have had to win political office.

Despite the opposition of influential men like Kitutu and Mutenio, and of Gunigina as well, the movement to split the union was gaining strength. In September 1963 the general meeting agreed, with DCD approval, that each crop should have its own cooperative. The coffee society, which kept the name Bugisu Cooperative Union, elected Waisi as its president. A separate cooperative, the Masaaba Cooperative Union, was formed to market cotton. Gunigina served as its president until 1979.

Party Politics and the BCU

With the coffee and cotton departments split, and Mugoya and Gimugu both fired, Waisi was by far the most influential man in the BCU. Mugoya's old post of general manager and that of his assistant were both abolished. Wakiro was appointed as secretary/manager, the newly established senior staff position. Unlike either Gimugu or Mugoya, Wakiro had never been in a political or leadership position; he had no other basis of power than his own job and showed no disposition to challenge the dominance that Waisi was asserting.

Waisi had achieved this position in large part by eliminating completely from the organization its other major foci of power. He either had defeated them entirely, as in the case of Mugoya, or had divided the base of power in such a way as to leave himself without competition, as in the separation of coffee and cotton growers. In contrast with Kitutu, who also was without important competition within the union itself, Waisi was in charge of an organization free of the Bugisu Coffee Board's control. He thus had much more freedom to implement his own policies. He had achieved this power through his interactions with and promises to the coffee-growing peasants, offering them the benefits of a stronger union and the solutions to their discontents. His ability to fulfill these promises, however, depended ultimately on the newly independent government's concession of autonomy to the union. His own and other committee members' participation in party politics and their occupation of the important and powerful new posts, which political changes had opened to the Bagisu, promised to give him that ability.

The most important of these posts were the memberships to Parliament. Control of these positions allowed a limited number of Bagisu a greater extent of power at a higher level of articulation than previously had been available to them. The existence of these positions made exchange relations with their holders a crucial secondary source of power, so that politicians at the district level were strongly opposed to each other either for direct control of parliamentary seats or in support of one of the candidates. The participation of national parties and their extension into district council affairs widened the basis of alliance between candidates and the supporters of each party in different areas and intensified the conflict between parties in each area.

The introduction of party politics and the rewards offered for electoral success created new conflicts and intensified old ones. Because many of the major figures in these conflicts also held positions in the BCU, it was inevitable that the BCU's internal struggles would reflect those that were going on outside and around it. Mutenio stood for MP in south Bugisu as an Independent in 1961 and as a member of the DP in 1962, losing both times to Wakholi, the secretary who had been dismissed from his staff position for signing an illegal contract for tin sheets in 1955. Mugoya stood as an Independent in 1961 for north Bugisu, losing to Muduku, and was organizing to stand again in 1962 but was finally discouraged. Waisi was becoming an important figure within the UPC, though he did not stand for office within it until he won the northern constituency chairmanship in 1969. He was closely allied to Wakholi, as well as to the other UPC MP, Kitutu's son Kimaswa, from Manjiya. He fought Muduku both on cooperative and political grounds and quite violently opposed any union officials who had connections, political or cooperative, with him.

These conflicts extended to the general membership as a result of Muduku's attempt to identify the BCMA as a DP organization, a ploy he needed to gain favor with the government under which he was trying to get a coffee selling and export license. This use of party connections made Mutenio's position as head of DP in the district especially problematic within the union itself. No matter how much he tried to keep the committee from a division along political lines, he himself was too vulnerable a target. The eventual defeat of the BCMA and the separation of the two unions were effectively UPC triumphs, as they brought a committee with close political ties to that party into power. It also left the breakaway societies that had joined the BCMA vulnerable to politically based reprisals when they tried to rejoin the BCU. As late as 1971, some of these societies had not been allowed to reincorporate, and their members were forced to sell through GCSs controlled by other lineages and located in other areas. The BCU could thus be used directly to reward political loyalty and to punish opposition. This gave the union's leaders a highly effective resource with which to negotiate within the national parties at the district level.

The struggles for power between committee and staff, as well as for control or position within committee and staff, also extended into the general membership as rivals sought to mobilize the peasants. As long as the structure that the state imposed on the union through statutory regulations and official decisions limited the power of cooperative roles, the committee and staff members had very limited resources for the expansion of their power through exchange and alliance. As soon as power was restored to their positions, individuals not only were able to engage in negotiations and exchanges in order to expand it, but also were in some cases obliged to use these means to protect their positions.

Mutenio had wanted to run the BCU like a modern business, but he was also much concerned with Bagisu rights and welfare. Both his personal beliefs and his other political positions in the district enhanced his sensitivity to pressure from the peasants and from other committee members to confront the state directly. Neal's insistence on ignoring Mutenio and his committee stimulated a tremendous resurgence of populist agitation against the state. Rival claimants to power were able to manipulate the strong political emotions of this resurgence to their own advantage. If Neal had not frustrated the Bagisu leaders so completely, neither Mugoya nor Waisi could have achieved the power they did, nor could they have used it in such disruptive ways. Subsequent chapters will recount how Waisi's use of the enormous personal powers he had gained led eventually to another disastrous confrontation with other Bagisu and then with the state.

The Effects of Conflict

Clearly, the conflicts in the union and over its control were costly to the efficiency of the union as a commercial organization. The particular issues behind which it was possible to mobilize the popular support that the Bagisu leaders needed in their struggles for power were not those that would have made the union itself more efficient or profitable. In this sense, these struggles can be seen as prejudicial to the Bagisu themselves if we assume that a cost-efficient union would have directly benefited them. The state's tendency to appropriate reserve and surplus funds, both in Uganda and in other African nations (see esp. Bates, 1981), makes this assumption untenable. Rather, it seems more plausible to conclude that the Bagisu peasants benefited because these struggles prevented either the BCU or the state from achieving clear or direct control over the coffee crop. They also moderated the extent to which the Bagisu themselves depended on commercial crops. The prices available through protest and the freedom from the extra work involved in carrying cherry to a central pulping station and in maintaining quality control left the Bagisu closer to a subsistence economy. This was finally the basis for any political resistance that they organized against the state or the commercial cropping system represented by the BCU. The peasants' concern with price and quality perpetuated a situation that individual leaders could exploit for their own power and profit, but only to the extent that they could maintain peasant support. In order to do this, they had to keep upward pressures on prices and to protect the Bagisu from excessive exploitation of their labor. Both of these imperatives left them susceptible to state intervention in the BCU, the basis for their own power, and ultimately to the risk of being debarred from office.

Because of its dependence on peasant agriculture, the Ugandan state had to balance its need for more revenues against the possibility of so alienating the peasants that they would cease or reduce their cash cropping or would lower their controls on quality. This exit option cost the peasants in terms of cash incomes, but it also reduced their opportunity costs by freeing up time for other kinds of economies. The state did not enjoy a subsistence option and so suffered effective vetoes on its own initiatives under this threat. This threat did provide local leaders with the possibility of enhancing their own power, but even these leaders' own strategies for power may have retarded, as in this case, the capture of the peasantry by reinforcing their resistance to lower prices, quality controls, differential prices, and so forth. The constant pressure on prices and the resistance to quality controls that the Bagisu leaders maintained in their struggles with the state and with each other limited the capacity of the union to appropriate surplus and thus limited the potential power of the BCU officeholders, while it made them susceptible to intervention by the state. The upward pressure on prices and the resistance to quality controls also limited the state's capacity to appropriate surplus value. The result of the struggles described here was that the Bagisu continued to grow coffee—but on their own terms. This reduced the economic importance and the demands of cash cropping and of its potentially disruptive effects on their own economies and social organization. The inefficiencies caused by struggles for power over the BCU were expensive, but they were also part of a struggle by which a freeholding peasantry resisted subordination to even more exploitative relations of production.

The peasants expressed dissatisfaction with the ways their leaders used their powers and positions in their own benefit, but they nonetheless resisted the state's attempts to reduce these leaders' powers. They rejected the state's invocation of cooperative principles as a justification for state intervention. Because of their discontent, however, the peasants could be mobilized behind competing Bagisu claimants to power.

Competition for market control kept the relations between the peasantry, local power groups, and the central state highly unstable. This instability prevented the formation of powerful local classes and preserved the political and economic integrity of peasant lineages and communities. The next chapter will show, however, that when local conflicts intensified, they directly undermined the autonomy of the only organizations able to articulate peasant demands to the state. The intensity of these struggles for local power also limited the possibility that a coherent national peasantry could emerge to defend its own interests against a centralizing state. The Bagisu, and other ethnic peasantries, could exercise a veto power against the state's intervention in local affairs, but their isolation meant that they could not affect policy in any constructive or positive manner at the national level. They and their leaders remained bound to local politics.[4]

NOTES

1. J. N. K. Wakholi had been dismissed as committee secretary, a staff position, for his part in the Patel contract (see Chapter 4), but was later elected to the BCU committee.

2. According to Mutenio, "Mr. Neal was asked to train the staff and the committee to take over when he left, but he despised them and did not inform them of anything. The committee continued to meet, but it was never informed by Mr. Neal." Interview, Mbale, April 1970.

3. My interviews with Mugoya were among the most frustrating that I have ever done. I was courteously received in his large, comfortable house, and he was willing to talk for hours. He managed never to tell me anything that I did not already know and was steadfast in recounting the past to shed favorable light on himself and unfavorable light on his opponents, even when this involved suppressing events or changing their sequence.

4. The intensely local nature of both politics and class action in Uganda helps to explain why ethnic identity figures so strongly and so disruptively in national politics (cf. Young, 1976, and Saul, 1976). Neither of these authors nor others who focus on ethnicity in Ugandan national politics have adequately recognized that this ethnic identity and the local nature of political concerns are profoundly rooted in the economic relations between the central state and local organization.

6

Struggles for Administrative Control
after Independence, 1963-66

George Waisi assumed the presidency of the BCU unencumbered by most of the restrictions that earlier committees had fought against. W. E. Neal had been withdrawn, and the Bugisu Coffee Board had been dissolved. The wealthiest sector of the union was now independent of the poorer but politically astute cotton growers. The staff had been prohibited from holding political office. Paulo Mugoya and A. G. Gimugu, the most powerful staff members, had been fired. Political uncertainties and a peculiar federalism in the newly independent state allowed more autonomy at the local level, and the DCD was loathe to exercise its statutory powers.

Waisi himself was extremely ambitious, both for himself and for the BCU. His ample use of the committee's freedom and power and his attempts to extend them brought to a boil the conflicts that had been simmering between different groups in the union and in the district. During his brief term, BCU policy set off a bloody border war between Bugisu and Sebei. Waisi's demands to control sales and expenditures personally led to intense conflict with and disruption of the staff. As in the previous fights for control, the popular leaders attempted to mobilize peasant support—and Waisi was extremely effective in this. This time, however, peasant mobilization was directed against other Bagisu in a struggle for internal power. The resulting vituperation and bitterness divided the union and the district. This conflict prompted the Bagisu staff members to appeal to the national level of the DCD for arbitration, thus finally breaking the united front of committee and staff against central state intervention. Thus, the autonomy that the BCU had so assiduously sought and defended, once gained, stimulated conflicts over internal power. In the resulting battles, some Bagisu were willing to compromise the union's autonomy to protect their own powers.

The independence enjoyed by the separate coffee cooperative led to much more intense interaction, manipulation, and negotiation among the power-holders who had access to its resources. That the union could no longer demand control over the Bugisu Coffee Fund had little real effect, as the Bagisu had never controlled the fund and as the BCU had only used it in its argument against the now-defunct Bugisu Coffee Board. Local power-holders had control over sales, the letting of contracts, buying, and the setting of prices. Even without the fund, the union's high annual turnover, its ability to get loans, and its great liquid assets were sufficient to provide a rich resource base to whoever could control it. Political groups, organizations, sections of the union, and individuals fought to control all or some part of this base. The strong members of the committee were able to achieve compliance from the other committee members through the sharing of power, favors, and spoils. They manipulated most of the staff through substantial salary increases or the threat of dismissal. Struggles between national parties were played out at the district level in the conflicts between the BCMA, which was allied with one party, and the BCU, which became increasingly associated with another.

Committee and staff activities and meetings became more numerous and more intense during this period. I felt slightly overwhelmed as I read through the lengthy legal proceedings, reams of correspondence, and voluminous committee minutes that were filed during these two and a half years. Much of the archival record documents charges, countercharges, defenses, and attacks based on highly idiosyncratic or opportunistic interpretations of cooperative rules. Any pretense of cooperation or effort at compromise was abandoned during the final stages of these struggles, with staff, committee, and government agencies all openly fighting to maintain the powers they claimed. I have simplified the strategic and legal intricacies of these fights as much as accuracy and comprehension allow for presentation in this chapter.

Both the internal power struggles and their outcomes reflected the rapidly changing balance of political force at the national level. The removal of a colonial state subject to direct British control had opened up national-level sources of power and wealth for which individuals and groups contended. The national state was up for grabs, and the groups that sought to capture it were often willing to forego economic considerations in their bids for power. National independence in 1962 created favorable conditions for building local power bases. The colonial government had granted extensive new powers to local administrations and their representative councils. The extensive decentralization of power during the final years of the protectorate government continued after formal independence was achieved. There was a net flow of resources toward all of the districts (Leys, 1967) as competitors for national-level positions sought support through alliances, concessions, and favors to local politicians.

Power Relations: An Overview of the Period

The separation of the two unions and the beginning of Waisi's presidency occurred less than a year after Uganda became fully independent. The new constitution provided for a federal structure of four kingdoms and ten territories. In order to safeguard their own prerogatives, the monarchies had resisted the establishment of a strong central government, so there was much more local autonomy in political and economic matters than there had been during the colonial period or than there would be during the more centralized republic that Milton Obote established and maintained from 1966 to 1971.

The competition between the three national parties also contributed to the greater local self-determination of these years. No national party had a clear majority, and until 1964 the UPC depended on its alliance with the Baganda royalist party, the Kabaka Yekka (KY), in order to stay in power. The national government and the parties were in a position very similar to that of the BCU committee during the years of its struggles with the Bugisu Coffee Board; all had to favor their constituents' wishes to build a strong following. Just as the BCU committee had been unwilling to implement unpopular programs of quality control, the central powers were reluctant to impose controls that might alienate support among local influentials. Because of these political considerations, agencies of the central government such as the DCD tended to act cautiously. Their own policies in the new situation of national independence were not clearly defined.

The committee took full advantage of the BCU's new freedom. For a time it was able to mobilize both staff and membership through the promise of a stronger, more profitable union. Various of its projects met with disapproval from the DCD, but the committee's usual response was simply to ignore DCD objections. The conflicts that eventually resulted from staff resistance to the committee's expanding powers and from both staff and committee attempts to mobilize popular opposition against the other finally precipitated state intervention and the imposition of much stronger controls, but only after a coup had resolved the struggles for power between the competing national parties and after internal conflicts had seriously split Bagisu popular leadership.

The Bureaucratization of the Staff and Its Alliance with the DCD

The Gretton report had started the isolation of the staff from power bases outside the union, and Waisi's success in having Mugoya dismissed completed the process. Senior staff members now held their positions on the basis of training and experience. Most, like Wakiro, had worked for the DCD; several had received professional training abroad.

The prohibition of staff participation in politics and the greater professionalization of staff members clarified the lines and functions between the staff and the committee. The committee no longer had political reasons to seek alliances and support from influential members of the staff, nor were individual staff members in a position to demand special favors from the committee.

The full-time and professional dedication to and dependence on their bureaucratic work, which resulted from the depoliticization of their positions, left the staff members more vulnerable to the kind of committee interference in routine operations criticized by Hyden (1970b) and Kasfir (1970). The overall efficiency of the staff increased, as they had no other resource than their own performance. Their only power against the committee was the legal or contractual definition of their roles and duties provided by the DCD. The only safeguards available to them against the committee were now based totally on power derived from the higher domain of national government, and they finally used this power to resist the power the committee was building up through a whole network of exchange-based alliances.

The Committee Expands Its Powers

The union went through its most turbulent and most dynamic period during Waisi's term, which lasted only from February 18, 1964, to August 12, 1966, when it was dissolved by government order and its current members were all forbidden to hold cooperative office again. The membership was probably more involved in the union's affairs than at any other time in its history, in part because Waisi took his ideas to them for approval and support, and in part because most of the various factions in the power struggles that developed during those years ultimately took their arguments outside of the union office building in Mbale to mobilize support for themselves and opposition against their competitors. Waisi's style was quite different from both the paternal, slightly evangelical style of Samson Kitutu, who urged the Bagisu to work together as brothers in order to stand equal to the Europeans, and the quiet, sober style of Mutenio, who urged that the union be run as an orderly and efficient business. Waisi flamboyantly insisted that the union itself was a rich and powerful body that should exploit all of its resources to become richer and more powerful and that he, as head and director of the union, should have a corresponding degree of authority to ensure that it realized this potential.

Whether the times suited the man or the man suited the times, Waisi's own character and background were strongly reflected in his policies for the union. The only one of the committee presidents from 1954 to 1983 who was not the son of a chief and a member of a relatively wealthy family, Waisi had less formal education before joining the union than any of the presidents except Kitutu, and his social and financial position changed drastically afterward. His personal career was as dramatic, turbulent, and ambitious as the policies he promoted.

Waisi was born in Buginyanya, the northernmost *gombolola* on the border with the Sebei. His father, a farmer, paid his school fees until he passed primary grade six, and then he worked to get through two years of junior secondary. When he left school, he got a job with Colin Campbell, the cooperative officer for Bugisu and Sebei, helping to organize the new GCSs in his home area. A year later he volunteered to join the British army, where he received further training, and rose to the rank of sergeant, serving in Libya and Egypt. He applied for work as secretary to the BCS while he was still in Libya. He worked for the BCS in a series of jobs, some in the main office and others in the field, traveling through most of the district in various capacities. Kitutu had been a friend of his father's, and the older man advised and helped him in different jobs, finally assisting him to get a scholarship from the BCU committee to the Longhborough and Consumer cooperative schools in England in 1956 and 1957. There he met other men from Uganda, two of whom were later to become UPC ministers in Obote's government. He worked briefly for the BCU, then quit to join the committee. Kitutu got him work in a company that sold the BCU much of its equipment so that he could learn more about merchandising and continue to earn a good salary while serving on the committee.

The committee selected him to take a one-month course on cooperative management in Israel in 1958 and later sent him to an agricultural cooperative school in Kenya for several months. As already mentioned, he spent six months in the United States studying cooperatives after his election as vice-president in 1962, returning through Israel and the Middle East. He then was sent back to England for a three-month course in coffee marketing at the end of 1963. After he became president of the BCU, he made other, shorter trips to Scandinavia, Germany, and Italy for study courses and later again to Italy, first for more courses, and then for direct investigation of the coffee market and the possibility of direct sale of Bugisu coffee to Europe. As early as 1962, he was helping to organize and was winning office in the national cooperative apex organizations that were then being set up in Uganda. He traveled extensively in this work and met with many of the new national politicians, some of whom, including Obote, he had met earlier on his various trips to Europe.

Waisi took over the presidency with a wide knowledge of the union and its proceedings, experience in the national cooperative movement and contacts with its other leaders, the acquaintance of most of the GCS leaders and of many peasants through his various coffee jobs and positions, and the prestige of his numerous study tours. He also came in with the knowledge that he probably had more training and experience in cooperatives than any member of either the staff or the committee, as well as more experience outside Bugisu and Uganda than anyone else in the union. Waisi was the first and the only president to rise to that position completely through his experiences in the union itself. He had been deliberately trained, with committee support, as an expert; and he had already shown himself to be bright, ambitious, and capable in his earlier pursuits. He assumed his new position eager to put all of his considerable energy into improving the union in ways he thought it should be improved. All of these ideas included his direct and active participation and control.

Staff, committee members, and the Annual General Meeting were all enthused at first by his aggressive and imaginative plans and were willing to support his intervention in the daily running of the union. They accepted his ideas about the changes necessary in marketing procedure, and most accepted his word that if he personally controlled marketing, he could establish direct sales in Europe and get much higher prices. Two of the other members of the subcommittee to investigate union problems had also been elected to the committee when Waisi was elected president. Part of the enthusiasm for Waisi and his committee came from the expectation that the firing of Mugoya and the subsequent rearrangements of the staff were first steps in the solution of the problems that Waisi had reported and that other reforms would follow.

Waisi came to power on promises to cut back the administrative expenditures of the union, make its operation more efficient, and utilize its reserve funds to establish a strong Bagisu role in the district's commerce. He claimed that all of these changes would bring more money to the coffee growers. Waisi did follow his program of expanding the BCU's more direct participation in the district's commerce, and he did make occasional moves in the direction of more efficient staff organization, but in addition to the grandiose schemes he outlined his term was characterized by increased expenditures by and special privileges for the committee members. He himself ended his term considerably and visibly more prosperous than he had begun it, as the owner of two expensive cars, a Mercedes Benz and a Land Rover, a large new house, and a well-capitalized business in Mbale. He manipulated committee privileges to reward the compliance most of the committee gave him, and he used his considerable powers to punish committee and staff members who opposed him.

Waisi's drive to increase the union's power was tightly entwined with his continuous struggle to increase his own sway over it. He clearly thought that the union had to be run as a tightly disciplined and unified instrument that would take and implement his ideas and orders quickly and efficiently. There was little room in this notion for dissension or disagreement. He did more and came closer toward achieving the acceptance, at least in principle, of central pulperies than any other person in the union's history. He finally backed off when it became clear that there was still so much resistance to the idea that many growers would participate only grudgingly at best, and that forceful or obligatory implementation would lead to widespread alienation and hostility among the peasants.

In addition to his advocacy of central pulperies and direct overseas sales, Waisi's most notable plans for the union were the construction of a large hotel and office building and of extensive new storage facilities for coffee. The DCD was firmly opposed to plans for the hotel, and it directly told the committee that it would not approve such expenditures. It was less directly critical of Waisi's plans to sell overseas. Waisi and the committee simply ignored or found ways to circumvent official opposition to the hotel plan. They arranged to employ architects and start construction with funds the union had in its own control, despite the commissioner's clear statement that he would not allow either the loans or the drawing of reserve funds that would be necessary to finish the project.

The committee also was voting funds for a training center for GCS officers and staff and for a large number of voting shares in the newly established Uganda Cooperative Bank. Waisi had been important in establishing the bank, and he was elected to a two-year term as its president in 1964. D. M. Kimaswa, MP, the BCU committee treasurer, and a close Waisi ally, was elected as the bank's treasurer. Waisi was also serving as president of the Uganda Central Cooperative Union, a post he had held since 1962.

Committee expenses skyrocketed during Waisi's term. Committee members made extended trips to address peasants on ways to grow and treat coffee. The original proposal was for Waisi to accompany district officials on these trips, but members of the committee thought that this was unfair and demanded that they all go on these expeditions. The expenditures budgeted for one of these expeditions in 1964 were as high as 10,000 shillings for subsistence and 10,000 shillings for travel.

Already in 1964 there were other indications of the committee members' willingness to spend union money on themselves. They increased the cash allowances they received for travel, for meetings, and for overnight stays on committee business, and voted that four rooms of the union's office building should be maintained for their own personal use when they were in Mbale on union business. They allowed Kimaswa to rent one of the union's houses, which were reserved at special rates for union employees, and gave another committee member an outright grant to help him build a house in town. There were some objections that Waisi had not used the money the committee loaned him to buy a car to tend to his duties, but the committee took no action on this issue.

The committee's expenditures were by no means limited to its members, however. It disbursed over 30,000 shillings in scholarships to Bagisu children each year, although there were some indications that the distribution of this money was determined more by political connections than by merit. It made loans to several GCSs for improving their facilities or expanding their services, in several cases by building maize mills.

Waisi was extremely popular with the general membership, and his relations with the staff continued to be generally good during 1965. There was talk on the committee about restricting travel and meeting expenses, but once again nothing was done to cut these back. The committee did, however, lodge a formal complaint in 1965 that the district cooperative officer was not cooperating with them, was attending none of their meetings, and was telling the Bagisu that the

BCU was cheating them. The growers, meanwhile, were confirming their enthusiasm for the BCU's new policies by bringing in the largest coffee crop in the BCU's history (see Appendix 1).

Waisi's aggressive, innovative plans for the union, his success in carrying discussion and debate about them to the general membership, and his ability to move from district-level to national-level cooperative organization manifested the extraordinary widening of political experience and understanding, both among the popular leaders and among the Bagisu peasants, over the two decades since the first sub-parish level cooperatives were founded. The content and the forms of political discourse and mobilization had changed radically; popular leaders confronted official agencies in technical discussions about the world coffee market and investment strategies, and the members of the GCSs were asked to support specific programs and policies far more complex than the formerly central issues of coffee prices, bonuses, and collection schedules.

Committee Interests and Separatist Movements

The BCU did confront serious problems during the first two years of Waisi's term. The Sebei, who had nine societies in the BCU, several of which contained many Bagisu who had migrated there before Sebei became a separate district in 1962, had finally established their own union.[1] The opinion of both the Bagisu and the DCD was that the new union had neither the membership nor the staff to be viable on its own. The developing ethnic consciousness of the Sebei and their resentment of Bagisu domination finally convinced the state that it would be wiser to allow the Sebei to set up their own coffee cooperative union, with continued rights to have their coffee processed at the Bugisu Coffee Mill. In March 1964 all but one of the Sebei GCSs indicated their intention to withdraw from the BCU, and the new union was formally registered in October 1964. The only society in Sebei that did not withdraw was the Bugimotwa GCS, which was close to the north Bugisu border and almost all of whose members were immigrants from Bugisu.

Waisi was the president of the Bugimotwa society. This position satisfied the condition that every member of the BCU committee had to be a member of a GCS committee and a delegate from that committee to the union's Annual General Meeting. Waisi obviously had a keen interest in keeping the Bugimotwa GCS within the BCU. The Bagisu members of the society not only wanted to remain with their fellow

Bagisu but also were unwilling to leave the prosperous BCU for the weak Sebei union.

According to the original terms of the Sebei union's registration, each society would choose which of the two unions it would join. In October 1964, however, a BCU driver for the Bugimotwa GCS was threatened by Sebei, and the next day the bridge to the GCS was destroyed. At a public meeting on October 31, the Kingoo, Sebei's constitutional monarch,[2] its secretary-general, and its administrative secretary all urged violence against both the BCU and the Bagisu living in Sebei District. Violence did break out soon after that, with Sebei killing several Bagisu, burning houses, and slashing coffee trees and banana plants. The Bagisu retaliated. They were heavily outnumbered, but their settlements, based on banana cultivation, were more densely populated than those of the millet-growing Sebei, who needed more land for subsistence. They therefore had a certain strategic advantage in what was essentially a series of terrorist attacks.

On November 14 Bagisu and Sebei leaders and cooperative officers met with government officials and agreed that they all would respect the vote of Bugimotwa GCS members about which society they wanted to join. The members voted overwhelmingly to stay with the BCU. The attacks from the Sebei continued, and the war was escalated. On January 5, 1965, the BCU committee, under strong pressure from the commissioner for cooperative development, voted that the Bugimotwa GCS should join the Sebei union and that the union be given a monopoly on coffee in its district.

By this time, however, the war had become a series of retaliations and vendettas between the Sebei and the Bagisu, and the fighting increased. The Uganda army sent troops in to police the area, but for the most part these soldiers refused to patrol at night, when most of the raiding took place, claiming that they would be no match for men who knew the paths much better than they did and could take advantage of the dark. The superior numbers of the Sebei started to tell, and many Bagisu were fleeing across the district line. The fighting continued in Sebei into 1966, with estimates of dead ranging fom 50 to 400.

Waisi himself had already moved officially to Buginyanya, where he was born and still had land, just across a valley from Sebei. He had enough power there to join the Buginyanya GCS, which called a special meeting and elected him president. In order to do this, Waisi supporters deposed and expelled the current president, Andrew Nandala, a prosperous and influential farmer, businessman, and former BCU committee member who was a local leader of the DP. Waisi's move brought party competition and considerable clan conflict to the Buginyanya cooperative and provided him with a large number of enemies on his home ground, but it allowed him to maintain his qualifications to be on the BCU committee.

The other problem the BCU faced was the continuing activity of the BCMA which, despite growing internal problems and the fact that it had not been allowed to sell coffee since 1963, still held meetings. The BCU had appointed a publicity secretary specifically to combat BCMA influence, but the cooperative officer, Bugisu, complained that his meetings were neither as frequent nor as effective as the BCMA's. Stephen Muduku opposed Waisi in every election during his term, at one time standing for each of the committee positions, but he never received many votes. His organization did, however, make the BCU leaders uneasy. In 1964 they wrote to the chief police agent stationed in Mbale that "subversive elements are fomenting and planning to cause trouble at the [Annual General] Meeting" and requested that he "take necessary precautionary steps before people's lives are put in danger." In 1965 Muduku challenged the procedure by which he had been defeated in that year's election. The BCU had to call a special general meeting under government supervision to hold the elections again, but again Muduku came nowhere near winning. He was certainly not helped by former BCMA officials who circulated a document charging him with misappropriating large sums of money (457,000 shillings) from the BCMA.

Some of the societies that had joined the BCMA in 1962 were suffering more serious problems. By law, they had had to dissolve themselves legally before they left the BCU, and when the BCMA trading license was revoked they could only sell their coffee through other GCSs. They were therefore trying to have their own GCSs registered in order to join the BCU again. This move was opposed by the GCSs in which they were selling their coffee, as the increased volume meant bigger dividends to all of these GCSs' members there. Their opposition rekindled the clan resentment that had led to violence in the BCMA's campaign, and there were a rash of beatings and at least one killing. Houses were burned and coffee trees were slashed. The antagonisms were exacerbated by some of the BCMA supporters, who continued to agitate against the BCU.

While neither Muduku's attempts to gain BCU office nor the sporadic violence between BCMA and BCU partisans constituted any direct threat to either the BCU or the committee, they were a continuing nuisance and concern to the union. Since Mugoya's firing, no one on either the staff or the committee could remotely be suspected of BCMA sympathies, but the tension of Muduku's continuing activities contributed in part to the great support that Waisi enjoyed within the union during the early part of his term.

Staff Resistance to the Committee: The Waisi-Wakiro Conflict

Waisi's rise to power and his expansive strategies as president depended on extensive popular contact and mobilization. His position in the BCU and the access to transport and audiences that it gave him were crucial to Waisi's attempts to expand committee autonomy from both staff and the DCD. These activities and his frequent successes allowed him to increase his personal influence and the power of the committee itself.

The committee presented its projects to the general membership as a means of engendering the local development that the Bagisu deserved in return for their labor and the use of their resources. Waisi's programs were enthusiastically supported by most of the Bagisu (Brett, 1970), but as the management staff started to see its own powers threatened, it joined the DCD in opposing these programs and Waisi's direct involvement in them. Staff members invoked principles of the bureaucratic division of functions, the role of expert knowledge, and the primacy of management efficiency to combat Waisi's attempts to expand representative powers and to diversify the BCU's economic activities.

Wakiro led the campaign against Waisi. He appealed to the commissioner of cooperative development, first for support, and later for arbitration, to enforce the management principles he was invoking. A long and bitter fight came to a head in early 1966, badly splitting the committee, in which a majority supported Waisi, and the staff. Waisi's faction invoked principles of ethnic unity and rights to self-determination and accused staff members of putting their own and the state's interests ahead of the Bagisu's as a whole. The DCD officers supported the staff, strongly criticizing Waisi and his committee throughout the district. They blamed Waisi for the various conflicts within and around the BCU, which they claimed were seriously threatening its economic viability.

The issue that finally brought chaos to the union and eventually led to the expulsion of both Waisi and Wakiro was Waisi's campaign to sell coffee directly overseas. This idea had at first been wholeheartedly supported by both committee and staff, and Waisi went on a promotional junket to England and Germany. He reported that the prospects were very favorable when he returned to Mbale, and he went on a second trip to Europe in 1965, this time accompanied by his wife. While he was there, the committee voted to send Wakiro along with him.

Cautious statements in committee minutes and my interviews with some committee members suggest that the committee was uneasy about Waisi's disposition of his expense money and his honesty in closing the contracts. Wakiro refused to go, saying it was an unjustified expense. He also stated that Waisi's second trip had also been unnecessary, as he, Wakiro, had already made arrangements to close the contracts with the European buyers' agents in Kampala. Various members of the union were concerned about who was paying for Mrs. Waisi's trip. It was unclear whether the money that Waisi had requested was also for his wife, whether the coffee buyers themselves had invited her and were paying her way, or whether Waisi had accepted money from both the BCU and from the coffee buyers for his wife's trip. Waisi himself maintained that his wife had paid her own way.

When Waisi returned, the chief cooperative officer for Uganda claimed that Wakiro as secretary/manager, rather than Waisi, should legally have signed the contracts for export. Wakiro complained that Waisi had not adequately informed him about the new arrangements. He repeated his objections to Waisi's trip and also to his having signed the contract. He also demanded a further accounting of Waisi's expenses on his European trip, even after Waisi's financial report had been accepted by the committee.

In February 1966 the committee voted to dismiss Wakiro, charging that he had disobeyed legitimate orders in refusing to go to Europe. Three of the eight committee members objected and subsequently left the meeting.[3] Within three days of Wakiro's dismissal, fourteen GCSs sent in a letter requesting a general meeting in order to consider the committee's reasons. The Umuinga, Bugisu's constitutional monarch,[4] wrote a harsh, insulting letter to Waisi, demanding that Wakiro be taken back, accusing Waisi of trying to wreck the BCU and to profit personally from it, and implying that Waisi had been directly responsible for the problems that arose in Sebei. He asked Waisi to refrain from causing serious problems in the district in order to achieve his own personal ambitions. Waisi answered the Umuinga in much the same tone, essentially telling him to mind his own business and mixing denials with his own insults and accusations against the Umuinga. Each had marked his letter confidential and included a list of twenty-two persons to whom copies had been sent.

The exchange between the Umuinga and Waisi set the tone for much of the long battle that followed. Charges and countercharges included detailed allegations about each participant's activities far outside the issues that had started the conflict between Waisi and Wakiro. Waisi was demanding the resignation of the three committee members who had left the meeting to protest Wakiro's firing, and Wakiro and Waisi were each complaining that the other was conducting a campaign of slander against him throughout the district.

A brief respite was achieved when four *basakulu*, a term which generally means elder but can also be translated as founder in the context of the union, requested to chair a meeting between the staff and the committee to iron out the differences between them. These four, who included Kitutu and B. B. N. Mafabi, a highly respected, sometime committee member who had made a name for himself as a persistent but fair-minded and astute critic of the union and was then working as personal secretary to the Umuinga, had until then remained neutral in the conflict. All had distinguished themselves in the early days of the cooperatives.

They made their bid as arbitrators in highly traditional terms, presenting themselves as "fathers" attempting to settle the differences between "sons." Because the Bagisu valued respect for their elders, any direct refusal to cooperate with them and deal reasonably with their suggestions would have made any of the competitors look very bad. The meeting itself, which took place February 25, was calm, orderly, and productive. The committee apologized to the *basakulu* for the disturbances that had occurred in the union. The members acknowledged that they had taken over the union from the older men and that they were running it for the advantage of all the Bagisu. They voted to reinstate Wakiro with a reprimand for his disobedience to their instructions. Everyone agreed that Waisi would have the power to sign contracts with foreign buyers. The *baksakulu* directed Wakiro to try to cooperate with the committee.

Waisi wrote the formal letter offering reinstatement to Wakiro the next day, but Wakiro refused his offer, claiming again that Waisi had been speaking against him in the district and that the dispute between them had not yet been resolved. On March 8, however, the day that Waisi had set as the deadline of his offer, Wakiro wrote Waisi that he had "accepted the persuasion of the Bagisu elders and founders" to return to the union; however, he demanded a new contract for his own protection and maintained that he would not accept the committee's reprimand "unless the award of the registrar or arbitrator so directs and is accepted by me."

The request for a general meeting was postponed until after the arbitration, which Wakiro now formally requested, and it was suggested that unless there were further difficulties the meeting could wait until the regularly scheduled Annual General Meeting. Colin Campbell, who was by then chief cooperative officer for Uganda, served as arbitrator, accepting lengthy depositions in which each side brought up all of their grievances and accusations.

Wakiro presented his case as being against Waisi. The committee members were now charging that Wakiro's refusal to act as they had directed had resulted in heavy trading losses both in Nairobi and abroad, and they added gross mismanagement to their charges against him. They rebutted each of his claims that he was not consulted on certain important decisions, showing from records that he had actually been present at the relevant meetings. They also enumerated ways in which they felt that Wakiro's demands and accusations demonstrated that he was overstepping his own authority and trespassing on the domain of the committee.

On April 7 Campbell submitted his decision that the committee's request that Wakiro go to Germany was unreasonable and that he was justified in refusing it, that there was no basis for the charge of gross mismanagement, and that the union should pay the cost of the arbitration.

Three and a half weeks after Campbell submitted his decision, the committee issued a letter to all staff and appropriate government officers announcing a reorganization of the management. The most significant changes were the abolition of the posts of secretary/manager and assistant secretary/manager and their replacement by the posts of secretary and coffee manager. Wakiro was to be the coffee manager, and his former assistant was to be sent to Mombasa as assistant general manager, to supervise the BCU's warehouses there. The new secretary was to be E. K. Gimadu, former publicity secretary and a friend of Waisi's from Buginyanya. The committee justified these changes with claims that certain posts were "overloaded," i.e., had too much work and too many responsibilities, and that the changes would allow considerable savings in staff expenses. Wakiro saw this as another attempt to remove him as chief executive officer.

Waisi assured him that he was still the chief executive officer, that neither his contract nor his salary was affected by the title change, and that he had all of the powers he had had before except those involved in the duties of the secretary. He did not directly answer Wakiro's objection that he would no longer have the power to co-sign all checks with the president. Waisi apparently assumed that this power had been Wakiro's by virtue of his secretaryship rather than of his managership. In any event, in the committee's new job definitions, the power to sign checks passed to Gimadu, who had by now clearly allied himself to Waisi.

On May 12 the former assistant secretary/manager, the mill manager, the accountant, and Wakiro filed a new declaration of dispute and a request for arbitration with the DCD. Wakiro also charged that Waisi had promised the peasants an unreasonably high second payment for coffee in order to gain their support. In a separate action the three dissident committee members whose resignation Waisi was trying to force filed a complaint that the meeting at which the committee decided to rearrange the staff had been held without their knowledge. On May 17 the deputy commissioner of cooperative development convened an informal meeting to try to resolve the dispute. According to the minutes of the meeting kept by an assistant cooperative officer, the committee agreed that Wakiro, as general manager, would have the power over check signing and that an assistant general manager position would be established.

In May 28 Gimadu wrote to J. F. Wanda, the former assistant secretary/manager and an ally of Wakiro's, saying that he was terminated because he had not kept his appointment to see the committee about his redefined position as assistant general manager. Wanda replied that he had told the committee that he would have to delay the interview as he had to take his wife to the hospital. The subsequent series of letters between Wanda and Gimadu give a clear impression that Wanda was willing to take the redefined job but that the committee, with Gimadu's encouragement, insisted that he had refused the job change so that they could justify his termination.

This impression is strengthened by a letter from Gimadu on the committee's behalf to the commissioner for cooperative development. Gimadu protested that the minutes of the May 17 meeting recorded by the assistant cooperative officer had omitted the agreement that the secretary was also to serve as assistant general manager. Gimadu's letter also protested that these same minutes recorded that all changes in the BCU management would wait to be reviewed and approved by the Annual General Meeting, while the committee claimed that it had made no such commitment and that the new organization was to be implemented immediately. The commissioner for cooperative development told the committee that there was no reason for haste in implementing their new order, but the committee insisted that it was already in force.

One of Wakiro's complaints during the May 17 meeting was that none of the committee members was conforming to the BCU procedures for committee expenditure—that they were spending money improperly and not giving him any accounting of what was spent. Wakiro had continued to demand an expense accounting from Waisi for his trip to Europe. On May 28 he sent all five of the committee members who had voted to have him dismissed in February letters "reminding" them that they had debts to the union, ranging from 7/60 for one of them to 864/= for another. He also pointed out that the bylaws prohibited their voting in any meeting as long as they were in debt to the union and that any vote they had taken during the period of their indebtedness was null and void. Wakiro signed this letter, as he was signing other letters during this time, as secretary/manager.

During these months, the committee had decided to change its Nairobi coffee broker, and it entered into negotiations with an Indian firm. It openly excluded Wakiro from these meetings. The committee also contracted for the construction of the coffee stores, which had been under discussion, and Gimadu sent a letter to the contractor authorizing him to start work before Wakiro had even seen the contract. The committee signed a five-year lease for the BCU-owned restaurant and arranged for the purchase of a large amount of building supplies, again without consulting Wakiro. All of this took place during May and June, when there was already talk of a possible commission of inquiry into the BCU. In June Wakiro instructed Gimadu to send a letter to the contractor for the stores to stop work, as the contract had not been properly signed. Gimadu did write the letter, but it was later discovered that the letter was not sent until six weeks later, during which time the construction work continued. On July 19 the committee fired Wakiro for the second time and locked him out of his office.

Government Intervention and the Loss of Autonomy

The repeated bids for arbitration and the obvious disruption of the union's functioning, together with the growing accusations of corruption against the committee, finally provoked major state intervention and ultimately led to a drastic restriction of not only the committee's but also the entire union's autonomy.

A commission of inquiry arrived in Mbale a few days after Wakiro's firing and demanded from Wakiro all of the documents, cash, accounts, and other official papers for which he had been responsible. On July 30 the committee refused to give evidence to the commission of inquiry. On August 12 the entire committee was dissolved on orders from the commissioner for cooperative development, and all of its members were barred from holding any cooperative office again.

Wakiro and Wanda entered a third bid for arbitration; Waisi and his supporters on the committee entered a suit against the DCD to enjoin its ruling that they could not stand for office; and the three dissident members of the committee submitted a separate letter disclaiming any connection with the majority decisions of the committee and petitioning that they be excluded from the ban on cooperative officeholding.

A government cooperative officer, A. K. Mulinde, was appointed as supervising manager under the same provisions and with the same powers as Neal. A new committee election was held, but the results were disallowed when Waisi's lawyers challenged the legality of barring him from office. In the second election, however, a ruling from the DCD confirmed that Waisi was not to be allowed to stand or even to be present for the elections. Both Wakiro's suit against the union and Waisi's against the government were lost. Mulinde carried on as supervising manager with a new committee headed by Enoka Musundi, a southerner, district council member, and influential in the local UPC.

Lack of clear precedent and ambiguities over whether the DCD was to have an advisory or supervisory role under the newly independent state had initially made it inconsistent in its arbitrations and cautious in acting on its own criticisms of Waisi. Waisi was enormously popular with Bugisu's peasants, and he was quite successful in mobilizing their enthusiastic support for local control as well as higher coffee prices (Brett, 1970:133; Young, Sherman, and Rose, 1981:77-79). Thus, the DCD's early reluctance to act against Waisi can also be interpreted as the state's unwillingness to contravene peasant preferences or to risk their opposition. Despite its publicly expressed opposition to BCU policies, the DCD did not intervene until after the Obote coup. The coup resolved a number of uncertainties at the national level and made executive control of the state much stronger. Obote was now less dependent on local support for the UPC and started to centralize local administration and marketing.

Waisi had strongly supported Obote's party. While the UPC was still involved in its struggles for national control, it depended on the kind of district-level support Waisi provided. Once the army-backed coup eliminated the threats to Obote's control, however, Waisi's support was no longer critically necessary. Thus, the BCU became subject to central government measures to reduce its autonomy and to eliminate the threat of further increases in the committee's power. Obote's coup strengthened the agencies of the central state and set the stage for a rapid reduction of local power across Uganda. Wakiro's suit provided the opportunity the DCD needed to use the power this new situation gave it.

Power and Privilege during Waisi's Term

Waisi's ambitious plans and his aggressive strategies to carry them out against BCU staff and DCD opposition were based on his own perceptions and the reality of widespread peasant support. The only one of his projects that he abandoned was the one to which the peasants clearly objected—the reestablishment of central pulperies. The turbulence his policies provoked in the district and in the union and the personal wealth and power he sought, together with the possible benefits his policies might have provided for the district's economy, raise again the question of how the struggles of local leaders against each other and against the state affect peasant welfare.

Waisi's drive to strengthen his own power within the BCU and his efforts to increase the union's financial and political strength relative to other institutions in Uganda each took force and cause from the other. Waisi was working to increase the BCU's control over the district's political and economic resources. All of his plans depended on concerted action from both management and committee. He was clearly interested in expanding his own power and wealth, but it would in no way be adequate to say that his actions to get rid of or rearrange staff positions, to force the resignation of his vice-president, or to attempt to get the resignations of the three dissident committee members during his fight with Wakiro were simply maneuvers to safeguard or to expand his personal position and his power within the BCU. On the contrary, Waisi was trying to introduce new processing and marketing systems. He wanted the BCU to plan and direct its own investments instead of having them managed by the DCD. He was spending a great deal of money in a hurry in the hopes of making a greater profit for the BCU. Instead of asking the DCD for greater autonomy, he was simply ignoring DCD objections to his plans. He felt the need to ensure swift implementation of his ideas to take maximum advantage of the often volatile international coffee market and of the rapidly shifting opportunities for political alliance at the national level. Success in his endeavors, of course, would have given him even greater powers in the union, but it is also quite possible that they would have generated revenues that would have flowed to the district, provided more employment there, and allowed higher returns to the coffee growers.

Waisi's own ascent enriched him personally, but it also strengthened the union. Because of his activities in the Uganda cooperative movement and also because of strong BCU participation in the national cooperative apex organizations under his guidance, Waisi and the BCU became very influential in the Uganda Cooperative Alliance, the Uganda Central Cooperative Union, and the Uganda Cooperative Bank. Not only did Waisi and Kimaswa hold offices in the bank, but also the BCU had bought more voting shares than any other union. Waisi's travels for the BCU itself, for the Bugisu Coffee Trust Fund to which he was the BCU's representative, and for the two apex organizations and cooperative bank gave him frequent contact with other staff and elected officers of cooperatives around Uganda and with national-level DCD officers. His relations with MPs, party officers, ministry officials, and other power-holders in the national domain strengthened his local power, which made him more useful to his national-level political and cooperative allies. This enabled him to argue BCU interests at a higher political level than would otherwise have been possible.

Through Waisi, the BCU gained a prominent position in national organizations that had considerable contact with and influence over the central government organizations that determined cooperative policy. This is not to say that Waisi was able to get his own way for the union or for the apex organizations he headed; he had enemies and was involved in struggles there. Rather, Waisi's apex organization posts moved both him and the union into the national domain with enough resources to compete directly for power there, instead of having only the recourse of appeal to higher authority in competitions for market control and investment autonomy at the district level.

The political situation in Uganda at the beginning of Waisi's term, the abolition of the Bugisu Coffee Board (BCB), Waisi's local and growing national standing, and the BCU's continuing prosperity all worked to allow Waisi a freer field to unify and strengthen his own power within the union. The DCD had advised and argued against many of Waisi's actions, but it lacked the precedents and the political strength to intervene directly in the union's activities. Waisi's prestige and influence in the local UPC and his friendship with national UPC leaders, including Kimaswa and Wakholi, increased his power in the BCU committee, where the majority were UPC members, and at the national level. This made it more dangerous for the DCD to intervene.

These connections strengthened Waisi's and his committee's ability to proceed with plans that were directly opposed by the DCD. Unlike previous committees, which had had to deal with the much closer powers of the BCB, Waisi's committee did not bother to protest government restrictions. It had the power to fight them fairly directly or simply ignore them, as it did in proceeding with their plans for the hotel. The ways in which Waisi strengthened the union, however, were offset by the committee's expenditures and by the conflicts with the committee.

Waisi's political strategies and his personal ambitions for wealth imposed extra expenses on the union, and these indirectly reduced peasant incomes. The extensive committee travel and meetings with

GCSs that Waisi used both to reward his supporters and to marshal GCS support for his projects were expensive, as were the special housing and transport privileges with which Waisi rewarded himself and his allies. Waisi also increased union expenditures to win staff support. Staff salaries were increased 33⅓ percent during his fight with Wakiro. He promoted and increased the salaries of his allies on the staff, and he arranged scholarships abroad for those staff opponents who were not fired.

I have not been able to determine whether the union paid extra costs on the various contracts that Waisi's committee signed. The financial conduct of the committee was not cited in the DCD's demand for an investigation, but it was an issue in the suits brought after the dissolution of the committee. It is certainly possible that some committee members were profiting personally from union contracts. Various of Waisi's opponents made this charge, but the government refused to bring against him the suit for misappropriation of funds that Wakiro's supporters demanded. As the commission of inquiry report was kept secret, it is impossible to know its reasons. Certainly the sudden rash of bids let and contracts signed at the end of the committee's tenure, many of which were later broken by the supervising manager on the grounds that they were disadvantageous to the union, suggests that there may have been personal incentives for the committee members' haste. On the other hand, all of these contracts involved projects that the committee had publicly espoused and defended during its entire tenure. It is possible that they hastened to conclude these projects, or at least to start them, in defiance of the growing resistance from Wakiro and from the DCD. Mulinde's claim that the contracts were unfavorable to the union may simply have been a reaffirmation of DCD opposition to the projects themselves, as Mulinde was employed by that agency.

Waisi was extraordinarily frank in a series of long conversations we had in 1970 about the ways he felt he had misused his position, but he defended the contracts and the ways the committee made them. He did admit, however, that he used his multiple activities to increase his wealth as well as his power. He was able to make a handsome profit from his expense allowances, which he convinced various organizations to give to him as a lump sum. As the necessities of travel for each post often overlapped, and as there was no legal hindrance to his staying with friends on his travels instead of in hotels, he had a tidy income on the side.

The extra expenses the committee incurred and Waisi's personal gains from them were dramatic and may have involved corruption and peculation; but they did not constitute a particularly significant share of the union's budget. It is quite possible that the committee's various projects would have generated far more revenues than the committee spent if they had been allowed to continue. The conflicts between the committee and the staff were far more damaging to the union than these extra expenses were. They seriously disrupted the union's management, and they served as a justification for a second, far more consequential intervention by the state.

The Staff-State Alliance and the Loss of Autonomy

Waisi needed unchallenged authority to run the union as he wanted, but his power became increasingly threatening to the staff, and especially to its chief officer, Wakiro. Wakiro justified his opposition to Waisi in terms of organizational efficiency and proper accounting procedures, but he was essentially defending the power and prerogatives of his own position. There is no question that Waisi's committee spent a great deal of money on itself, more per year than any other committee, but its use of funds in this way never became an issue until Wakiro challenged Waisi's right to sign contracts.

The only difference between the title of coffee manager, which Wakiro would not accept, and the title of general manager, which he did accept, was that the latter gave him an assistant and power over check signing, which the former did not. The addition of an assistant was agreed to primarily at the deputy commissioner's urging, so it is probably fair to say that Wakiro's main stake in that particular struggle at least was over his power to sign checks. Waisi was not going to be able to operate as flexibly or as rapidly if a man who was generally opposed to him had this power over expenditures. Wakiro's power over expenditure was his own strongest guarantee that he would be consulted and considered in the committee's and Waisi's decisions. The additional discussions of the extent to which it was proper for the committee to involve itself in the running of the union and the extent of the secretary/manager's right to information and consideration or his power to refuse to carry out committee instructions all revolved around the basic question of who had what rights in making decisions and who had what power in implementing those decisions.

Wakiro had no power base other than the definition of his own job in the BCU bylaws and in the national cooperative legislation. These definitions gave him formal control over union accounts, but they did not specifically state whether he was merely responsible for assuring that money was indeed spent in accordance with committee decisions and that the committee properly recorded its expenses, or whether he had the power to obstruct expenditure that he felt was unwise. The committee, in fact, had the power to make this interpretation as it saw fit. Thus, the only way that Wakiro could successfully oppose the committee was with the support of the DCD or other government officials.

Staff opposition to committee autonomy was motivated by personal and group strategies to maintain bureaucratic authority, but this opposition coincided with the interests of the state and of the DCD. Staff-committee opposition had earlier been moderated by their allied interest in conserving local power against the claims of the state. The conjunction of political uncertainty at the national level with expansionist organizational and individual mobility strategies and successes at the local level had vastly increased the power of committee members and other popular representatives. In order to redress the growing power differential, Wakiro and his allies were willing to sacrifice local autonomy in exchange for DCD protection against further loss of power and authority.

Wakiro's interests were very similar to those of the status group from which he had been recruited, the civil servants. Unlike Mugoya and other staff members during the first two committees' tenure, Wakiro had no independent power base. He and the rest of the staff under Waisi were barred from holding political office. They could not, therefore, form the alliances with or gain the concessions from the committee that had made earlier staff members so powerful. Waisi's committee did not need such alliances anyway; they had gained the autonomy from the BCB they sought, and the BNA itself had very little direct authority over them. Cooperative supervision had passed entirely to the the central state's DCD. Waisi's political alliances at the national level and the enthusiastic support of the peasants at the local level gave the committee a power base sufficient to its needs. It could therefore ride roughshod over the staff, and even over its own minority members, until a restrengthened DCD intervened.

The committee was acting to move the BCU into a position where it could act autonomously in the national sphere. To combat it, Wakiro appealed to the DCD to enforce the cooperative laws that emphasized that the union was a district-level organization that derived its power from the national state.

Recourse to law to settle a conflict over the tenancy of power positions necessarily implies that the authority of these positions is delegated by a higher authority. Wakiro had no recourse other than cooperative law in his fight to preserve his own power, but his appeal for arbitration by an agency of the central state implicitly denied the autonomy of the BCU and the legitimacy of the Bagisu leaders' claims to that autonomy, i.e., that the BCU's authority derived from independent power granted by the Bagisu growers rather than from dependent power derived from the DCD.

It is not clear whether this was the reason that the committee refused to appear before the commission of inquiry or whether, as was claimed by the management disputants, committee members refused to do so out of fear that their personal peculations would be discovered. In any case, the appointment of the commission of inquiry, with its mandate to inquire into all aspects of the BCU's operation, effectively ended the committee's claim to autonomous power. In this, even though Wakiro lost his particular claim, management essentially won its battle, as the committee was reduced to a competition subject to DCD arbitration at the district level whenever it fought management.

The appointment of the commission was a clear indication that the DCD was returning the committee to a subordinate position and not allowing it the power to make its own internal decisions. Though Wakiro was not rehired, the committee was unable to reclaim the autonomy that it had had; the role of the secretary/manager was vastly strengthened as he and the committee both had to approach the DCD for approval or for action. Both now functioned on the same level, subordinate to the DCD. The union and the Bagisu in cooperative matters were once again directly subject to the state's wishes and programs. The committee, which justified its expanded powers under Waisi by the claim to represent the BCU's members, now operated under a set of rules that emphasized the subordination of the members themselves and therefore of the committee to national decisions and policies.

Wakiro's insistence on maintaining his own powers within the BCU thus led directly to a major reduction in the power of the BCU itself. If, through agreement, collusion, or more power, Waisi had been able to forestall the conflict with Wakiro, it is likely that he could have maintained the union's autonomy and completed his own projects, since without Wakiro's protests there would not have been clear ground for the DCD's intervention. Wakiro's interests, however, demanded that he protect his own powers. To do this he had to appeal through legal channels to the very power from which Waisi was trying to establish his independence. Waisi's inability to marshal and control completely or sufficiently the local organization over which he was attempting to gain and legitimize power permitted the state to reestablish its authority over the BCU.

Peasant support was crucial to Waisi's committee, and the DCD had been cautious not to provoke peasant protest by intervening in the projects it opposed. When both Waisi's and Wakiro's factions were carrying their grievances to the peasants, and when other influential Bagisu leaders became involved in the conflict, there was no longer a consensus among the popular leaders. The divisions among the leadership meant that when one of the competing parties formally called in the DCD, it could act with more impunity.

Significantly, Waisi was the only BCU president who did not have a district council position. His main alliances to political figures were through the UPC. This served him well while he was able to negotiate directly at the national level, but was of little use when the UPC no longer needed local support as urgently as it did before the Obote coup and when Wakiro succeeded in redefining the BCU as a local institution subject to national regulation.

The three-way battle between Waisi, Wakiro, and the DCD shows again how upwardly mobile Bagisu were subject to the simultaneous need to mobilize the peasants and satisfy the state. Waisi gained peasant support by invoking principles of ethnic dignity and rights of producers to a fair price and to control over the sale of their products and the reinvestment of the profits. The state and management countered this invocation by appealing to other principles, such as business efficiency, bureaucratic rationality, the separation of personal and private rights, powers, and property, the primacy of "modernity" and national development, and the principle that the representatives of the people should not benefit unduly from their positions. The state's agents were unable to forge an alliance based on these principles with the peasants, because the peasants' basic interests were opposed to the state's revenue-gathering imperative. The professional staff, however, shared enough common interest with the state to form an alliance with its agents when the committee threatened its bureaucratic prerogatives.

The aggressive and imaginative activities that Waisi used to expand the union's and his own powers, his ability to exploit the uncertainties of power struggles at both the district and the national level, and his sensitivity to the discontents and the demands of the peasants who provided the ultimate basis of his power provide illustrations that peasant politics may involve far more constructive work than mere resistance of exploitation and avoidance of state power (cf. Lonsdale, 1981). The repeated cycle of expanding autonomy interrupted by state intervention but then regained through peasant mobilization and amplified by political bargaining until it provoked another state intervention was driven by the opposed interests of the state and the peasants. Analysis of the responses of the peasants as a struggling class (cf. Cooper, 1981a) must, however, be complemented by examination of the interests, alliances, and activities of members of opposed status groups that did not form a class at the local level. These status groups all derived power by mediating between the state and the peasants, but their competition with each other exacerbated the struggle between the peasantry and the state and directly affected its outcome.

Mobilization and manipulation of peasant support had finally allowed the BCU to compete directly with national-level agencies, but the conflict between members of different local status groups so divided local power groups that the state was able to reassert control. The BCU and the peasants finally lost much of their own power because of struggles for ascendancy between these groups and because the weaker side found it convenient to invoke its bureaucratic role as intermediaries for the central state (cf. Spittler, 1983). These internal struggles also prevented the emergence of the politicians as the independently powerful group they might have become if Waisi's programs had succeeded. The contradictions between the two sources of power from which all local status groups derived their own continued to restrict the degree of differentiation and the potential for class formation in Bugisu. In this instance, they had also seriously limited the claim for local power against the central state and left the peasants far more susceptible to central state control.

Contradictions in Cooperative Ideology

In Bugisu, as in other East African peasant economies, agricultural cooperatives emerged as a vehicle of challenge to the state's control over the commercialization of crops. Their egalitarian ideology, with its stress on producer self-determination, served the campaigns for local autonomy well. Their control over the commerce of the major sources of income provided important resources for local groups that aspired to upward mobility in an economy where control of the means of production was fragmented and dispersed. Their identity as business operations, however, served the state by emphasizing efficiency and rational bureaucratic procedures. Furthermore, the state could use the doctrine of member equality to remove cooperative officeholders who became powerful enough to challenge state supervision. Finally, the ideology of bureaucratic specialization and efficiency that the state promulgated provided the professional management with a lever against the powers of the representative committee. The staff's use of this lever inevitably weakened the local campaigns for organizational autonomy from state supervision.

Goran Hyden has pointed out that cooperative societies in East Africa tend to be controlled by local elites rather than by ordinary or typical members and are "very often ruled on the basis of already existing 'patron-client' relationships" (1970a:64). Various local groups define positions within the cooperatives as an opportunity for enrichment. This poses a serious problem not only in the egalitarian terms of the cooperative ideology but also for a state that relies on cooperative societies to implement its development programs and revenue collection at minimal cost.

Because of the access to wealth that committee membership may offer, the elected committee is usually the center of opposition to government intervention. For much the same reason (i.e., the broader the powers of the committee, the greater opportunity there will be for personal advantage) many East African cooperatives have been troubled by continued conflict between the elected committee and the professional staff over the division of their respective powers and duties.

The relationship between the elected committee and the appointed management staff is crucial in East African cooperatives. The legal fact is that the cooperatives are owned by the peasants whose crops they buy and sell. The ideology underlying the cooperative movement is that they will be run not only in the peasants' interest but also according to their wishes as far as economically and legally possible. Executive committees are supposed to be representative bodies which put into action the desires of their constituents.

A large cooperative is a highly sophisticated operation demanding a wide range of specialized skills and knowledge, from an understanding of commercial and business practices within the organization to the ability to understand world market, storage, and transport conditions and to deal with government laws and regulations. The demand for representative or popular participation in decision-making is in direct and irreconcilable opposition to the state's need for an efficient and unified business operation that can maximize taxable return on resources. There has been a strong tendency in many East African cooperatives for the committee to use the argument of its representative legitimacy to try to control practical decisions in the daily running of the cooperatives (Hyden, 1970b) and thus increase its members' base of power. The committees' demands for control have frequently limited the professional managements' capacity to run the cooperatives efficiently. On the other hand, management-oriented definitions of efficiency are biased toward profit or surplus maximization, which peasants see as benefiting the state at their expense (Bates, 1981). Peasants are opposed to inefficiency, waste, corruption, and favoritism in their co-

operatives, but their preferred solutions to these stress maximum redistribution of crop proceeds to the growers rather than maximum
capital accumulation by an institution that can be directly and indirectly
taxed by the state.

Most of the writing on East African cooperatives tends to focus either
on autochthonous cultural patterns that interfere with bureaucratic
rationalism or on purely organizational problems. The authors most
concerned with organization tend to compare a management ideal of
how a cooperative should be organized with observed patterns of
organization in actual cooperatives. Because they tend to assume ideal
organizational patterns from a managerial (and thus implicitly, from
the state's) perspective, they have generally not considered organizational problems as the result of conflicting interest and incompatible
demands for power by opposing groups. (See, e.g., Hyden, 1970a,
1970b, 1973; Brett, 1970; Kasfir, 1967, 1970. For contrasting views, see
Lamb, 1974; Kitching, 1980; Young, Sherman, and Rose, 1981.)

The different Bagisu's strategies to achieve and expand their own
power and their competitions with each other were greatly influenced
by the activities of a state whose primary interest was in controlling
crop production and commerce to maximize its own appropriation of
surplus. Management used the central state's cooperative ordinances
and acts to gain and protect its own power against the committee; the
DCD found the staff to be a useful ally in its attempts to promote a
kind of economic efficiency that favored the state's ability to collect
revenue with as little protest or opposition as possible. Representative
power-holders, however, opposed this tendency, appealing to the principles of local autonomy and popular participation to protest both
central state control and management dominance. The ideological principles used by the various claimants to power overlapped considerably,
but the ways in which these principles were invoked reflected the
shifting power relations forged by the opposition and conflict between
local and central power systems, on the one hand, and competition
for local power, on the other.

The state maintained that the surplus accumulated by efficiently run
cooperatives would assure their continued operation and that this would
serve the peasants' interest and welfare. Bates (1981), however, has
shown that the surplus realized from the marketing of peasant crops
in Africa tends to be appropriated by the state for its own political and
economic projects, which do not serve the peasants' interests. Bagisu
peasants correctly perceived the results of what the state defined as
management efficiency as limiting their own incomes. In most instances,
therefore, they defined their own interests as being best served by

representative rather than specialized control over decisions. At the same time they realized that the potential for extravagance, corruption, or embezzlement by their elected representatives could also reduce their own incomes. They were therefore responsive to the invocation of the different ideological principles that the state and the local power groups used.

The fluid alliances and oppositions between groups with both overlapping and conflicting interests continued to limit the power of the state or of the cooperative to exploit the peasants, but they also continued to prevent the peasants from developing a coherent political program of their own. The manipulation of ideological principles was crucial in the formation and dissolution of these alliances and oppositions. The peasants controlled the most vital component of these struggles and campaigns, that is, they could increase or reduce their production of cash crops. They had also learned a great deal about both the potential advantages and the possible abuses of cooperative management and politics in the years since the union's founding. They demanded more of their local leaders and judged their performance more critically. They were concerned to defend themselves against both local power groups and the agents of the state. All of the competitors for market control in Bugisu—state, staff, and elected committee— had to take their concerns into account, but they could also attempt to manipulate them to their own advantage.

The opportunistic manipulation of ideology and of the peasants' economic concerns by these three competitors for market control impeded the development of a coherent political consciousness among the peasants. I discussed earlier the ways that the popular leaders' focus on local processes and their own power within them prevented the emergence of national class-based organizations to promote or defend the common interests of the different Ugandan peasantries. The subordination of the peasants' political education to the short-term strategies of the different competitors for power heightened the effects of this political insularity. In the absence of a nationally or even locally coherent political program, peasants' political actions continued to revolve around their own short-term economic interests. They could no longer intervene positively or effectively in the struggles for political control that increasingly affected their own economic environment, especially as the locus of these struggles shifted more and more to the national arena. The next two chapters will show how much the peasants' loss of political influence damaged both the national and the local economy.

NOTES

1. Sebei was originally part of Bugisu District. Much poorer than the Bagisu, the Sebei had long felt they were treated as a minor adjunct of the district and that both the Bagisu and the administration discriminated against them.

2. At independence, it had been agreed that as each of the four kingdoms had a monarch, each district should have the option of electing a "Constitutional Monarch." Bagisu and Sebei both chose to have such a figure, but even before the Republican Government of 1966 abolished this system, the Bugisu District Council had resolved that the post should be discontinued.

3. Of these three committee members, one was also a Mubeza, i.e., a member of the same major lineage as Wakiro, and another was Wakiro's affine. Lineage and kin relations continued to define the lines of conflict.

4. See note 2, above.

7

Cooptation and Control under a Single-Party Regime, 1966-71

The fights between different Bagisu to control the BCU had divided and weakened the local groups that had previously organized and directed peasant protest against the state just as a greatly strengthened UPC was preparing a major initiative to centralize economic and political control under a new constitution. The conjuncture of these events was devastating to the union and its ability to defend the interests of Bugisu's peasants and of local status groups. The imposition of the second supervising manager and the tenure of the committee that replaced Waisi's coincided with a major shift in the policies of the now consolidated central government. As this regime withdrew autonomy and budgetary strength from district administrations (Leys, 1967), the Bagisu leaders saw one of their major power bases diminished. The central state also pushed for greater managerial control over agriculture by a rapid increase of its extension services and bureaucracy and for central administrative control over the cooperative unions (Okereke, 1970; Uganda Republic, 1968). Growth of the state bureaucracy and subsequent strengthening of the UPC at the local levels further reduced the options available to local leaders (Bunker, 1975:367-81; Young, 1979:319-320).[1]

The tendency for individual and group competitors for national power to subordinate the economic needs of the state to their own political strategies and to claim greater powers for the state than were possible in an economy based on freeholding peasant production became increasingly evident. During the period described in the last chapter, national politics revolved around different parties' struggles to gain full control of the state. Milton Obote and the UPC achieved this goal in a coup backed by the military. During the period described in this chapter, Obote and the UPC attempted to consolidate their political control by subordinating administrative and economic processes to the central control of a state whose bureaucracy was increasingly subject to interference by individual politicians. Obote used the state and its resources to reward his allies and to strengthen his party rather than to fortify its own revenue bases (see also Saul, 1976). As a result, the state under Obote was much less sensitive to peasant demands and to the threat that they might withdraw from export crop marketing.

Local political autonomy was stifled, so there was little evidence of the dynamic challenges to the state that characterized earlier periods. In fact, though, the national state was extending itself beyond its own organizational and economic capacities. Major tensions and inefficiencies emerged during this period. The Amin coup occurred soon after the major statutory changes toward direct national control of crop marketing, but the high costs of directly suppressing local organization were already evident.

Government Centralization, National Party Supremacy, and the Realignment of Power

The centralization of government functions and the growing power of the UPC heightened the importance of the politicians at the district and local levels. The abolition of all opposition parties in 1969 was the beginning of an intense drive to build a strong UPC with administrative and development powers from the *muluka* to the national level. Each of these changes introduced new competitors into the chiefs' and civil servants' domains and rearranged the structure of power relations among the politicians. Local political leaders had increased control over development programs, but they were themselves much more directly subordinate to the national party than they had previously been. They also were in a position to mediate between the people and the government in a way which formerly only the chief could do and with more influence than the chiefs had had. The party, however, lacked the administrative discipline and competencies of the district administration and the civil service. This meant, first, that the party used the chiefs and civil servants for actual program implementation and, second, that the reduction of chiefly powers left local administration much more susceptible to political negotiation, bribery, and inefficiency. Local politicians became more wealthy, but less autonomous. The increased centralization of party power and discipline reduced the impact of peasant demands and protests on national policy and on local administration.

The erosion of the chief's powers and functions and the compromise of his status and prestige by specialized government agencies and officers had started well before independence, but the declaration of a one-party state and the subsequent UPC drive to strengthen its local efficacy suddenly introduced a powerful and threatening new force into the chiefs' domain. The party was gearing up for elections to be held in 1971, and competition for the influential constituency chairmanships was intensifying. Control of the constituency chairmanship required control of the majority of the constituency branches. These branches had been reorganized in 1969 on the *muluka* level rather than on the *gombolola* level, so political conflict followed precisely the boundaries of the lower-level chiefs' jurisdictions. Constituency boundaries did not follow county boundaries exactly, however, so that a *saza* chief might have to deal with more than one contest in his own area. His conduct in these contests could have profound effects on his career, as constituency chairmen (CC) would all be strong contenders for election to Parliament; and even if they did not succeed to Parliament, they had great power under the reorganized party system.

The reorganized party gave the CC tremendous patronage and administrative powers that he could use as a resource in exchange for compliance from the chiefs, local influentials, and party subordinates. The connection between the *muluka* branch chairman and the CC allowed for a direct report or accusation against chiefs to the CC, who was assumed, probably correctly, to have access to powers greater than the district commissioner or the administrative secretary and who could therefore effect a chief's transfer or dismissal. Relations with politicians had always been problematic for the chiefs. The MPs, like the district councillors, were "the people's representatives," and therefore had a legitimacy that the chief could not claim. They also had supervisory and accusatory powers over the chiefs and could receive the people's complaints against them. Before 1969, this had meant essentially that the district council members could threaten the chiefs, but the sanctions on which they could directly rely went no higher than the Bugisu district administration. The institution of local powers in a strengthened UPC meant that the chief could now fear repercussions from party officials influential enough to effect his dismissal through their UPC connections. The relation of the *saza* chief to the CC was analogous to that of the *muluka* chief to the branch chairman, except that the powers of the CC were considerably greater. Proposals that low-level chiefs should be elected, though not implemented at this time, left these chiefs feeling very insecure.

The time between the declaration of the one-party state and the coup was too short for these powers to be tested or for the chiefs to learn their limits, but the CC and the branch chairman were in a position to exploit the ambiguity of the situation, and the prudent chief dealt carefully with them because the limits of their powers were so indefinite. Thus the chiefs acquired a new set of masters who, like the administrative agencies, called upon them to lend their prestige, expedite projects, and answer for the people in their areas. This greatly reduced the administrative effectiveness of the chiefs and thus undermined the district administration's organizational and developmental capacities in the rural areas.

The UPC Rural Development Program (RDP) provides a clear example of the administrative problems that followed from direct party dominance over the chiefs and civil servants. The RDP was instituted in 1969. The UPC provided each CC with 100,000 shillings out of Ministry of Finance funds to pay for local development projects. Local communities were to decide what projects were needed, but the CC made the decisions about which areas would get the funds and had the ultimate power over the choice of projects. In Bugisu in 1969 all of the CCs were MPs, although there was a dispute between George Waisi and Stephen Muduku about the election in north Bugisu, which led to problems there for the party and the RDP.

The funds were issued to the district commissioner, who in turn disbursed them to the CC. The district commissioner was responsible for ensuring that proper accounting procedures were followed. In this he could call on the chiefs for reports. The chiefs were also expected to be actively involved in the projects in their own areas and to attend the district commissioner's meetings with the CC. The projects were to depend on free labor from the community; it was the chiefs' responsibility to mobilize this labor and to call meetings at which each project was to be discussed.

Both the district commissioner and the chiefs were in many ways less powerful than the MPs whom they were meant to supervise. In one case, an MP to whom the district commissioner had refused to issue money because he had not accounted properly for the last disbursement went directly to the Ministry of Finance and drew the money himself. In north Bugisu especially, work went slowly, and large sums of money were not properly accounted for. The chiefs in the north were in an uneasy situation because of the dispute about who was the proper CC. To act at all was to appear to take sides; not to act subjected them to threats from the district commissioner's office. Following the 1971 coup, the district commissioner's office reported that the chiefs had not submitted useful or accurate reports because of the threats they received from the politicians in their areas.

The chief was not the only person immobilized by political conflict. There were reports throughout the history of the RDP that people were not working because the projects had come to be associated with particular political factions or because they were seen as the property of particular politicians. There was little point in starting a project without prior assurance of funds from the individual politicians who controlled them. Work was supposed to be free, but the positions of headman or director of the project were valuable rewards that the politician could use to assure and strengthen support and compliance, and some fund money was often used to feed the workers. Again, however, it was the chiefs who were held responsible if the people in their area did not turn out to work on projects or if the projects went too slowly.

The UPC politicians were also using the civil service apparatus to accomplish party programs. The UPC had to depend on the civil service because it was incapable of managing the development programs it now controlled. Because party officials and MPs had more actual power than the civil servants through whom they were working, the portions of the civil service involved in the RDP, especially the district commissioner, the chiefs, and the Ministry of Finance, were all compromised. Both the district commissioner and the chiefs were forced to deal with political issues in civil service terms, and the chiefs especially were too vulnerable to political retaliation to function effectively. The district commissioner was more secure, but still powerless to perform his function effectively in the RDP.

The district commissioner's impotence and the confusion of his own position made the chiefs' position more difficult because they could not get a clear mandate from him. One example of a district commissioner's correspondence to the county chiefs should suffice to show the chiefs' dilemma. His letter about the monthly progress reports on RDP projects, in which the chiefs were to include the reasons why projects were not on schedule or had not been started, ended thus: "You need to make your investigations wisely. You should, however, not behave as inspectors, or detectives. You can get all information correctly if you are keenly interested and involved in the promotion of the rural development scheme by working together with the MPs or assisting them." In other words, the chiefs were to file accurate reports on the shortcomings of the projects, which would reflect against the MPs, but they were not to take an adversary role in doing so. However, they did receive the blame if they did not report fully on what was going wrong with the project or if they themselves did not get involved in the project.

The resulting demoralization of the district administration and civil service and the concentration of power in the hands of a few politicians who directly depended on the national party provoked considerable resentment, but little effective opposition. The patronage that the UPC made available to its own representatives and the UPC monopoly over political positions effectively closed all alternative channels to political power.

Obote had instituted what he called the "move to the left," a rhetorical ploy to justify the acts and initiatives that were placing more and more of the economy and the government under direct central control. The UPC was persecuting and suppressing the DP; various DP and dissident UPC members were known to have been jailed without charges. The move to the left and the need for and priority of "nation building" were given wide play in the press and the radio, and there was a general feeling that opposition to the government was not healthy.

Local departments of the national government were also becoming increasingly strong and active in the district, taking over many of the functions formerly handled by the district commissioner, the chiefs, and the district council. The district council itself was in eclipse; it could only be called into session by the Minister of Regional Administration. In May 1970 it met for the first time in over a year and then was allowed to meet only one day. Many of the local politicians and leaders, including some of the BCU committee, were feeling helpless and useless. The UPC-central state monopoly of power disrupted administrative efficiency and became increasingly costly.

The BCU's Relations with the State and the Move toward National Party Control

Only certain powerful ministers in the UPC now stood in the way of the strong centralization of the economy and administration favored by Obote, and the cooperatives were not a strong force within the party. There were thus no pressing political reasons for the government to allow the cooperatives the autonomy that Waisi's committee had enjoyed.

The trend toward centralization continued through the entire period of Obote's regime, with progressive loss of autonomy for the nation's cooperatives. This loss was especially notable in the BCU, which, because of its wealth and success and because of the special nature of the coffee it handled, had generally received special privileges from the government. The growth of the UPC's power and the consequent decline in the power of local representative institutions such as the district council centered more and more political and economic resources in the party and in the national administration. The Rural Development Scheme and other party-controlled funds and programs put enormous patronage power in the hands of the CC, MPs, and their supporters. As a result, the party became the chief means of access to resources for upward mobility, and party loyalty became a more important consideration than the union's autonomy in individual strategies for the accumulation of wealth and power. When the BCU lost even the right to arrange its own sales, the committee members' dependence on and subservience to the party made them extremely cautious in their appeals to the government. They took great pains to avoid any suggestion of opposition or serious objection to the new party-controlled and centralizing state.

The new direction toward central government control of the cooperative movement was spelled out in the 1968 Produce Marketing Act and in the 1970 Cooperative Act, which superceded previous cooperative legislation (see Uganda Protectorate, 1946, and Uganda Government, 1963). Both of the new acts were introduced specifically to increase "government powers in the guidance, direction, and control of Cooperative Societies" (Uganda *Argus,* July 7, 1970). They gave the DCD new powers and centralized the workings of the department itself. The Cooperative Act of 1970 required all societies to submit annual estimates of income and expenditure to the department for approval by the minister; no expenditure could be made on any item until the estimates were approved. If the minister did not approve the estimates, he stated what estimates he did approve; these were binding on the society. This act also gave the minister power to amalgamate or divide societies, to dissolve committees and appoint supervising managers without first conducting an inquiry, and to appoint any other officer (see also Young, Sherman, and Rose, 1981:61-65).

In various speeches about the bill the minister stressed that the central government needed "powers to regulate and standardize union marketing and accounting systems, staff qualifications and committee activities," and control over all union and society expenditures because "such was the essence of nation building and the new political culture" (Uganda *Argus,* July 7, 1970; Uganda *Coop News,* Nov. 1970). Any move to standardize the cooperatives and subordinate them to central control inevitably conflicted with the ideals of membership control of each society and union. These ideals were still expressed in various public statements by DCD ministry officials. The DCD made no attempt to reconcile the statements that it made about the need for national coordination and individual sacrifice for the common good, on the one hand, and its continued insistence on the cooperative principles and the responsibility of the cooperative leaders to the members of their cooperatives on the other. All efforts to appeal the new decisions were met by answers that the good of the country had to come first.

The Produce Marketing Act of 1968 had given the DCD the power to set the prices paid to farmers for all controlled produce, which included coffee, and to prescribe how and to whom the processed crop was to be sold and at what price. The BCU was instructed to sell all of its coffee to the Coffee Marketing Board (CMB), a parastatal body under the Ministry of Marketing and Cooperatives. The BCU appealed this instruction, claiming that it would lose a great deal of money under this agreement. It was given a year's grace (1969-70) to continue marketing its own coffee, but despite BCU efforts all of the 1970-71 crop was sold to the CMB. The BCU committee pointed out that the CMB had previously dealt exclusively with Robusta coffee, a lower-grade strain requiring different and less exacting handling procedures, with different market and price structures. The committee members maintained that the BCU, as the only Uganda organization with any experience in handling Arabica coffee, was the agency most qualified to sell it.

The 1970-71 season got off to a very inauspicious start when the CMB declared a single pricing system for all Uganda. It simply ignored or rejected the fact that Arabica not only brings much higher prices per pound on the market but also requires much more intensive cultivation and processing, thereby reducing the amount that an individual or family can raise and increasing the cost of processing. A separate price was finally established for Arabica coffee after the committee, the secretary/manager, and the senior cooperative officer all met with the minister, but other problems soon arose.

The board transported and stored the Bugisu coffee in the same way that it had always handled Robusta, and the more delicate Arabica deteriorated in quality because of the long storage period in Mombasa— which is hot, humid, and at sea level—rather than in Nairobi, which is much higher and cooler. Communication between the CMB and the union was so poor that the union did not learn of buyers' complaints until six months after they were made. The CMB was not moving the coffee from Mbale as quickly as the union had been able to do, so the mill's storage space was full. No new coffee could be processed, so no new coffee could be bought. Many GCSs had full storage sheds for several months, and many peasants had to keep their coffee at home. This backup not only caused a severe shortage of cash in some parts of the district, but it also increased the danger of theft and deterioration for both the GCSs and the individual peasants.

The committee claimed that the margin between the coffee prices to be paid to the peasants and the prices the union was to receive would be so small that the union would inevitably lose money. The redistribution of union profit to the peasants had great significance in the district, especially as it occurred during the off-season when peasants had no coffee to sell. The members' attitudes toward the union tended to reflect the absence or presence and size of bonus payments each year. Union leaders foresaw immediate problems if there was insufficient profit during the season to provide for a bonus, and long-range problems for the whole Bugisu coffee industry if the deterioration in quality continued, as the price received for coffee on the world markets depended heavily on its reputation. That the coffee, which had already been bought from the peasants and had already been processed, was not being bought by the CMB also left the union paying high rates of interest on the short-term loans it took out each season to pay coffee advances. This money could usually be paid back quickly, as the coffee was sold in Nairobi; the delays caused by the CMB increased the interest paid far beyond what the union had budgeted. The staff had already estimated that the price that the CMB had agreed to pay them for the processed coffee would be far less than enough to pay their operating expenses. They negotiated with the minister of marketing and cooperatives after the commissioner for cooperative development had refused their plea for higher prices. Even though the minister finally agreed that their figures were correct, and that they would indeed lose money, he still responded simply that the Bagisu must be prepared to make sacrifices for the national good and that no one could be exempt from the demands of the new politics of central control.

Thus the state ignored the management and efficiency principles that had been the main ideological stay for the defense of its appropriation of revenues by controlling crop markets. Instead, it invoked principles of national development enforced by the strictures of party discipline. In doing so, it more openly acknowledged that the peasantry was being taxed to support the state and its projects and that many of these projects would not benefit the peasantry directly but would support trends to increased industrialization and central control of social services. Rather than deny its appropriation of peasant surplus production, it called on the peasantry to sacrifice for the national good. To the extent that the party was seen as a part of the national government and at the same time the distributor of local goods and services, this was a much more difficult ideological principle for local leaders to use against the state than were the cooperative principles, the egalitarian ideals, or the management models that they had combatted earlier. Even though the state was justifying CMB control as a local sacrifice required for the national development that all Ugandans would later benefit from, the commissioner for cooperative development and other DCD officials continued to invoke cooperative principles when they exhorted members to participate in meetings, to increase production, and to promote efficient management (BCU Annual General Meeting, minutes, 1969, 1970).

The Committee Abdicates Power

The BCU committee was left with no real power in the union, and the union itself was more and more subject to harmful control by the government (see Figure 3). The question of autonomy was no longer relevant; the problem was how to intercede with the government to change decisions damaging to the entire Bugisu coffee industry.

The increasing centralization of power in the hands of party leaders and the increasing importance of party membership for political power in the district limited the strategic options of individual committee members. The new committee members were politically influential and economically successful, but their income and prestige were signifi-

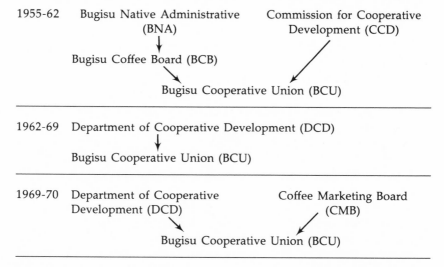

Figure 3. The Changing Hierarchy of Coffee-Marketing Organization in Bugisu, 1955-70

cantly tied to party positions, which restricted their freedom to defend the BCU's interests. Seven of the twelve men who served on the committee between 1968 and 1971 had been members of the district council; five of the seven were still members while they were on the committee, and the other two had had to resign when teachers were barred from holding political office. All but one of the twelve were or had been members of the DP or the UPC, and all but one of these eleven had held party offices. Two of the four men who had belonged to the DP had been that party's candidate for MP from their own area. Three of these four later joined the UPC, one in 1965, the other two after the prohibition of the DP. Rather than giving them independent bases from which to criticize CMB policies, however, these positions, especially those in the UPC, gave them vested interests in not publicly opposing official policy. Party positions were becoming more and more important points of access to power and money in the district, and the yearly competition for them was fierce. A BCU committee member who was publicly speaking against party policy would be extremely vulnerable to effective attack within the party both from higher-level position-holders and from other contenders for the position he held.

The committee members were cautious to the point of being obsequious in their relations with government about the CMB, even though they were highly disturbed about its implications. The value of "toughness" in politics had completely disappeared. Orders from Kampala were seldom opposed, for Kampala was handing out all the favors through the UPC, whose local officeholders could distribute them in return for political loyalty.

The district council had also been incapacitated as an effective center of power and could not be counted on to help present the union's case against the government as it once did. It was only through the party that one could accomplish anything, as the CC and the MP, who were usually the same man, came to control more and more of the political power in the district. Despite the promises of assistance that the committee received from the two MPs with whom it had good relations, those men either did nothing or had no effect. This is not surprising, as the MPs were under similar pressure to conform to party directions at the national level as were their counterparts at the local and district levels.

The new committee had started off under the total control of A. K. Mulinde, the supervising manager. Rather than regaining power as it had at the end of W. E. Neal's term, the BCU, and especially the committee, continued to lose autonomy even after Mulinde was removed in 1968. The DCD exercised even more direct control over the

BCU than it did over other Uganda cooperatives, because the BCU was a "record" union, having been the first in the country to be placed under a supervising manager and the first in the country to have been placed under a second supervising manager. It was also by far the union most important to state revenues. The new cooperative legislation and the special controls placed on the BCU transformed the committee from a primarily decision-making body to an advocatory one, whose representative function was to plead its own and the Bagisu's case to the power that held ultimate control over all major decisions. The committee's powers were now delegated from the higher levels of state and party rather than allocated by a mobilized peasantry. There was little space for the types of bargaining, alliances, and political exchanges that previously had characterized the struggles for control within the union and between it and the DCD.

Only two of the nine new committee members had ever served on the committee before. The new committee became the stablest of all during the union's history, lasting seventeen years; only three new men joined it, two members having resigned to take other employment and one having lost his eligibility when he failed to be reelected to the committee of his GCS.

The new president, Enoka Musundi, was thirty-five years old, had been trained for a month as an agricultural instructor after completing six years of primary school, and had worked two years for the Department of Agriculture. The son of a wealthy and respected *muluka* chief who had bought a lot of land from his neighbors before they realized how valuable it would be some day, he returned home to take care of the land and crops when his father died in 1953. He was elected to the district council in 1956. He was elected vice-chairman of his GCS in 1957 and chairman in 1958, after having investigated the problems caused by an earlier committee and bringing about the imprisonment of most of its members for embezzlement. His management of the GCS had been very successful; it had prospered, expanded, and been the first in the district to build its own maize mill. He had become prominent in the south Bugisu constituency of the UPC, of which he was treasurer, and was known as an impressive speaker both in the district council, where he held a number of committee positions, and in the union's Annual General Meeting, where he had been a delegate since 1958.

A large man, slower and gentler in speech and movement than other Bagisu leaders, Musundi was nonetheless capable of violent anger when he felt that the loyalty, respect, and decency owed to the elders of his own lineage or to the union he headed were being violated. He saw himself more as a conservator of the organizational legacy of the union's founders than as a leader or innovator. He responded to criticisms and challenges in both his GCS and in the BCU with statements that he would only serve as long as the members wanted him, and in fact he did not campaign actively to get or to keep either post. He came to the BCU presidency with strong political support from members of the UPC and the district council. Noted among the district's politicians for his moderation and his ability to arbitrate and pacify, he was described to me by Waisi as a "wise fool," a man who understood less of the political and economic complexities of the union than many other cooperative leaders but who was highly successful in accommodating and integrating the powerful conflicting forces that had done the union so much harm in previous years. His fellow committee members also credited him with doing more than any of his predecessors to alleviate the regional jealousy and rivalries that had afflicted both the committee and the staff.

Once again the Bagisu appeared to have chosen a BCU president whose temperament fitted the times. Once again, however, the times changed faster than the committee. Musundi's long presidency, which started with submissive accommodation of supervision by a central state that was apparently growing stronger, would continue through that state's violent decline into economic chaos and political instability. As the state collapsed, there was little that Musundi or anyone else could do to maintain the BCU's economic integrity or its political efficacy.

Relations between Mulinde, the supervising manager, and the new committee were, from the start, much better than those between Neal and the Mutenio committee had been. In part, the situation was probably easier for Mulinde because he was coming in after a fight that had seriously divided the union's leaders. More important, from the beginning he consulted the committee frequently and involved them directly in the work of restabilizing the union.

The committee was extraordinarily subservient to its new master. One of Musundi's first official acts was to submit to the commissioner for cooperative development a long letter of recommendations for changes in the union that would avoid a recurrence of the difficulties that had arisen during Waisi's term. Submitted on behalf of the committee and the union, the letter had resulted from and been much influenced by collaboration with Mulinde and listed many of the changes that Mulinde put into effect, especially those that defined committee-staff relationships.

Musundi's letter suggested that committee powers be limited drastically. It proposed that committee meetings be fewer; that transport allowances be more rigidly supervised; that committee members receive a fixed allowance instead of one based on meetings; that they receive an incentive bonus in order to "increase their spirit of working for greater profits"; that staff posts and salaries be reduced; that all appointments should be subject to the CCD's approval; and that the commissioner for cooperative development have ultimate control of all contracts let and of all coffee prices. This remarkable document was an almost complete reversal of all previous committees' policies and attitudes. Not only did it propose that some of the committee's power be removed, but it also suggested that much of the control of the union should pass directly to the DCD. The only proposal included that was in any way advantageous to the committee itself was the one asking for an incentive bonus.

Musundi's description of this letter was that it had made a very good impression on the department at a time when the BCU's reputation with that agency was very low indeed and that it had thereby filled an important need. There can be no question that such a letter would impress the DCD; if the committee continued to act as the letter indicated it would, the DCD had a clear guarantee that it would have a free hand and almost no problems with the BCU. It is a little difficult to see, though, why making a good impression on the DCD was so vitally important. The department had no intention of ending the BCU, nor was there any talk about ending its monopoly, either. The supervising manager had already been appointed, and it was clear that that was to be the official solution. Musundi's letter simply gave away as much as or more than the DCD would have or could have taken away from the committee by fiat. The letter did indeed put the committee in a very amiable relationship with the supervising manager, and it assured that the relations would be harmonious between both sides. However, it put the committee in a weak position that would eventually hurt both it and the union. By 1970 Musundi was lamenting the loss of autonomy that he had earlier proposed.

It is, of course, possible that Musundi saw the chaos of 1966 as a result of the committee's having excessive rights and liberties and wanted to prevent similar problems in the future, but in fact he had supported Waisi until the committee was dissolved. Another possible explanation is that Musundi wanted not only smooth coordination with the supervising manager but also a guarantee of his own and his committee's continued tenure and ample benefits and was thus making the best of his situation. Why Musundi so totally abdicated all of the claims and efforts of previous committees was a question which only he or the other committee members could have answered, but I was never able to get a convincing explanation from any of them.

Mulinde consulted the committee and explained to its members what he was doing. He also acted through and with them, so that the changes that he made in the early months of his tenure were presented as joint decisions of the supervising manager and Bagisu leaders. This reduced the likelihood of committee dissent and also strengthened the supervising manager's position in the district considerably. Waisi's supporters were still numerous and vociferous; he and his committee continued to dispute the DCD ruling that barred them from committee office, and they decried most of Mulinde's actions as illegal, bad business, or based on prejudice against the Bagisu. Acting in the name of the committee and with its obvious support made Mulinde much less vulnerable to such criticism. In fact, though the criticism continued, it was never sufficiently well organized to have any impact on the union or its members.[2] Finally, there was never any of the criticism that had been directed at Neal because of his neglecting to train the Bagisu committee and staff to take over from him when he left.

The Management Staff's Subordination to Direct State Control

The position of the staff was reinforced by the policies and the training programs that Mulinde established. Close DCD supervision further strengthened it in relation to the committee after Mulinde's term was concluded, but the changes in cooperative law made the staff more subordinate to direct government control. Because of the close relation between the secretary/manager appointed after Mulinde was removed and the chief DCD officer in the district, the secretary/manager came to occupy a crucial position, both as adviser to the committee and mediator between it and government.

Much of Mulinde's early work was aimed at undoing the projects and decisions of the Waisi committee. All planning on the hotel and office building was halted, although, ironically, Mulinde and the committee had started plans for a large office and shop building in Mbale, with the full support of the DCD, before his term ended. The contract that Waisi had signed with the new broker for coffee sales in Nairobi was broken and the CMB was hired as coffee agent for the union. Mulinde cancelled the contract with the company that had already started work on the clean-coffee store buildings. The company brought suit, but the BCU won the case, even though it did have to pay for the work already done. Mulinde also cancelled a large contract that

Waisi had arranged with a local supplier to repair some of the BCU's real estate in Mbale, and he cancelled the five-year lease of the coffee shop and restaurant. As the latter contract had been with a Mugisu, and as Mulinde re-let the contract to an Indian, this action became a strong basis for claims that Mulinde was anti-Bagisu, but nothing more than a fierce letter-writing campaign came out of this. The union lost some money over the broken contracts, but at the end of his term Mulinde was able to claim that he had all of the work done for much less money than Waisi's committee had agreed to, even after paying off the legal fees and costs incurred in legal contests.

Mulinde also cut staff posts and salaries. He reduced the salary increases the Waisi committee approved during its last months, and he eliminated the new positions it had created. He also changed some posts that had existed for a longer time. As Waisi's bid to sell coffee overseas had been scrapped completely, the three marketing officers whom he had appointed were either reassigned or sent to other organizations. The general manager, secretary, and committee clerk positions were all abolished, as were several others that Mulinde claimed the Waisi committee had established in order to justify salary increases to staff who supported it. In all, Mulinde abolished thirteen posts with combined annual salaries of 167,925 shillings and cut remaining salaries by a total of 20,220 shillings. He added nine new posts with annual combined salaries of 64,700 shillings. He made a fairly consistent attempt to get rid of former Waisi supporters among the staff, particularly those he felt Waisi had favored, but otherwise men whose jobs had been abolished were reassigned, though usually to lower-paying jobs.

Mulinde's other money-saving policy change was to convert the BCU's extensive real estate holdings from housing offered at a loss to BCU employees, and in some cases to friends and members of the committee, into profit-making rentals, or increasing the proportion of the employee's salary that went back to the union for rent. Formerly, this had been in some cases as low as 1 percent of a salary. Mulinde also rented out the five rooms in the BCU building that the Waisi committee had reserved for its own use for a total of 9,800 shillings a year.

Despite the various economizing measures Mulinde took during his first year in power, the union lost money during that coffee season, primarily because the price to farmers for high-grade coffee had been set higher than the world market could support, and in part because of late payment by some of the overseas buyers. Waisi's committee had already set the prices for that season, but the buying had not yet started when Mulinde took over, and he had the right to reset the prices. He showed no reluctance to change other decisions by the former committee, but he was still reluctant to risk the protest that a lowering of prices would have provoked.

Mulinde had the BCU bylaws changed to allow the union to take over direct management of any GCS that was in financial difficulties due to mismanagement. The BCU secretary/manager could decide to take over a failing GCS and appoint a secretary/manager there with power over the GCS committee, a miniature model of the supervising manager arrangement for the union. The union took over twenty societies during Mulinde's tenure, and all of these were making a profit within a year; most were returned to local control within two.

Mulinde announced at the Annual General Meeting held in July 1968 that the DCD had intended to return local control to the union. He had recommended strongly to the department that this be done only on the condition that the present committee, which had worked with him and "actively participated in the making of the present policy, and as such are the only people at present competent to see that the same is furthered or continued," be kept in office (BCU Annual General Meeting Minutes, 1968). He also had recommended that the BCU bylaws be amended to extend committee terms to three years, with one-third of the committee retiring each year. The committee then had already held office for two years without an election, as the state of emergency maintained after the coup had prevented the meeting the year before. The committee was returned again without objection from the meeting, and the amendment for three-year terms was approved.

Mulinde also said: "The post of Secretary/Manager was split into that of General Manager and Secretary and other jobs created for reasons of offering employment to friends of influential committee members and also to restrict the authority of persons holding key positions. In order to avoid this recurring in the future, I am recommending that no changes will be allowed to be added to the present structure without the prior approval of the Commissioner for Cooperative Development." He went on to announce that the post of secretary/manager had been reestablished to replace his role as supervising manager. The new post was to be filled by J. G. Wagunyanya, a Mugisu whom he had recruited as a DCD officer and had been training in the BCU for the past eighteen months.

All of Mulinde's conditions and pronouncements were accepted by the Annual General Meeting. The bylaws were amended to limit committee power to change staff structure or make appointments except with prior approval. The committee's power to set prices passed to the commissioner, who would receive but was not bound by the committee's recommendations, and the district cooperative officer retained Mulinde's power to approve all union expenditures. The secretary/ manager was to have control of all appointments below the senior staff level.

The cooperative relations between Mulinde and the committee had done nothing to give the committee more power. Rather, they emphasized the committee's acquiescence to its own loss of power. Its good relations with Mulinde simply assured the continued tenure of its members and a much higher rate of direct remuneration from their positions. The 1968 Annual General Meeting at which Mulinde announced the conditions of his removal formalized the loss of most of the committee's political and patronage powers and the limitation of many of its past functions. The incentive bonus that Musundi's letter had proposed two years earlier was initiated with effect for that season; the president received 5,500 shillings, the vice-president and treasurer each received 5,000, and the rest of the committee members each received 4,500. They all continued to receive their set allowances of 100 shillings per month. There was one objection from the floor that the committee had not had sufficient power during the year to merit such a reward, but the supervising manager replied that the amount had already been decided and figured into the balance sheet.

The union continued to work much as it had while Mulinde was in charge. The secretary/manager and the district cooperative officer attended all meetings. The majority of business and proposals came from the secretary/manager; they were for the most part already carefully worked out and explained, and his proposals were generally approved by the committee. In other cases, where the issue was simple but politically delicate, as when the local branch of the UPC was well behind on the rent for the office they used in the BCU building, Wagunyanya would simply inform the committee members of the problems, and they would decide what to do about them. The committee served occasional ritual functions, such as meeting government officials at public events and on special days; it handled as well some of the political aspects of the union's business, which were fairly minor. Its members served as peasants' representatives only insofar as they could claim to see problems as peasants rather than as technicians.

When I asked one of the committee members what kind of disputes had come up in the committee and how they had been handled, he said, "We never fight, because we have nothing to fight over." The committee, Wagunyanya, and the district cooperative officer all got on well and courteously; Wagunyanya's personal secretary also served as secretary to the committee and was married to the district cooperative officer, a pretty symbol of the close and open relationship among the three.

Remarkably, the committee that held office after the imposition of the second supervising manager, with fewer powers and less freedom to act or to agitate, was much better paid than any committee before it, and its pay increased as its powers and responsibilities declined. From 1954 until 1960, committee members received 10 shillings per meeting; from 1960 to 1963, 15 shillings per meeting; and from 1963 to 1966, 20 shillings per meeting. From 1966, committee members received 100 shillings a month; their incentive bonus was increased by 1,000 shillings each in 1969, the same year that the committee lost any power over or responsibility for the sale of coffee. Stripped of their powers, the committee members were left a sinecure that could be revoked by order of the minister should he decide to dismiss any or all of them. The leaders were in an uncomfortable bind, because the membership also had the power to remove them, and they feared this would happen if their prediction that the CMB had left them an insufficient margin was correct. If the union lost money, the growers would receive no bonus, and the committee members were likely to lose their positions.

The committee had acquiesced in the loss of many of its local powers and had received a secure tenure and a sizeable gratuity instead. By 1970, however, the changing political structure and the continuing centralization of power over the BCU were starting to threaten the viability of the union. The forced sale of coffee to the CMB would bring a loss that year. The BCU committee's loss of power was accompanied by a steep decline in both leader and general membership involvement with the union. Committee meetings, after the withdrawal of the supervising manager in 1968, were held less frequently than they ever had been and tended to be pro forma approvals of decisions made by the secretary/manager and the senior cooperative officer. While the committee did still function to receive complaints from the membership, these were acted on by the secretary/manager. In contrast to the frequent meetings held or visits made in the rural areas by other union committees, the Musundi committee never held a meeting other than in its Mbale offices. Education in cooperative practices and issues was left to the DCD; education and supervision in improved coffee cultivation were left to the Ministry of Agriculture. The union was evolving into a branch of the government rather than an autonomous agency, and its committee into quasi–civil servants with narrowly defined functions.

The leaders and many other people in the district were angry and apprehensive about the effects of the forced sale of coffee to the CMB, but the government's strategy of cooptation successfully prevented organized resistance or open opposition to the new policy. The well-paid committee restricted itself to unpublicized, but frequent, meetings with and appeals to the ministry. Moreover, direct and open opposition to government policy was more dangerous and less profitable than it once had been. Since criticism was seen as disloyal and politically dangerous, discontent was no longer a possible focus for organization and involvement.

The BCU committee members repeatedly expressed their fears that they could not satisfy their constituents' demands under these conditions. I attended several GCS elections where BCU committee members defended their incumbency by explaining the new restrictions on the BCU and by emphasizing that they were continuing to serve their constituents' interests through their positions on UPC committees and other political positions they held.

The committee members were threatened by the loss of their positions and their large bonuses whether they opposed the state or acquiesced to its policies. Most of them ended with a pessimistic quietism, feeling that they had exhausted all possibilities of avoiding a serious loss that year and that their work on the committee was essentially useless. One said to me, "The committee can do nothing now. Wagunyanya makes all the decisions, and even he has to check with the Cooperative Officer." Several of the committee members talked of resigning. None did resign; the new political structure of opportunity and their dependence on the DCD both for their tenure and their rich bonuses effectively neutralized the committee.

Idi Amin's coup of January 1971, though it put many of the committee members in danger for their past UPC activities, brought some hope that the cooperative rules would be changed. Amin had specifically mentioned many of Obote's policies as justification for the overthrow. This hope was soon dispelled, however. When Musundi presented a plea for independent marketing to General Amin and a group of his ministers on their first visit to Bugisu, the new minister for cooperatives and marketing answered him harshly, saying that his talk had mixed politics and cooperatives and that there was to be no consideration of exempting individual cooperatives from central control.

The three officers whose turn it was to resign were returned to office in 1971, despite the huge deficit for that year. The GCS delegates were by then as aware as the committee members that the committee and the union could do nothing about the impossible margin of operation that the CMB had left them. Under Amin, the CMB ran Arabica prices down closer to those set for Robusta and forced the union to assume extensive debt. Coffee production fell drastically (United Nations, 1981:10-14), although less than official figures indicate, as there was considerable coffee smuggled across the border. Processing machinery deteriorated in the absence of capital and spare parts.

The Amin regime provoked what previous centralizing regimes had avoided—a withdrawal from the market economy or at least from the official crop-buying agencies. Whether the Obote regime would have been forced to relax its central control by a similar withdrawal is impossible to tell directly, but the outcome under Amin strongly suggests that the DCD's and the BCU committee's fears of peasant resistance were well founded. Obote's strategies effectively immobilized the politicians, but the peasants did maintain their exit option. Under Amin, they proved that they could carry out their threat.

The Bagisu's bargaining position was stronger than that of other ethnic groups, but much of the literature on cooperatives in Uganda and Tanzania suggests that local peasantries in both countries have been able to sustain effective challenges to central state directives (see Kasfir, 1970; Hyden, 1980). The state under Obote was attempting to bring about changes that the dispersed economic and administrative structure of Uganda effectively impeded. The crises that Obote's move to the left provoked within the Ugandan state resulted in part from state programs overrunning limited state powers. The national civil service was demoralized by the UPC's ascendancy, and peasant discontent was general. Obote had successfully preempted the local powers that had previously communicated peasant demands and protests to both local and national agencies of the state. While these outcomes may have had no direct influence on Amin's decision to take power, they were certainly evident in the initial enthusiastic reception of the coup. It is certainly possible that Amin would not have attempted his coup or that the considerable military resistance to the coup would have been more effective if Obote's policies had not already engendered widespread opposition.[3]

Whether or not the increasing concentration of state power, the UPC's disruption of the civil service, and the suppression of peasant-based local organization made Amin's coup possible, they did start a process that led to massive peasant withdrawal from controlled export markets. Local organization, which had served to mobilize peasant production as well as peasant protest, became weaker and weaker and had less and less effective contact with the peasantry. The infrastructure of crop collection, storage, processing, and transport deteriorated. The social welfare projects that peasant production had supported also declined. Uganda's peasant-based export economy and the prosperity that it had maintained disintegrated. The highly repressive Amin regime was primarily responsible, but I will argue in the next chapter that the peasants do use their withdrawal option against states that stop responding to their demands. Obote's government attempted to ignore the peasants' power, at great cost to his own regime and to the peasants' economy. Without effective local organization to direct, focus, and communicate it as a threat, the peasants' exit option is only a veto, a negative and destructive threat without constructive power. When the central state attempted to concentrate power, it provoked this veto and both demonstrated and increased its own fundamental weakness.

The centralization of power ultimately disenabled the local intermediaries, the state bureaucracy's only effective linkage with the peasants. By attempting to exceed the limits imposed by its dependence on freeholding peasant production and diverse local systems of authority, the state brought about the collapse of its own bureaucracy. Spittler (1983) argues that when the bureaucracy of the peasant state can no longer function, the state relies increasingly on violence. Uganda's recent history shows how this violence further weakens the state. Violence, and the threat of violence, characterized the actions of the Uganda state after 1966, proceeding slowly at first, with political arrests as the UPC strove for hegemony through an accelerating vortex of murder under Amin to the chaos of an undisciplined national army fighting equally undisciplined guerrilla armies in a war that continued to kill mostly civilians, even after the second Obote regime was overthrown.

The collapse of the Ugandan state less than eight years after it achieved formal independence can be attributed, at least in part, to its attempt to exercise more power than the society and economy it rested on would allow. This explanation, however, simply raises another question—why was the state so driven to an impossible attempt to expand and strengthen itself? One answer is that the colonial state did not in any sense emerge from immanent forces of social and economic change or from struggles that brought about such changes. Rather, it was a foreign structure imposed by Europeans who depended on local collaborators to perform the highly limited functions of maintaining order and appropriating surplus, with little intervention in the social relations and processes of production. As long as this state was subordinate to the colonial office's external control of succession, which guaranteed the tenure of governors until it replaced them, there was no internal pressure for the state to exercise power beyond that necessary for limited intervention in production (primarily through agricultural extension, which worked more through suasion than coercion) and an equally limited appropriation of surplus. Once the external control over succession to control of the state was removed, however, the state became a prize for which multiple claimants competed. This competition required the formation of alliances that were held together only by distribution of the surplus appropriated as spoils. The formation and maintenance of alliances were themselves competitive processes that required an ever increasing supply of spoils for distribution. Gaining or holding control over the state thus inevitably required increased exploitation of the peasants, which was impossible, for all of the reasons that I have already described. States thus became what Lonsdale (1981) has called "despairing kleptocracies." Holders of power required expanded revenues simply to maintain power, but their attempts to gain these revenues ruined the limited bureaucracies capable of appropriating them. The revenues that were still available were increasingly devoted to the political and military projects of maintaining power, so that the social and physical infrastructure necessary to appropriate surplus in a routine and predictable fashion deteriorated ever more rapidly. Violent appropriation and violent maintenance of power thus became the state's only means of survival, but these were inevitably self-limiting means. The state declined in a series of coups and attempted coups.

The collapse of Obote's first regime, the relatively long survival of Amin's regime, and the economically destructive policies of the second Obote regime all demonstrate that the weakness of the state emerges primarily from the political weakness of the peasantry, its inability to form a national class, and the consequent absence of a national society. Ethnically and regionally separate peasantries have been able to challenge the Ugandan state and to veto its projects at the local level, but they have not been able to unite across ethnic and administrative boundaries to create a political project of their own. They cannot, therefore, deter the groups and individuals who subordinate economic imperatives to their own campaigns to capture and use the state; their veto power can work constructively only when the state's concerns are primarily economic, and even then only at the local level. In the absence of political and social linkages between these peasantries, there is no social or political force capable of restraining the military and political competitors for national power. The following chapter will show how these unrestrained contests for control of the national state destroyed both the national economy and polity, and why the continued suppression of effective peasant organization impedes programs to reconstruct them.

NOTES

1. The Uganda Public Service, excluding teachers and military, was expanded from 16,896 to 25,603 between 1962 and 1969 (Uganda Republic, *Uganda Statistical Abstract*, 1970).

2. The successful cooptation of the BCU committee and the growing power of the UPC are the best explanations of the lack of effective organization on Waisi's behalf. It may also be significant, though, that Waisi, alone of all BCU presidents, never held a district council position. Rather, his political power bases were almost entirely within the union, the party, and the national apex cooperative associations.

3. See Saul (1976) for his own and others' interpretation of Amin's coup. All of these interpretations emphasize ethnic conflicts and struggles between national-level politicians, soldiers, and bureaucrats. These are all significant, but they cannot be properly understood without analyzing the extent of the state's dependence on the peasants. By incorporating too directly the notions of the relative autonomy of the state without realizing that the European experience from which this concept derives differs fundamentally from Uganda's, Saul neglects the crucial links between economic relations and political action.

8

Centralization under Violence and Dependency, 1971-83

Uganda continued through most of the 1960s in steady, though relatively simple, economic expansion. In comparison with other African economies, it maintained impressive growth rates both in internal consumption and in exports and a generally favorable foreign trade balance. Most of the economy remained agricultural, with coffee and cotton providing some 80 percent of foreign revenues, but a small manufacturing and industrial sector was expanding to provide substitutes for petty commodity imports.

The Idi Amin coup of 1971 and the destructive political system that it instituted shattered this apparent progress, but political struggles over class, ethnic, regional, and religious privilege were already jeopardizing Uganda's continued development and stability (Saul, 1976). In 1969 Milton Obote's regime had instituted a series of economic and social reforms that aimed at concentrating economic and political power in the central state. Following the Tanzanian example, the single legal party was to provide most of the impetus and organization for a series of development programs, while nationalization of banks and large industry was to enhance national independence. As explained in the last chapter, export crop sales, crucial for foreign revenues, were to be coordinated by centralized marketing boards, and essential services were to be controlled by central state agencies. This experiment generated considerable apprehension and opposition among the peasantry and bureaucrats, but it was cut short long before its consequences or viability could be assessed. Amin's coup simply precipitated a crisis in the growing tensions between an ambitious, centralizing state and the regional and subregional organizations of a highly diverse population and an extremely decentralized economy. As the state ultimately depended on local systems for almost all of its revenues, it was too weak to achieve the central control to which Obote aspired.

The devastating effects of political struggles to capture and strengthen the weak state now became fully evident. Amin's regime, and the war that ended it, left the national economy in shambles. Physical infrastructure, markets, and currency reserves had all deteriorated badly by 1980; growth rates had been negative for several years, and inflation had spurted to over 100 percent. Much of the population had survived by turning to subsistence farming or by smuggling crops out of the country. There were numerous reasons for this decline, but chief among them was the drastic reduction of crop prices in relation to those of consumer goods. I will argue in this chapter, however, that the suppression of local political organization under both Obote and Amin played and will continue to play a major part in the deterioration of the economy.

Amin maintained his power through direct and highly expensive favors to the armed forces. The army was expanded by 25 percent almost immediately, and arms purchases abroad soared. Military personnel were given control of key ministerial and marketing board posts, and there was little attempt to control corruption. The Coffee Marketing Board (CMB), in particular, became a trough from which various politically favored individuals were allowed to extract a great deal of money. Military officers entered, violently and aggressively, the private sectors vacated when the Asians were expelled.

Amin's government kept crop prices more or less stable in nominal terms until 1976, and then let them rise, but more slowly than prices of consumer goods. Rapid inflation undercut real peasant income, especially after 1977, when coffee prices on the world market lost the gains that the Brazilian crop losses had caused (Table 17).[1] The government also taxed the cooperatives heavily, both directly and indirectly. Imported goods became increasingly scarce as the real value of the shilling dropped; crop processors could not get necessary spare parts

Table 17. Real and Nominal Average Coffee Prices Paid to Ugandan Farmers, 1974-79

Prices	1974	1975	1976	1977	1978	1979
Nominal prices[a]	1.19	1.25	1.40	2.50	3.50	3.50
Prices in constant terms[b]	1.55	1.29	0.99	1.11	1.04	0.86

SOURCE: Bates, Hahn, and Kreag (1981:16), taken from Seers et al. (1979:62).
[a] In Ugandan shillings/kilogram.
[b] In Ugandan shillings/kilogram; 1975 = 100.

for their machines. Peasants all across Uganda increased subsistence cropping. Because of the inefficiencies in collection and payment by the CMB, and because the producer prices in neighboring Kenya and Tanzania were so much more favorable (Table 18), much of the coffee that was grown was smuggled out of the country (Table 19). The decline in crop volume aggravated the economic difficulties the cooperatives faced.

Any possibility of local organization or protest was effectively quashed. Arbitrary arrests and political murders were commonplace; soldiers in the various garrisons prevented or punished whatever—or whoever—they felt was subversive. The numerous attempts against Amin's life and the various abortive invasions by Ugandan exile groups maintained

Table 18. Average Producer Prices for Coffee in Uganda, Kenya, and Tanzania, 1975-80

		1975	1976	1977	1978	1979	1980[a]
A. Producer Prices[b]	Uganda	15.8	18.2	30.2	41.3	63.9	86.5
	Kenya	78.0	145.1	200.7	153.8	158.7	153.8
	Tanzania	47.4	79.2	89.1	73.7	na[c]	na
B. Average export values[d]	Uganda	49.1	88.3	188.0	124.7	138.7	136.8
	Kenya	63.8	131.8	237.3	170.5	172.5	155.1
	Tanzania	52.0	119.7	223.1	144.5	142.1	143.8
C. Proportion of export value paid to producers[e]	Uganda	32.2	20.6	16.1	33.1	46.1	63.2
	Kenya	122.2	110.1	84.6	90.2	92.0	99.2
	Tanzania	91.1	66.2	39.9	51.0	na	na

SOURCE: Bates, Hahn, and Kreag (1981:15).
[a] Third quarter figures.
[b] In US cents/pound, green bean equivalent; from International Coffee Organization, *Quarterly Statistical Bulletin on Coffee* 4, nos. 2-3 (1980), Table IV-25 (p. 84).
[c] na = not available.
[d] In US cents/pound, green bean equivalent; from ibid., Table IV-18 (p. 76).
[e] A ÷ B × 100.

Table 19. Ugandan Coffee: Production and Smuggling, 1970-78

	1971-72	1975-76	1976-77	1977-78
Coffee production[a]	183.7	137.1	155.9	121.3
Coffee smuggling (estimated)[b]	—	25-30	50.0	45.5

NOTE: Data are given in thousands of tons.
[a] IBRD/World Bank (1982:150).
[b] Seers et al., 1979, cited in Amman (1980).

an atmosphere of tension and threat against the regime. This in turn inclined the soldiers to deal quicky and brutally with anyone they perceived as dangerous.

Occasional letters from the cooperatives to the DCD and the CMB outlined the problems that state policy was causing, but their language was very restrained, especially in relation to the gravity of their situation. It was dangerous to object and certainly out of the question to name the corruption and inefficiency at the root of the problem.

The district councils had been completely disbanded when Amin took power. The district administrations were subordinate to military supervision. Chiefs were elected after 1973, but most men were afraid to stand unless they had the direct support of the military regime. The elected chiefs were given military training, and those who did not pass this training were replaced by soldiers.

The powers that the DCD had gained between 1968 and 1970 were enhanced and were used extensively. The department assigned supervising managers, usually political appointees, to run numerous cooperatives.

Both the DCD and the CMB, as well as the Ministry of Agriculture, were used to absorb the rising number of professional school graduates who could not find employment elsewhere in the declining economy. DCD staff increased from 650 in 1970 to 1,500 in 1979 (Amman, 1980). The CMB's main processing plant, designed for 924 staff members, was working at well under half of capacity by 1979, but its staff had expanded to over 2,000 (interview, CMB, 1983). Actual performance of DCD field supervision and auditing and CMB crop collection and processing, however, declined precipitously.

The growing corruption and inefficiencies of the state's crop marketing boards delayed the crop purchases from and payments to the cooperatives. Delayed payments to the cooperatives delayed payments to peasant farmers. Finally, the breakup of the East African community in 1977 left most of the rolling stock of the East African railroads in Kenya. Political tensions with Kenya increased the difficulties of access to the Port of Mombasa.

The inefficiencies of the Ministry of Agriculture, the DCD, the CMB, and other marketing boards hurt the cooperatives and their members, and the suppression of local organization prevented any effective protest against these problems. The state's agricultural pricing policies had even more disastrous effects, as they simultaneously pushed the peasants into subsistence, decapitalized the cooperatives, and contributed to the further expansion and corruption of the state marketing boards.

The Bagisu coffee growers and the BCU were more severely affected by these developments than were the growers and cooperatives in other areas. The long-standing price differentials between Robusta and Arabica had reflected the difference in world prices and also that Arabica was sold partially processed. The differential was also a necessary recompense for the extra land and labor that the cultivation and processing of Arabica required. When the BCU had made its own marketing arrangements and fixed its own prices to farmers, the price differentials had emerged quite directly out of the different price-setting mechanisms for the two types of coffee on the world market. When the CMB was put in control in 1970, Bagisu leaders had had to plead with that agency to avoid a single pricing policy for the entire country. Under the Amin regime, and with the increasingly arbitrary powers of the CMB, the price differential was steadily whittled away, from approximately 4 to 1 down to 2 to 1 (Table 20). Thus the impact of the price decline that afflicted all Ugandan coffee farmers was almost exactly doubled for the Bagisu.

The Bagisu's response was even more pronounced. Robusta sales to the CMB dropped 58 percent, from 232,500 tons in 1969 to 98,300

Table 20. Minimum Agricultural Producer Prices for Robusta and Arabica Coffee in Uganda, 1966-80

Year	Robusta, Unhulled	Arabica, Parchment (Bugisu I)
1966	0.88	3.74
1967	0.88	3.74
1968	0.88	3.30
1969	1.06	3.65
1970	1.06	4.46
1971	1.19	4.46
1972	1.19	4.46
1973	1.19	4.46
1974	1.25	4.46
1975	2.50	4.55
1976	2.50	5.86
1977	3.50	8.50
1978	3.50	10.50
1979	7.00	15.00
1980	7.00	15.00

NOTE: Data are given in Ugandan shillings/kilogram. Bugisu I = highest standard grade of Bugisu Arabica.

tons at its nadir ten years later. Arabica fell 88 percent, from 18,400 tons in 1969 to 2,300 tons in 1978 (Table 21).

The decline in actual production, however, was much less. Official statistics record an increase in actual Arabica acreage (Table 22). On the basis of my own observations and interviews in 1983, and given the general disarray and disorganization of the Ministry of Agriculture field staff under Amin, I do not believe these figures are accurate. At the least they are misleading. Numerous Bagisu farmers were already abandoning or neglecting their coffee plantations by 1978, and the nurseries that would have been necessary for this expansion simply were not functioning at this time. It is clear, however, that the Bagisu were smuggling enormous amounts of coffee into Kenya.

Peasants told me of arduous foot trips over Mt. Elgon in which men and women would carry from forty-five to sixty-six pounds of coffee to the improvised markets across the border. There they would exchange the coffee for a variety of goods, from agricultural implements to pots and pans, unavailable in Uganda. The round trip could take as much as four days. Amin's soldiers constituted a major hazard for these smugglers; a number of Bagisu, as well as some soldiers, died in confrontations on the way to the border.

Many of the army officers based in Mbale were also smuggling coffee. By using bribes and connections the officers could use the main roads

Table 21. Production of Coffee and Cotton in Uganda, 1968-81

Year	Coffee[a]	Robusta	Arabica	Cotton (Lint)
1968	133.4	119.2	14.2	60.4
1969	250.9	232.5	18.4	78.2
1970	201.5	187.4	14.1	86.4
1971	175.7	159.5	16.2	84.8
1972	183.7	162.9	20.8	74.8
1973	213.7	195.7	18.0	74.5
1974	198.6	180.5	18.1	50.0
1975	198.5	183.5	15.0	31.9
1976	137.1	123.1	14.0	24.7
1977	155.9	151.6	4.3	13.8
1978	121.3	119.0	2.3	20.2
1979	103.8	98.3	5.5	14.8
1980	135.2	130.4	4.8	13.3
1981	134.0	125.0	9.0	4.6

SOURCE: IBRD/World Bank (1982:150) taken from Ministry of Planning and Economic Development, Statistical Department; Ministry of Agriculture.
NOTE: These are figures for official purchases only. Data are given in thousands of tons.
[a] Figures are for crop year ending in September of year shown.

Table 22. Production and Export of Ugandan Coffee, 1971-72 to 1979-80

	Acres		Production			
	Robusta	Arabica	Robusta	Arabica		Exports
Year	(000 Ha)		(000 MT)		Total	(000 MT)
1971-72	228.9	28.2	162.9	20.8	183.7	142.6
1972-73	227.8	28.7	195.7	18.2	213.9	220.6
1973-74	205.7	28.3	180.5	18.1	198.6	197.0
1974-75	192.3	30.1	185.3	15.0	198.5	171.7
1975-76	190.6	32.6	123.1	14.0	137.1	145.9
1976-77	190.8	33.0	151.7	4.2	155.9	147.0
1977-78	190.9	33.0	119.0	2.3	121.3	104.6
1978-79[a]	190.0	33.0	114.5	5.5	120.0	na

SOURCE: Bates, Hahn, and Kreag (1981:3), taken from Ministry of Agriculture and Forestry, Planning Division, *The Uganda Coffee Industry: A Brief Survey of Uganda's Coffee Industry 1973-1978* (Entebbe: Ministry of Agriculture, 1979), Table II.2.
NOTE: 000 Ha = thousands of hectares; 000 MT = thousands of metric tons; na = not available. Arabica figures include production from Kigezi.
[a] Estimated.

for large truck loads. Some of them allegedly worked in collusion with BCU staff. Some buyers from Kenya also made illicit arrangements with border guards to come by truck to buy coffee. People told stories of pitched battles between rival buyers, one of which left over fifteen bodies along the back road to Kenya.

Smuggling opportunities declined after 1978. Kenya attempted to limit this activity because it had enough coffee to fill its export quotas under the international coffee agreements. Bagisu farmers were left with large stores of coffee that they could not sell in Kenya and would not sell in Uganda. The Bagisu chiefs were ordered to force the growers to deliver their coffee to the GCSs. Under the threat of violence, the growers complied, but they delivered much of their coffee improperly cured and still wet, so it deteriorated very quickly in storage.

The BCU was by this time in nearly total disarray. Because of the decline in production and the smuggling, its volume had so diminished (Table 23) that it was suffering severe operating losses (Table 24). The private truckers who had previously collected the crop were mostly out of business. Many had sold their trucks because such a visible sign of wealth was simply too great an invitation to murder and robbery by soldiers eager to find some excuse to do away with them and take the trucks. The deteriorated roads discouraged those few who still had trucks. The BCU had bought its own fleet of ten trucks in 1973, but it could not maintain them in the face of its own losses and the absence

Table 23. Total Tons of Coffee Purchased and
Processed by the BCU, 1970-82

Financial Year	Coffee Purchased	Coffee Processed
1970-71	12,955	12,300
1971-72	12,076	11,103
1972-73	15,097	15,217
1973-74	11,421	12,787
1974-75	12,312	10,762
1975-76	11,634	11,084
1976-77	2,315	4,416
1977-78	652	623
1978-79	5,760	4,007
1979-80	6,965	6,055
1980-81	2,661	3,886
1981-82	19,388[a]	10,764

SOURCE: Bugisu Cooperative Union (BCU).
[a] This figure reflects the purchase of coffee stored by
farmers and GCSs from three previous seasons.

Table 24. BCU Operating Balance, 1969-79

Financial Year	Profit (Loss)	
1969-70	4,781,971	profit
1970-71	(1,143,849)	loss
1971-72	(1,306,561)	loss
1972-73	1,008,056	profit
1973-74	(19,003)	loss
1974-75	(978,078)	loss
1975-76	(817,776)	loss
1976-77	(3,224,818)	loss
1977-78	(3,607,401)	loss
1978-79	(5,648,261)	loss

SOURCE: Bugisu Cooperative Union (BCU). Accounts
for subsequent years have not yet been approved, but
have also entailed losses. Prior to 1970-71, the BCU
had recorded losses in only two financial years, 1954-
55 and 1958-59.
NOTE: Data are given in Ugandan shillings.

of spare parts. Furthermore, the CMB had not paid for much of the coffee it had taken from the BCU, so the BCU could not pay the GCSs. For all of these reasons, the coffee, already deteriorating, remained in the inappropriate stores of the GCSs, where it continued to deteriorate at the same time that it prevented the GCSs from receiving more coffee from the growers. Coffee started to pile up in the even less favorable storage conditions of the individual growers' houses.

The DCD had effectively stopped functioning in the rural areas, so the GCSs were audited sporadically, if at all. Under the pressure of the chiefs, much coffee was delivered on credit, as the BCU had long since exhausted its crop advance monies and had to wait for the delayed CMB payments. Accounting systems broke down, and various GCS secretary/managers stole from coffee stores or absconded with whatever funds eventually came in. Numerous GCSs ended up deeply in debt to their own members. The BCU, in turn, owed the GCSs about 40 million shillings.

There was very little the BCU committee members could do about this situation. Their few mild complaints by letter about CMB delays or about the improper handling of the crop, which was worsening Bugisu coffee's already deteriorated international reputation, were simply ignored or rebuffed. The committee did take advantage of the commissioner for cooperative development's obligatory ritual appearance at Annual General Meetings to repeat their complaints more forcefully, but the commissioner usually responded with platitudinous statements urging the Bagisu to support the cooperative because it had been founded for their benefit and because their efforts would contribute to national development.

The committee also used the general meetings to explain to the delegates why the union was doing so badly. In addition to presenting accounts of CMB delays, they twice accused the staff of absenteeism, smuggling, and theft, though they also pointed out that these activities were motivated by the inflation that had drastically devalued staff salaries.

The committee continued unchanged through 1982 except for two retirements. Various committee members told me that they had continued serving against their own wishes. They did not receive incentive bonuses because of the BCU's losses, and their allowance lost value because of inflation. Two of them said that they were closely watched because of their positions, so they had to deliver their crops to the GCSs at the low official prices and suffer the effects of delayed payments. Their trips to town exposed them to harassment at the improvised roadblocks the soldiers used to complement their salaries. Conspicuous business activities attracted the dangerous attention of the soldiers; both of the committee members who had commercial vehicles sold them at very low prices in the early years of the Amin regime. There were no political positions left to link profitably with the BCU positions. All in all, there was little attraction or benefit left in the committee memberships. DCD representatives, however, implied that it would not be safe for them to resign, so the committee continued at a very low level of activity and with no effective power. Members were frequently absent from meetings, often because they had gone into hiding in Kenya while soldiers were looking for them.

All of Enoka Musundi's committee did survive, but members of George Waisi's more active committee were not so fortunate. Three of them were arrested or disappeared soon after the coup. Waisi was arrested several times but rejected his family's urgings to leave the country. He was arrested again on the second anniversary of the coup and murdered soon afterward.

The BCU remained virtually immobilized by the end of the Amin period and the war that finally overthrew him. The war coincided with a severe drought that left many Bagisu hungry and sick.

Amin was overthrown in 1979 by a coalition (Uganda National Liberation Front, UNLF) of exile organizations of quite divergent political persuasions backed by the Tanzanian army. The war itself was brief, but the looting that followed left Kampala and a number of smaller cities in shambles. There was relatively little fighting in Bugisu, and Mbale was spared the destructive looting that other cities suffered, although most of its few remaining vehicles were commandeered by one army or the other. Many of the Sebei soldiers who had served under Amin fled home with their weapons, and soon after the war began attacking settlements across the Bugisu border. Returning Bagisu soldiers responded in kind, and several communities on both sides of the border were devastated. Members of both ethnic groups took advantage of the strife to loot each others' houses, farms, and businesses, as well as an agricultural experimental station.

At the same time, Karamojong from further north, also heavily armed, started raiding cattle in Bugisu. The Tanzanian army created a people's militia in Bugisu, but discipline was very loose, and its members soon started using their weapons to assault and rob other Bagisu.

The UNLF government was as unstable as its component groups were diverse. Yusufu Lule, its first president, was removed soon after he was installed. In early 1980 David Oyite Ojok, the general who led the UNLF forces in the war, and Paulo Muwanga, a Muganda who had been powerful in the first Obote regime and had remained in

Uganda until shortly before the war, led a coup against Godfrey Binaisa, the second president. They invited Milton Obote, who had been excluded from the meeting in Tanzania that formed the UNLF, to return. They started to rebuild the Uganda People's Congress (UPC). The Tanzanians oversaw national elections, which a team from the European Economic Community (EEC) monitored, late in 1980. The EEC team certified that the elections were fairly run, but there were numerous allegations that it was very difficult for anyone but UPC candidates to register in many parts of Uganda, and the leaders of several different factions within the UNLF started guerrilla movements shortly after the UPC victory. Although none of these groups was strong enough to overthrow the government, they made communication and transport dangerous, increased Obote's already considerable dependence on Ojok and his military forces, and provoked the large, undisciplined, and underpaid army to brutal and destructive repression, especially around Kampala.

Peasant Responses to the New Dependency of the Ugandan State

Goran Hyden's (1980) "uncaptured peasantry" thesis focused primarily on the ability of the Tanzanian peasantry to veto unpopular state initiatives by withdrawing into subsistence agriculture. Hyden maintained that this "exit option" weakened the state, reduced its developmental capacities, and even allowed the peasants to "capture" the bureaucrats. Market withdrawal is indeed a possibility for freeholding peasants with enough land to sustain themselves through diversified cropping, but many peasants are so dependent on commodity exchange that such an action would seriously diminish their living standards. I have argued in this study that the exit option is not necessarily a simple veto, but rather can be used as a bargaining lever against the state. Rather than simply weakening the state, this lever can be used by local political organizations to gain concessions on crop prices and marketing conditions from the state. These concessions may actually serve to stimulate increased peasant production. Furthermore, peasants may be able to use this leverage symbolically. Even if actual crop reduction would be very costly for them, this threat can be effectively manipulated to bargain with the state if the state's agents believe that withdrawal or significant crop reduction is a real possibility. Thus the exit option is not necessarily a restriction of the state's power, as Hyden argues, but may enhance the peasants' capacity to communicate with the state in ways that maintain cash cropping as a viable option for the peasants and thus indirectly sustain state revenues.

Bagisu peasants were able to bargain effectively with the state until 1971 because the state depended on them to achieve its political and economic goals. I believed that the attempts of the second Obote regime to resuscitate agricultural exports would stimulate renewed flows of power back to locally based, peasant-supported organizations. I found, however, when I returned to Uganda during the summer of 1983, that this regime was far less susceptible to local political demands than the first Obote regime or any of the previous national or colonial governments had been. The reconstruction programs that the Obote regime had undertaken created major new dependencies on international agencies, and the state's first concern was to satisfy these agencies. Also, it used its dependence as an argument against peasant demands for high prices or the cooperatives' protests that they could not operate within the pricing margin that government policy allowed them. In the rest of this chapter I analyze some of the effects of this new dependency on peasant agriculture and political organization in Bugisu District.

I spent the first three weeks of my return trip interviewing officers of the World Bank, the International Monetary Fund (IMF), the U.S. Agency for International Development (U.S. AID), and the EEC in Nairobi and in Kampala. In Kampala I also interviewed the minister and various officers of the Ministry of Cooperatives and Marketing, as well as of the CMB and DCD. The atmosphere in Kampala was extremely tense; there were heavily armed soldiers everywhere and a great deal of shooting at night. I felt quite apprehensive during most of my time there and was somewhat more discrete in my questions to certain officers than I would have been in a more secure situation, but I was granted almost all of the interviews I requested and was quite surprised by the openness of most responses to my questions. Travel in Bugisu itself was somewhat dangerous because of marauding by the undisciplined local militia, but there again I was able to get around reasonably freely. The difficulties of communication and travel in the district meant that it was impossible to schedule interviews in advance, so the actual choice of informants in each area followed access and convenience. Furthermore, records of agricultural production and sale had in many cases not been kept at all, had been kept so badly as to be useless, or had been lost or destroyed, both in the government offices and in the cooperatives. Most of the data from Bugisu presented here therefore come from interviews with officers of various ministries and of the district administration, cooperative committee members and staff, and coffee growers, as well as from direct observation.

While the Bagisu could, and did, ignore a state that was even weaker than it had been in 1971, the state continued to offer considerable rewards to local influentials who were therefore interested in organizing the Bagisu in ways that enhanced their own individual power. In order to do this, they had to satisfy the state to some degree without antagonizing their local constituencies. The nature of the state's own dependence, however, and therefore of its power, had changed considerably.

Until 1971, the state was externally dependent on world prices for its exports and imports, but this dependency was moderated by a consistently favorable trade balance. The state was internally dependent on freehold peasant production, which left it highly susceptible to the political and economic demands of local peasantries.

The looting that followed the 1979 war, the continued guerrilla opposition to Obote, wide-flung black market systems (see Green, 1981), renegade deserters from Amin's armies, and a large, undisciplined military continued to destabilize political and economic processes. Nonetheless, Obote's programs to reconstruct Uganda's agricultural export economy attracted, and became highly dependent on, international agency loans and grants. As a result, the IMF, the World Bank, and the EEC, together with a number of national agencies such as the U.S. AID, exercised considerable control over policies that affected crop prices, capital investment in crop processing, quality controls, and rural extension programs. Though still dependent in the long run on peasant crop production, the Ugandan state's more immediate need was to satisfy the demands of these agencies. Both the Obote regime and the major donor agencies agreed in their basic premises that Uganda would need large injections of foreign capital over the coming years. Because of the continued levels of violence and insecurity, both private banks and bilateral aid agencies had expressed reservations about further loans to Uganda. As a result, the Ugandan state was particularly anxious to maintain IMF approval. Until 1985 its policies satisfied the IMF, which concurred with several reschedulings of the national debt. Uganda was, however, in arrears with its principal payments, and the national debt had risen rapidly since 1980. The debt service ratio rose from about 17 percent in 1980 to over 50 percent in 1981, and it was anticipated that it would continue to climb.

The Obote regime was anxious to establish its own revenue base, and levied heavy duties and indirect taxes on coffee exports that forced down both farm gate prices and processing margins. The regime found IMF strictures convenient, as it could use this agency's demands to justify policies that both the peasants and the cooperatives opposed.

It could also invoke the need for national reconstruction. The state's alliance with and direct reliance on the IMF thus restricted the possibility for effective local intervention in policy formation and program implementation. The second Obote regime did not manage, therefore, to mobilize the peasants behind the state's most pressing long-term need, that is, the production of foreign-revenue generating crops.

Bagisu Response to Economic Crisis after 1980

As I explained earlier, Amin's policies and the reduced market for smuggled coffee in Kenya had led to coffee hoarding in growers' houses and in GCS stores. Soon after the UPC victory in 1981-82, the BCU and the DCD mobilized all available transport to collect coffee stored throughout the district to the mill. Much of this coffee had by then deteriorated even further. The CMB refused to pay full prices for it, and the BCU refused to accept the lower prices, maintaining that the CMB was responsible for the delays in purchase and shipment that had caused the coffee to deteriorate. This impasse further increased the backup of coffee in BCU storage; the excessive weight actually destroyed internal walls in the main warehouse. It also aggravated the BCU's debt, as it was paying interest on coffee it had already purchased but still had not sold. Three hundred sixty tons of this coffee disappeared, presumably by theft. The shortage of funds to pay for the coffee once delivered increased further the BCU's debts to the GCSs. Partial payments were made in some cases, usually months after delivery. GCS secretary/managers could therefore not pay for the crops when they were delivered and had to parcel out whatever money did arrive between different farmers. There were no set rules about how this money was to be distributed, so that there were ample opportunities for the secretary/manager to favor his own kin or to embezzle part or all of the money himself. The coffee growers had no reliable way of knowing whether or how much money had been delivered, or whether they were to be paid at the rate prevailing at the time they had delivered their coffee or at new rates which might have been set subsequently. This system of payment put additional strains on the accounting systems of the GCSs and increased farmers' suspicions that the GCSs would not pay them. As a result, many GCSs split along lineage lines.

By 1983 the total number of GCSs had doubled. This meant that more untrained managers were running GCSs, that meager supervisory resources were stretched even further, that collection schedules became even more complex, and that total administrative and overhead costs of the GCSs doubled.

After Obote returned to power in December 1980, he initiated contacts with numerous international development organizations. In addition to the arrangements with the World Bank and the IMF, under which the regime renegotiated its short-term debts and started incurring substantial long-term debt, it concluded bilateral loan and grant arrangements with a wide array of aid agencies. Much of this aid was directed at reestablishing commercial agriculture. Hoe manufacture had virtually ceased in Uganda; the EEC and U.S. AID instituted programs to import and distribute hoes and chemical pesticides. There was considerable graft and inefficiency at the distribution end. The impact was limited because most of the hoes and other supplies reached growers well before the reestablishment of marketing opportunities for commercial crops. Some farmers sold these implements to raise cash.

The direct aid to farmers did not last long, in any event. Subsequent aid programs were focused much more on the reestablishment of capital intensive infrastructure and high-level marketing and administration facilities and on stabilizing currency and commerce. A major EEC program was aimed at reestablishing coffee mills throughout the country. Under this program, the BCU was pressed to incur a debt of 650 million shillings to expand its processing capacity to 40,000 tons, which BCU officers believed was ten to fifteen tons over the maximum coffee production then possible in the district. The union would have four years to pay the debt.[2] The U.S. AID was training cooperative technicians at the higher ranks, both in Uganda and the United States. It was preparing to channel a planned US$20 million cooperative credit grant through the Uganda Cooperative Bank (UCB), even though a report it commissioned warned of the UCB's near total disorganization. (Implementation of this plan was halted after objections by a visiting evaluation term. After eighteen months of further searches and intense negotiations with the minister of cooperatives and marketing, who still wanted the UCB to control the funds, U.S. AID decided to route a US$32 million credit plan through the Uganda Development Bank. Preparations to establish independent channels to the farmers were interrupted by the 1985 coup, when U.S. AID suspended its programs and withdrew most of its personnel.) Other international agencies mounted programs to reestablish urban and transport infrastructure, with loans and grants tied to specific projects. There was little effective communication or coordination between these agencies. Neither the state nor the IMF, whose agents effectively filled executive positions in the budgeting, banking, and planning agencies of the state, had complete or consistent figures on loan disbursements or applications. This meant there was no way to monitor precisely the rapidly growing national debt to which these agencies were contributing. Furthermore, international agency personnel interacted primarily with their high-level national bureaucratic counterparts. As the lower levels of the national ministries were starved both for salaries and operating budgets, these bureaucrats had little notion of local-level problems and processes or means of assessing the impact of state policy. Finally, military expenses absorbed about one-fourth of the national budget and much of its foreign revenues. Political demands from the military kept agencies like the NCTU (National Cooperative Transport Union) and the CMB subservient to corruption and interference. Inefficiency, corruption, and pressure from the military all distorted the programs the international agencies supported.[3]

Vast numbers of trucks were imported, both under loans and through direct barter for coffee. These barter arrangements enhanced the opportunities for corruption in the CMB. IMF policies stimulated importation of a wide array of goods, including luxury items such as private cars, clothing, liquor, and electronic devices. This encouraged smuggling of imported luxury goods to Kenya. In Bugisu, however, as in other parts of Uganda, peasants were unable to purchase more hoes to replace those that quickly wore out through intensive use, could not purchase the coffee-pulping and -drying equipment that they needed, and had no access to chemical fertilizers and sprays. There were not enough gunny bags to transport or store the coffee harvested, so much of it was piled directly on mud or concrete floors, subject to pests, dirt, and moisture, which reduced its quality.

Coffee prices set by the government under World Bank and IMF supervision rose, but at rates below the rate of inflation. The World Bank's representatives pushed for higher prices, but Obote's ministers used an IMF-supported system of dual exchange rates and the IMF's economic prescriptions to keep prices down. The separate rates of exchange, one for essential imports and agriculture, the other for non-essentials, were used to justify very low real prices to the farmers (see Uganda Republic, 1982:24). The state used the Window I, or essential goods rate, to maintain its claim that farmers received about half the world price for their coffee. The CMB was reimbursed at this rate for the coffee that it sold. Theoretically, the farmers should have been able to buy agricultural implements imported at the Window I rates on which their coffee prices were based. In fact, in the absence of these implements, all of their purchases were at rates closer to those of Window II, which exchanged 2.5 to 3 times the number of Uganda shillings to the dollar. The state appropriated the foreign exchange that came in from coffee and sold it at Window II. It reimbursed the CMB in shillings at Window I rates. This meant that it was the state, rather than the growers or the CMB, which benefited from the differential exchange rates. The growers were effectively being paid less than 18 percent of market prices. Corruption and inefficiencies in the CMB, which operated under Ojok's supervision until his death in December 1983, slowed down coffee purchases and payments to cooperative unions, so growers usually could not sell their coffee when they wanted, and often had to wait for partial payment of these low prices.

The CMB continued to control all coffee exports despite opposition from the cooperatives and continued criticism from various aid agencies. In addition to providing attractive opportunities to groups and individuals who supported the Obote government, the CMB provided jobs for a vastly inflated staff. It also was a key component in the state's strategies for appropriating crop revenues (Bates, Hahn and Kreag, 1981; see also Bates, 1981, for comparative data on state control of crop marketing). The government was therefore most reluctant to move toward its abolition or reform, despite clear evidence of its inefficiencies. In Bugisu, CMB delays aggravated the BCU's and the GCSs' financial and organizational difficulties and the growers' discontent with the cooperatives.

The DCD had effectively taken control of both staff and committee appointments in the cooperative unions, so the committees were no longer sufficiently autonomous, nor, in Bugisu at least, did they have sufficient following to organize effective demands for higher prices or more rapid payment. Surprisingly, however, DCD control of staff appointments had not achieved the degree of quiescence that the DCD may have aimed at. Most of the senior staff appointees were from DCD ranks, but many were appointed to their own ethnic areas. In the case of Bugisu at least, these senior staff members adopted many of the political behaviors of the earlier elected committees. They participated indirectly in local political activities and used the union as a focal point for local organization. Their contacts within the DCD and their knowledge of its operations helped them to defend local interests. In Bugisu it was the secretary/manager, rather than the committee, who led the campaign to force the CMB to pay full price for the spoiled coffee. This issue was finally resolved in the BCU's favor by a presidential commission appointed after the secretary/manager simply shut down the coffee mill for three months, alleging that it was impossible to buy more coffee until the old coffee was sold and removed.

Francis Nagimesi, the BCU's secretary/manager, had worked both as a senior DCD officer and in the Uganda Central Cooperative Union (UCCU). He was connected by kinship and marriage to families who had been powerful in both the BCU and the district council, and he collaborated closely with Y. Wambosa, George Waisi's younger brother. Wambosa had worked first for the BCU, which gave him extensive formal training, and then for the UCCU, before returning to Bugisu after Waisi was killed. In Bugisu, Wambosa had worked on the MCU staff, and had been elected in 1980 as the MP for north Bugisu. Nagimesi and Wambosa collaborated both in BCU matters as well as in the self-help and other projects that Wambosa was pushing through the district. By using the BCU's resources and prestige to back politically based development projects, Nagimesi was overcoming the political weakness and isolation of the staff. He became politically more active and powerful than the representative committee. Nagimesi traveled frequently to Kampala, where he used his extensive ties in the DCD to argue for higher prices to Bagisu farmers, a wider operating margin for the BCU, accelerated CMB collection and payments, and a return of the BCU's right to arrange its own foreign sales.

While the secretary/manager's intransigence was reminiscent of the early struggles between the Bagisu and the state, it was not sufficient to raise coffee prices to satisfactory levels. The DCD itself was almost without power in budgetary and pricing decisions,[4] so the BCU staff's influence there was limited primarily to questions of crop-purchase credits and collection schedules. For the moment, at least, the Bagisu had lost their ability to bargain with the state. Not only was the state able to deflect pressures on it by invoking its dependence on the IMF and other agencies, but the BCU itself was no longer cohesive enough to mobilize effectively against the state.

The BCU committee had become even weaker than it was at the end of the first Obote regime. The minister assumed the power to impose educational and political criteria on the committee elections. In 1982 he disqualified all of the current BCU committee members from standing for reelection. The Bagisu remained sufficiently rebellious to elect the old committee three times in three days. The minister finally admitted partial defeat in order to conclude the overlong Annual General Meeting. He said that the BCU could elect the old committee, but that he would refuse to let it convene. Faced with the prospect of having a union without a committee, the meeting elected a new committee, primarily composed of men with few remaining ties to agriculture. The chairman, S. W. Magona, had worked for years in Kampala as national sales manager for Mobil Oil Company and then ran a gasoline station in Mbale, two members were headmasters of schools in Mbale, one was a retired policeman, one a civil servant, and another an MCU staff member.

All were influential UPC members, and most held other political office. The strong UPC discipline, however, continued to mean that the political activities of the BCU committee members enhanced their political subordination rather than their ability to challenge central control. It was also symptomatic of the growing problems in and weakness of the BCU that there was a strong campaign in this Annual General Meeting to divide the union into separate cooperatives for the north and the south.

The subordination of the committee to direct ministerial approval, the fragmentation of the GCSs, the disillusionment of members with the long history of deferred and partial payments for their coffee, and their fears that GCS managers might not pay them at all limited the BCU's capacity to mobilize the peasants against the state. The low operating margin that state-set prices left the cooperatives meant that the BCU continued to operate at a loss. The only possibility for solvency was accidental and unpredictable; because of rapid inflation and frequent devaluation, the BCU occasionally bought from peasants at one price and sold later at a much higher price. Inflation also greatly reduced the real value of the BCU's debt to the NCTU for the trucks it had recently acquired, but the high taxes on cooperative profits reduced whatever relief this economic instability provided and created a strong incentive for the BCU to redistribute as much of these random gains as possible back to the peasants. Central state restrictions on bonuses and second payments made this difficult, however.

The peasants' responses to low coffee prices and to the BCU's organizational and financial difficulties weakened their own bargaining position against the state. The reality of coffee crop reduction limited its utility as a threat. The combination of low prices, inadequate agricultural inputs, and the uncertainty of payment schedules and values stimulated many coffee growers to diversify, not only into a wider range of subsistence crops, but also into a number of cash crops.

While I was in Bugisu, I traveled through all of the coffee-growing areas and interviewed growers as well as staff and committee members in thirty-seven different GCSs. In several of these areas I also had long discussions with groups of GCS members. I was able to compare coffee plantations in 1983 with those of areas I had known well in 1969-71 and in a few cases was able to confirm my own written notes and memory from the earlier period with photographs I had taken then. In many areas coffee trees were neglected so that labor and land could be used for expanded subsistence cropping of peanuts and corn or for plantains, carrots, cabbage, tomatoes, and onions for the Kampala and the Kenya markets.[5] In some areas coffee trees had been slashed down to make room for these alternative crops; their owners said that they would wait the next three or four years for the trees to grow back before deciding what to do with them. In a smaller number of cases growers had taken the more decisive step of uprooting coffee trees to make way for other kinds of cultivation.

The higher volume to value and greater perishability of these food crops imposed considerable marketing problems in a mountainous area where what was never more than a rudimentary transport system had deteriorated badly, but many farmers told me that the quick returns and multiple harvests per season compensated them for these additional problems. More serious problems resulted from lack of knowledge about what were, for many of them, new crops. They complained of lack of fertilizers and sprays. Most were still experimenting with different systems of intercropping and spacing. They had already learned about the effects of altitude on different crops and used this knowledge in attempts to prevent pest infestation. These manipulations of different ecological and climatic niches were increasing the diversity of crops between different parts of Mount Elgon. This diversity contrasted strongly with the homogeneity of coffee cultivation before 1971 and may further restrict the potential for district-wide organization and mobilization to regain control over crop marketing. Such cooperatives and other collective organizations as do emerge are more likely to be limited to fairly small localities, rather than develop the district-wide power base that the BCU's commercialization of a single crop gave it.

Another consequence of the diversification of both subsistence and cash cropping and of the collapse of effective state control was extensive invasion of the forest preserve, which formerly protected all slopes above 7,000 feet of elevation. In addition, land pressure stimulated cropping on steep slopes. Population is estimated to have increased by over 50 percent since 1969 (Uganda Republic, 1985). Erosion has always been a danger in Bugisu; mud slides occasionally eliminate entire hamlets there. Coffee trees protect the soil and slopes better than short-season crops that necessarily denude the ground several times a year, and erosion is likely to become an even greater problem than before.

Few growers abandoned coffee altogether. They were aware that vegetable markets were uncertain and that vegetable crops were highly susceptible to blight and pests. Coffee does not have to be sold immediately and therefore serves as security against emergency cash needs and as savings for large periodic expenses such as school fees. Vegetable crops were a favorable substitute for coffee under current conditions, but they did not, nor can they, provide the returns that coffee did before 1971.

The market for vegetable crops was favorable in part because of military violence and looting in the rural areas of Buganda that had previously supplied Kampala's food. If and when peace is established, the Bagisu vegetable growers would depend primarily on the Kenya market, which is subject to the vagaries of agriculture there, Kenya's own crop exports, and the relations between the two countries. If the Kenya market closes down, the Bagisu could very quickly saturate their remaining marketing options. On the other hand, if Kenya continues to export most of its own crops, its domestic market could present expansive opportunities for Bugisu crops.

The Bagisu became more self-sufficient, even though less prosperous, as they diversified into other crops. They were less vulnerable to market and other forms of economic breakdown than in the past. Except for the threat of armed violence and deterioration of public health systems, they were not physically endangered by Uganda's continuing economic problems. They and other Ugandan peasants could maintain themselves with minimal access to markets. Under such conditions it was highly unlikely that they would grow the controlled export crops in the volume that the state needed for its own ongoing expenses and to pay off its long-term debt.

State planners and the aid agency personnel who influenced their decisions had inadequate means of learning peasant responses to their pricing and marketing policies. Local organizations that until the 1970s provided means of bargaining with the state were too disorganized to communicate peasant demands effectively. The government bureaucracies no longer had the resources necessary to maintain the communication with the rural areas that they had before 1971. The resources they did have were flowing primarily to training and rehabilitation at the higher ranks. In 1983 cooperative and extension field agents in Bugisu had not received travel allowances for over two years. Their inability to move from the rural areas to district headquarters impeded both the efficiency of their own work and the flow of information between peasants and government. It also limited effective supervision of what activities they did carry out in the field and has thus allowed them to collude with dishonest GCS managers and further disillusion the peasants.

Conclusion

Uganda now depends on coffee for 95 percent of its foreign revenue earnings, but little of the foreign revenues generated are going back to coffee growers. As a World Bank economist said, "Coffee is obliged to finance the entire budget." When I answered that this was impossible, he answered, "Well, we are printing money." Uganda was indeed printing far more money than projected in its IMF-approved plans, and the resulting inflation only worsened the coffee growers' already difficult situation. In Bugisu coffee growers responded by starting to raise crops that will not generate foreign revenues. At the same time, the state was increasing its long-term debt, and encouraging the coffee-marketing cooperative unions to incur debts to expand their processing capacity.

The peasants had lost most of their bargaining power against the state. Because they had implemented their long-term threat to reduce coffee production, this threat was no longer the effective bargaining lever it once was. In the short term, the state could ignore the peasantry and take shelter in its relation with the various donor and lending agencies. In the long run, however, it was undermining the only basis available to repay the debts it was rapidly accumulating. Returning to Uganda, I did not see the resurgence of local political organization that I had expected the reconstruction programs to stimulate. Instead, I saw a state that was attracting large loans for programs to reconstruct its economy while it effectively ignored the producers on whom that economy is based.

In 1983, in an interview in Kampala, an IMF representative claimed that Uganda's debt was comparatively small and that it was therefore justified to continue making new loans. I pointed out to him that not only was the debt growing very fast, but also that very little of the credit was being applied in ways that would increase the peasants' production of the export crops required to repay the loans. He responded that Obote's government had been very amenable to IMF conditions for the continued extension of credits and for rescheduling the debt payments. I replied that Obote had to be, because he depended so largely on foreign credit to keep his regime in power. I predicted, however, that when the debt became too great, as it would, the IMF would impose conditions that Obote could not accept.

Obote was, in fact, unable to keep the budget within the IMF guidelines, in part because he could not control the expenditures of powerful political figures who ran various ministries. A rise in world coffee prices had given foreign revenues a badly needed boost in 1984, but nonetheless the government had had insufficient revenues to meet its recurrent expenses. It forced various parastatals, including the CMB, to purchase treasury bills. This further depleted the CMB's already scarce funds and further limited its ability to collect or pay for coffee from the unions. The BCU accumulated huge stores of coffee, despite the decline in production.

The government allowed Window I rates to rise rapidly in 1984 and finally merged Window I and Window II. It imposed exchange restrictions in an unsuccessful attempt to control inflation, and black market rates were soon running at more than twice the official rates.

Aid agencies did renew their programs to get implements and pesticides to the farmers, but the CMB actually purchased less coffee in each year after 1982. Ministry offices claimed that International Coffee Agreement (ICA) quotas prevented them from purchasing more, but, in fact, quotas went up slightly. In principle, the CMB should have exported as much Bugisu Arabica as possible. ICA quotas are set by volume, so it is advantageous for Uganda to export whatever coffee brings the highest prices on the world market. Nonetheless, CMB purchases of Arabica declined proportionally even more than its purchases of Robusta coffee, from 14,600 long tons in 1983 to 10,100 long tons in 1984 (Uganda Republic, 1985).

Total indebtedness mounted, and foreign reserves were drawn down. Obote's inability to control his budget (due to the pressure of the various political allies on whom he depended) forced him to reject IMF conditions for renewed credits in the summer of 1985. Within a month he was overthrown by a military coup, apparently because he passed over high-ranking officers of other ethnic groups to promote Langi officers whose ethnic loyalties he felt he needed. I can only guess about whether Obote's difficulties in renegotiating the credits that sustained his political control contributed to the dissolution of the political-military coalition that kept him in power. It is clear, however, that the two processes were concurrent. The 1985 coup did not end the violence in Uganda, nor did it solve the problems of the huge external debt that Obote's reliance on foreign agencies incurred. That debt further diminishes any possibility that the state can find either the funds or the political space necessary to stimulate the production of export crops or to reestablish the processing, marketing, and transport infrastructures on which it depends.

The Bagisu's search for new crops and new markets suggest possible refinements to Hyden's (1980) analysis of how an "uncaptured" peasantry may respond to unfavorable state policies. The Bagisu, as many other African peasantries, have come to depend on numerous commodities, both for consumption and as implements of production. They were able for many years to use the threat of withdrawal from or reduction of participation in export-crop markets to bargain with the state, but actual implementation of this threat would have been extremely costly to them. When they were no longer able to bargain with the state effectively enough to gain favorable prices and marketing conditions, they did not withdraw completely into subsistence, but diversified into a mix of cropping. This mix varied according to ecological conditions, but generally included some coffee, subsistence crops, and food for domestic markets. This strategy to some extent offset the losses they sustained from falling coffee prices. The net result for the state, however, was approximately the same as a withdrawal into subsistence, that is, it could not guarantee sufficient foreign revenues to satisfy its own political or economic needs.

Peasants in Bugisu have not withdrawn into subsistence cropping alone; they are actively exploring alternative crops and markets free from direct state control. They are able largely to ignore the export-promotion policies of a state that needs their land and labor to generate foreign revenues. The turn to production for local consumption or for subsistence poses a major problem for the Ugandan state, as well as for those of other African countries such as Ghana and the Ivory Coast, where a similar flight from export agriculture is occurring. This withdrawal reflects peasant responses to both national and international economic crises. It directly debilitates the national states and contributes to prolonged political instability.

NOTES

1. Young, Sherman, and Rose (1981:53) point out that the apparent prosperity that the 1976-77 boom in coffee prices produced masked the weakness of an economy that had become almost entirely dependent on coffee for its foreign revenues.

2. The EEC had originally proposed that construction costs would be paid as direct grants to the cooperatives, but the government insisted that the grants be transformed into rotating credit funds. As one EEC officer said, the Ugandan government has a long history of diverting agricultural funds to other, less productive purposes. The EEC, however, agreed to the government's demand.

3. An officer of one of these agencies told me, "On paper, nobody officially recognizes the incompetence or corruption which will keep these plans from working" (interview, Kampala, 1983).

4. I was present during a chance encounter between the minister of cooperatives and marketing and the minister of finance at the time the parliamentary debate over the budget was going on. Their initially guarded discussion became quite heated, as the minister of cooperatives and marketing claimed that the proposed farm prices and processing margins would wreck both the farmers and the cooperatives and complained that no one was taking his figures into account. The minister of finance replied with the standard

invocation of the need for sacrifice during a period of national reconstruction. The minister of cooperatives and marketing later said to me privately that his ministry had very little leverage.

5. As far as I could see, men had become as dominant in the cultivation and sale of commercial food crops as they were in the cultivation and sale of coffee.

9

Conclusion: Suppression of Local Organization and Decline in Peasant Marketing

African agricultural production per capita has declined precipitously over the past decade and a half. Economic decline is aggravating the already notable instability of numerous African states. The economic chaos that Uganda suffered during and after Amin's despotic rule was extreme but did demonstrate the results of two incompatible processes in much of Africa. On the one hand, African states have attempted to appropriate large portions of the peasants' production with relatively little return in social or economic services to them (Bates, 1981). On the other hand, African freeholding peasants have demonstrated that they can withdraw from cash markets if their product is excessively taxed (Hyden, 1980; personal communication, 1983). I have argued in this book that local groups can achieve power by mediating between these tendencies. The state, however, perceives their success as a threat to its own control and revenues. I believe that much of the decline in African agricultural production can be explained by the unrestrained struggle of competing factions for political control of the state and the related attempt by holders of state power to increase political control over and exploitation of peasants. This attempt induces the state to suppress local organizations, which are as essential to effective organization of local production and marketing as they are threatening to central state control.

Indirect Rule, Agricultural Development, and Peasant Politics: A Summary

The only way the Ugandan state could increase its revenues from Bugisu was to increase coffee production and improve coffee quality without paying higher prices to the farmers. As elsewhere in Uganda, state strategies to increase revenues were effectively limited by the peasants' subsistence option. The Bagisu coffee growers, however, posed an especially acute dilemma for the state. The high market value of Arabica coffee made it particularly important to the state's export strategies. The central state's dependence on small-hold export agriculture in Bugisu for a significant share of its revenues made threats of popular mobilization to reduce or withhold coffee production an effective means of reversing or diminishing actual central control and opening up new avenues to power and wealth for local groups. These groups had to exert pressure for higher coffee prices and reduced quality control in order to keep peasant support. This set them against the state. Each time they won concessions from the state, they expanded or strengthened the institutions, such as the BCU and the district council, which they could use against the state. These institutions emerged from the Bagisu's struggles for local control, which were fortified by similar struggles in the rest of Uganda, such as those which pushed the colonial state to enact the 1946 Cooperative Societies Act and the 1955 African Local Government Ordinance (see Brett, 1970; Mamdani, 1976).

The colonial state had superimposed a district-wide hierarchy—the Bugisu Native Administration (BNA)—over the existing acephalous lineages. It had coopted lineage heads as government chiefs and then used them to organize and regulate the production and exchange of agricultural commodities. This arrangement left traditional social organization intact as viable political and economic units and established overarching administrative links (i.e., county chiefships and later district council positions) between the lineages. The British thus created a politically viable "tribe" that could organize political and economic resistance to central state authority (La Fontaine, 1969). Indirect rule served the colonial state's interests by reducing administrative costs, but it also increased its dependence on Bagisu administrators and agents who could use their bureaucratic and political positions to press for greater Bagisu participation in and control of district agencies and the local departments of national bureaucracies. It also provided a means of communication and created common interests that could be used to mobilize the peasants in opposition or protest against low prices and against the central market control that the civil servants and politicians claimed kept prices low.

The British imposition and use of the chiefly system gave rise to an educated group of Bagisu. This group in turn used its crucial administrative position to press for increased Africanization of the economy and the administration. Even though this Africanization initially benefited only the members of a small, privileged group, it did establish the basis for later, more general claims by the Bagisu for participation in the higher levels of their own district's affairs.

The BNA's investment in and administration of coffee sales was costly and increased its dependence on the Bagisu. As the economic importance of the coffee crop increased, so did the Bagisu's opportunities to make demands about how the crop was handled. The effectiveness of such demands, however, depended upon the size and power of the groups making them.

The small group of civil servants and bureaucrats that emerged from the chiefly families had to mobilize the Bagisu peasants behind their own demands for increased Bagisu participation and status in the administration of the district and in the organization of its agricultural commodity markets. The success of this mobilization, however, stimulated far more general demands for political participation. The forces that the civil servants engendered contributed to the emergence and growing power of a group of politicians, more directly representative of the peasants and less dependent on the bureaucratic forms and disciplines that limited the civil servants' direct opposition to the state. All three groups — chiefs, civil servants, and politicians — competed for power with each other even while they allied themselves against the central state. All three groups continued to exercise various forms of power in the district, but the relative power of each and their relations with each other shifted as the institutions that emerged from the conflict between the peasantry and the state increasingly favored first the civil servants and later the politicians.

The Changing Nature of Authority in Bugisu

The political and cooperative positions, which provided channels for the politicians' upward mobility, emerged and expanded as the politicians mobilized the peasants to pressure the colonial and later national states for increased control over the state's administrative and crop-commercialization apparatus. The criteria for these positions and the bases of their power were quite distinct from those of the chiefs and civil servants who had previously held power. The chiefly families' power depended on their greater wealth and on power derived directly from the state. The chiefs' male descendants maintained their predominance in the civil service and other professional posts because of their relatively high level of education. As business was almost totally dominated by the Asians, the avenues for acquiring either wealth or power were almost entirely closed to the rest of the Bagisu.

The new institutions allowed men with relatively little education, who were much more typical of the majority of Bagisu, to achieve positions of formal authority and power. Many of them used these positions to accumulate a level of wealth that was formerly impossible for them. Much more than in the case of the chiefs and their sons, the continued success of these new position-holders depended on their satisfying their Bagisu constituents. But since their positions were established by the state, they were also dependent on the government. Thus, they derived their power from two sources, and the relative influence of the two sources of power over the representatives varied according to the organization and structure of power within the colonial or national system as a whole and within Bugisu. The entire sociopolitical and economic system, however, continued to depend upon the peasants and on the production that they controlled. The politicians' strategies for gaining and expanding their power required them to mediate between the peasants and the state.

The power of the politicians against the state and the capacity of the state to implement its own revenue gathering and developmental plans, therefore, can only be understood in terms of the conflict between the peasants and the state, and this conflict in turn can only be understood by analyzing the ways that each struggle changed the relations between different groups and the institutional forms through which the struggles were carried out.

Each time the state coopted Bagisu leaders, it created new institutional and organizational bases from which members of peasant communities could increase their control over vital administrative and economic resources. Peasant demands that the leaders gain higher prices intensified the leaders' pressures on and resistance to the state. At the same time, the very logic of cooptation meant that the coopted leaders risked the loss of privileges and powers that they derived from formal positions within the state apparatus if they conceded too much to their peasant supporters. It bears repeating that the politicians were thus constrained to satisfy two opposed constituencies: the peasants, who resisted exploitation, and the state, which depended on the surplus appropriated from the peasants.

The resulting contradictions faced by the leaders coopted into formal positions within the state created opportunities for rival claimants to power who could mobilize peasant demands against them. If these rivals achieved a sufficiently large following, the state could either coopt them into new institutional positions or allow the groups already coopted to make more concessions to the peasants. The first alternative increased the number of institutional avenues through which the peasants' representatives could bargain with the state; the second increased the power of already coopted groups against the state. By 1969 these two outcomes had combined to create multiple power domains at various levels of articulation (cf. Adams, 1975) through which the peasants could communicate and bargain with the state (Figure 4). Some of these domains limited the absolute power of the state, as they allowed the peasants and their local representatives to intervene in state policy. These domains also provided the state with means to mobilize and organize the production and sale of the coffee (and cotton) the peasants grew. More important, they guaranteed that the state would respond to peasant pressures. When the state finally attacked these limits to its power by radically reducing local autonomy and institutional access, it made inevitable the local resistance and crop reduction it feared.

In Bugisu the threat of crop destruction was effective until Milton Obote and Idi Amin effectively suppressed local organization. Even though actual destruction of coffee trees occurred infrequently, the state had consistently moved slowly against local claimants to power. Some property destruction and withdrawal from the market had happened, but these incidents were only a particularly violent manifestation of a continuing struggle between the Bagisu peasants, the state, and the local leaders who mediated between the state and the peasantry.

The Manipulation of Peasant Protest

The issue of who wins and who loses when peasants protest is difficult to resolve, in Bugisu as elsewhere. The forms of protest there were directed and orchestrated by local political leaders, themselves still cultivating as peasants, who mobilized other peasants to achieve greater power for themselves. In the process they themselves became wealthier; this wealth was ultimately extracted from the peasants' production. At the same time, however, these political leaders, by using protest, crystallized and strengthened peasant resistance to the state, and this reduced the rate at which the state could appropriate value from the peasants. This, then, diminished the revenues that the state could use for its developmental initiatives and thus contributed to the conservation of a peasant mode of social and economic production.

Peasant mobilization against the state was used to gain local autonomy, but fights between different factions over the resources that this autonomy made available divided both the peasantry and the local power groups able to mobilize them. The peasants were in no sense fully allied with their representative leaders. The willingness of some of them to follow B. B. N. Mafabi's and Stephen Muduku's dissident

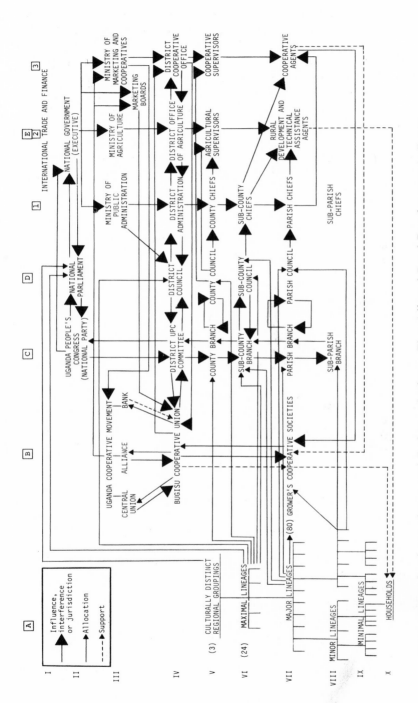

Figure 4. Levels of Articulation and Exchange Linkages That Affected Rural Development in Bugisu

Rows I-X indicate levels of articulation. Columns A-E3 represent separate but interacting organizational sets; A, autochthonous local; B, cooperative; C, political party; D, representative; E1, 2, 3, ministerial-administrative.

movements and the complaints of at least a few of them to the Gretton commission and to George Waisi's commission of inquiry indicate resentment against the ways the BCU leaders exploited their own powers and privileges. However, their suspicions of and resentment against the state and the fundamental discrepancies between the state's interests and their own frustrated the state's attempts to form an alliance with the peasants against the local leaders. The peasants' suspicions of and resentments against their own leaders did allow rival aspirants to power to mobilize some of the peasants in dissident movements. These mobilizations — or the potential for them — further reduced the leaders' power and made them more sensitive to peasant demands and criticism, but they also left local institutions susceptible to state intervention.

Local struggles for power severely disrupted the economy and administration; they threatened public order and state revenues. They also weakened local resistance to state intervention. This combination of threat and opportunity enabled the state to recover the control it had lost. The ambitions of different local groups to expand their own power thus weakened the peasantry's, and their own, bargaining position against the state.

The leaders' dependence on peasant support and their susceptibility to state intervention prevented their emergence as a separate class. Their wealth and power depended on the combination of economic and political activities that their positions enabled them to exploit, but these never constituted an independent economic base. Their powers did enable them to represent the interests of the peasants as a class against the state, at the same time they served essential functions for the state. By suppressing local autonomy, the state also sacrificed these functions and suffered the revenue reduction it had attempted to avoid.

Peasant Power against the State

Political and military struggles to capture a weak state and to extend its powers led to an increasing and dangerously destructive willingness by the power-holders in the state to ignore the economic threat of the peasants' exit option. The Obote coup, the centralization of power and of resources under a one-party regime, and the cooptation of local bureaucracies to serve as extensions of the national bureaucracy severely restricted the options of local leaders and representative institutions in Bugisu. The distribution of power in 1970 was such that advocacy of local interests against central bureaucratic authority directly threatened individual officeholders' economic and political positions, especially as the centrally controlled Uganda's People Congress (UPC) provided the most significant opportunities for individual advancement. The Amin coup in 1971 led to further loss of local power by making any political activity, especially opposition, physically dangerous, and Obote's subsequent dependence on international credit and development agencies allowed his regime to ignore peasant needs and demands.

However, it would be a mistake to assume that a particular point in time, especially a point as fortuitously chosen as one that coincides with a particular researcher's field work or analysis, is necessarily the culmination of processes that have somehow evolved in linear fashion. Recent studies of bureaucratic centralization in East Africa do appear to make such a linear evolutionary assumption (Mamdani, 1976; Shivji, 1976; Samoff, 1979). In the case presented here, however, analysis of center-local power relations shows that these relations have been cyclical, that both extreme centralization and extreme decentralizaton have provoked reactions in the opposite direction, and that local opposition to centralization has occurred both within and without officially established bureaucracies.

The long trend to increased Bagisu control was interrupted by the establishment of the Bugisu Coffee Marketing Company, by recompositions of advisory and governing boards, and by dismissal of Bagisu supervisory employees. Each of these reversals stimulated Bagisu opposition, which eventually brought new concessions from the state. A combination of resistance from within the BCU and a major challenge from the Bugisu Coffee Marketing Association brought significant pressure for a return to local autonomy after central state intervention in 1958.

When political conditions allowed campaigns from within state-sanctioned institutions to expand the resource base of local officeholders, these campaigns were played out within the boundaries of formally recognized organizations. Examples include the campaign to satisfy enrollment requirements in the GCSs, the Kitutu committee's efforts to wrest power over certain decisions from the Bugisu Coffee Board, and the Waisi committee's campaign to expand the BCU's economic and political influence. When, on the other hand, there was insufficient access to formal power at the local level, leaders have gone outside the recognized organizations, mobilizing the Bagisu against the Bugisu Coffee Scheme, organizing opposition to the first supervising manager, and establishing a rival organization to the BCU. In all of these efforts, the threat of reducing coffee production or of uprooting coffee trees gave leaders a crucial edge on a state that was constantly concerned with its export revenues, a major share of which depended on coffee.

In some of these efforts, especially after independence, national level politicians' need for local support also increased opportunities for autonomous local organization. Until 1970 local forces were consistently able to gain concessions, even to wrest a considerable degree of control and effect deep changes in the administrative apparatus, due to their control of the resources upon which the local economy and administrative apparatus were based. They only lost this ability as the competitors for control of the state abandoned considerations of economic development and administrative efficiency in their quests to gain, maintain, and expand political power.

The resources available to both local and national systems had increased greatly by 1962, providing bases for Waisi's campaign to extend local control of coffee revenues far beyond their previous limits and for the state's eventual use of patronage in a national party system to coopt more securely potential sources of opposition. The new patronage systems and the resulting dominance of political figures over the entire district administration, however, seriously disrupted development programs in the district. Furthermore, the centralized Coffee Marketing Board did not have the expertise to handle the delicate Arabica crop and allowed it to deteriorate in storage, causing a major loss of revenue. The Amin coup ended this attempt at central control before the state was forced to take its high cost into account, but it is conceivable that these costs would have strengthened the hand of the BCU committee, which was already appealing to the Ministry of Cooperatives and Marketing to recover control of sales and prices when the coup occurred. Significantly, the senior cooperative officer/Bugisu was encouraging and counseling committee members in these efforts. I was in close contact with both the committee and the Department of Cooperative Development (DCD) and was impressed by the urgent efforts by both sides to change ministry policy and the apprehension of both that these policies would provoke spontaneous popular protest.

Enoka Musundi's committee was restrained from militant action by UPC discipline and patronage, by the DCD's powers to remove its members, and by the large bonuses that made their positions so rewarding. If the Amin coup had not occurred, however, alternative organizations might have emerged, as they had before, to increase pressure on the committee and on the state. On the other hand, political pressures on Obote from both his allies and his rivals would have made decentralization far more difficult to achieve than it had been before and just after independence. The inexorable logic of state expansion as a strategy to accommodate competition for control of the state and access to its revenues had already locked the state into contests that it could only win in the short run by measures that would further destabilize it in the longer run.

The Amin coup made protest and mobilization impossible, and the Bagisu did finally withdraw into smuggling and subsistence. The second Obote regime showed no inclination to respond to peasant demands, and the coffee growers continued their flight from export crops. As control over the state becomes even more tenuous, and as the Bagisu have to implement the threat that served as their most effective lever against the state, it becomes even less likely that they will eventually be able to organize sufficiently to bargain with the state or that the state will finally respond constructively to the fact that they are no longer growing as much coffee as they did. If the state can or does attempt seriously to stimulate coffee cultivation again, I expect that the Bagisu would quite quickly organize to take advantage of their new opportunities.

The case of the Bagisu lends support to the proposition that leaders who can mobilize freeholding peasantries who contribute significantly to export economies can effectively challenge central state control. Even though the central state controls vastly more resources than local organizations can, and even though the local power groups may weaken themselves in internal struggles in which the weaker contestant may appeal to central authority, the central state apparatus continues to be dependent on local organization. The effective cooptation of local leaders may temporarily immobilize local opposition, and a centralizing dictatorial state may impede the emergence of alternative, extra-official organization to bypass the coopted local leaders, but examination of past cycles of center-local power struggles suggests that these are likely to be temporary rather than culminating resolutions.

I have shown in this study that the peasants' bargaining position affects the ways that the national economy is incorporated into the world economy and that this position evolved from and with peasant struggles to limit the rate at which the state appropriated their product and the strategies of different ascendant groups whose own mobility was dependent on peasant support against the state. The dynamic of the struggles described here reflected the particular social organization of the Bagisu themselves, the ecology and location of Uganda, and of Bugisu within it, the historical conjuncture of British colonial conquest and administration in Uganda with crises in the world-system—particularly those after World War I but also economic and political conditions attendant on World War II—the end of direct British colonial control, and the current crises in the world economy. Particular as these events were, however, they clearly warn against the assumptions of unilinear trends to national state hegemony within a capitalist world-system or of increasing socio-economic homogeneity under this control.

Issa Shivji's (1976) and Mahmood Mamdani's (1976) assumptions of the hegemony of a national bureaucratic class in Tanzania and Uganda simply do not take into account the political and economic power of peasant communities and of local power groups capable of mobilizing these peasants against the state. These two authors seem to have transferred the Latin American dependency model, where large landowning classes, a dispossessed and vulnerable peasantry, and strong central states have indeed created conditions in which a dominant class fragment could maintain and improve its position through strategic alliances with international capital, to the very different East African situation. The history of peasant organization in Bugisu suggests that their assumption of a strong state in Uganda or in Tanzania is highly questionable. These states cannot control production, and they can only control appropriation indirectly and tenuously, through intermediaries whose powers, statuses, and functions are deeply embedded in autochthonous local social organization. Such a state is necessarily weak.

Lonsdale (1981), Cooper (1981a), and Spittler (1983) provide far more useful guides for understanding the political relations and processes that weaken the state and prevent it from expanding its control over or its exploitation of the peasants. Even these authors, however, do not adequately consider the ways that the peasants can discover and exploit the state's weakness to create political space within which they can construct their own associations and programs. These associations, though they challenge the state's political control and reduce the rate at which it can appropriate surplus, are essential to increase and sustain the mass of production from which the state can appropriate surplus. The two most significant and dramatic surges in coffee production occurred during the two successful mobilizations for BCU autonomy, those led by Kitutu and by Waisi (see Appendix 1). The state's imperative to tighten its political control and to accelerate its rate of appropriation impelled it to restrict these movements rather than to attempt to work with them. The peasants' retreat from the market was slow, partly because coffee trees continue to produce for a long time, partly because other alternatives did not immediately present themselves, and partly because world market prices lessened the impact of the state's increased rate of appropriation, but the withdrawal from the market became pronounced after 1977. The threat of violence by the state increased delivery somewhat, but the coffee delivered was of low quality. The actual destruction of coffee trees was beginning by the end of 1982. In the absence of effective local organizations that could communicate with the state, the state had no means of knowing what the peasants were doing until after the affected harvests were collected and recorded.

The Bagisu's capacity to organize effective resistance to the demands of the central state derived in large part from their direct control over land and the means of production of a major export crop and their capacity to withdraw into a subsistence mode. Numerous sub-Saharan African peasantries enjoy similarly favorable circumstances; many have used them to organize effective communal action outside of the framework of central state control (O'Brien, 1975; Peel, 1976; Hyden, 1980) and as a brake on central state power (Amin, 1964). Their Asian and Latin American counterparts (and obviously the peasants of, e.g., South Africa and Zimbabwe) do not contribute such high proportions of either gross domestic product or of exports and are far less secure or independent in their access to lands (Zaman, 1975; Scott, 1976; van Binsbergen, 1977). Their political autonomy and their capacity for confronting the state is consequently much reduced (Brokensha and Erasmus, 1969; Bunker, 1979, 1981).

Within Africa as well, the economic and political positions of peasant groups varied between and within countries, as well as over time (Saul and Woods, 1971). The Bagisu's favored position depended in part upon the high value of their crop, the very value which stimulated the state to extra efforts to control what the minister of cooperatives and marketing called Uganda's most important and most difficult cooperative (interview, Mbale, 1970). Nelson Kasfir (1970:207-8), Goran Hyden (1970a:66), and E. A. Brett (1970) document and discuss effective challenges to central authority in other, poorer East African cooperatives, though the conflict between local and national power systems is obscured in the debate over participation versus efficiency in much of this and other specialized literature on cooperatives.

A freeholding peasantry's capacity to restrict central state power and to maintain a partial local autonomy affects a nation's developmental capacities in two very different ways. On the one hand, local power can brake the extreme exploitation and repression of peasants by the state. On the other hand, local power can also brake state initiatives and programs aimed at increasing production. Thus, a freeholding peasantry that participates significantly in the national economy, and especially in its exports, is likely to maintain equity at the expense of growth. As Hyden's (1980) study of the Tanzanian peasantry makes clear, "peasant power" stabilizes and preserves peasant modes of production and therefore restricts the amount of capital and labor available for the development of other modes of production. This result clearly moderates some of the worst dislocations—especially those of concentrated land tenure and excessive urban growth—that rapid industrialization and commercial agriculture have brought about in other parts of the world. It also limits the state's capacity to increase social services and, in the long run, to deal with problems of population growth that may exceed the absorptive capacity of peasant economies.[1] Most important, however, it creates an ineluctable restriction on the expansion of the state itself. To the extent that the independent state must expand to survive, the state finally ruins itself in violent attempts to overcome this restriction. The peasants retreat from the markets that sustain the state and endeavor to minimize their contacts with its representatives. Any program to reconstitute or restabilize the peasant state, whether undertaken by the state itself or by external development agencies, must allow for this fundamental contradiction between the state and the peasants and for the disastrous consequences of the state's attempting to overcome it by either force or fiat.

Central state power presents both advantages and dangers for development; peasant power offers an obverse set of dangers and advantages, but a state like Uganda's is not strong enough to choose between these two options. The attempts of a weak state dependent on peasant agriculture to increase its rate of appropriation from the peasantry by suppressing local organizations are ultimately self-defeating. Such a state can only increase its revenues from the peasants by offering them something in return. If it uses its superior force to suppress local organizations, without maintaining satisfactory prices and marketing conditions, the peasants will exercise their exit option as an economic strategy rather than manipulating it in symbolic political strategies. The state finally loses much more when the peasants actually do withdraw. Thus, the option between satisfying peasant demands or accumulating capital for development projects that discriminate against the peasants does not really exist for Uganda. It continues dependent on the peasantry, and it ignores its demands and suppresses its autonomous organization at its own risk. It must accede to peasant demands or face continued economic decline and political instability.

The economic and administrative bases for sustained peasant resistance to the state and the resulting tensions between state political aspirations and state political capacities contributed to the chaos, strains, and inconsistencies of Obote's "move to the left," as well as to the political instabilities that preceded it and ultimately brought the Obote regime down in 1971. In Bugisu at least, Obote's attempt to control local opposition by converting the UPC into a conduit for political patronage from the national directly to the parish level severely disrupted the district administration and civil service.

The Amin regime abandoned the developmental strategies and the export promotion programs that had created and maintained the state's dependence on the peasantry. The resulting decline of export agriculture and, in frontier areas like Bugisu, the smuggling of much of the export crops that were grown devastated Uganda's economy. The Amin regime effectively smothered any possibility of local attempts to control the state's bureaucratic apparatus, but peasant reaction to this confirms the real basis of earlier threats to withdraw into subsistence. Indeed, the subsistence option was apparently crucial to the survival of rural populations and to returning urban migrants (Young, Sherman, and Rose, 1981).

It remains to be seen whether a state with sufficient stability to reorganize the national export economy can emerge from the chaos that has followed Amin's overthrow, but if such a reorganization were attempted, it would succeed only if it could create the conditions for a renewed flow of power to local systems. If the state decides to increase its dependence on agricultural exports, it will also increase its dependency on peasant production and administration, thus revitalizing the peasants' bargaining position against the state. The policies of the International Monetary Fund (IMF)—which created the illusion that peasant demands could be ignored—made this outcome unlikely. They also stimulated continued flows of credit, which temporarily fortified the alliance that controlled the state.

The second Obote regime's access to large loans to reconstruct its economy allowed it to ignore the peasants on whom that economy is based.[2] Peasants in Bugisu have responded by expanding their subsistence crops and exploring cash crops and markets. They can thus largely ignore the export-promotion policies of a state that needs their land and labor to generate foreign revenues. This directly debilitates the national state, increases and will prolong its dependence on foreign aid, and may lead to persistent political instability. The national debt has grown rapidly, and Uganda is now suffering the experiences of other countries; the flow of credits has started to dry up, and the IMF is no longer so free about the rescheduling of payments. Total debt increased faster than export values. In this sense the state made itself dangerously dependent on allies whose direct support diminished rapidly, leaving the state without effective internal support and very short of the revenues necessary to build that support. In the meantime, the state's refusal to provide adequate prices accelerated the decline of peasant-based political and economic organizations and thus reduced the state's ability to mobilize or even communicate with the peasants on whose production it ultimately depends.

The recent history and present crises of Uganda are particularly dramatic, but Uganda is not alone in suffering from low farm prices, deteriorated infrastructure, political instability, and a growing debt. The exit option that provided an "uncaptured peasantry" (cf. Hyden, 1980) with bargaining levers against the state now functions less as a political threat and more as an economic reality as local communities struggle to survive the economic and political decline presently facing many African nations. This withdrawal, in turn, aggravates the crises that the state confronts and limits its ability to implement effective economic and social policies. In Tanzania (Hyden, 1980, personal communication, 1983; John Harris, personal communication, 1983), Ghana, the Ivory Coast, Senegal, and various other West African nations, peasants appear to be withdrawing from cash markets, especially those controlled by the state. All of these states depend in significant degree on revenues from peasant crops. All of these states have contributed directly to peasant flight from export crops by imposing pricing and marketing policies aimed at promoting urban and industrial development and at maintaining their own political bases and organizations (Bates, 1981). Even if they had the political strength to reorient their agricultural policies, present world economic conditions and their own economic difficulties would make it very difficult for these states to reestablish cash cropping for controlled markets as an attractive option for peasants. The political crises that afflict these states and the states' growing dependence on international credit make it appear even less likely that these states have either the political will or strength to make such decisions. The peasantry, having withdrawn significantly from the market, does not have the political strength necessary to demand these changes. Unless the peasants are allowed the political space necessary to organize and bargain effectively with the state, however, I believe that economies and states like Uganda's will remain in crisis.

Whether or not Uganda can or does take the necessary steps to entice peasants back into the agricultural export market, the balance of power between the peasants, local power groups, and the state is likely to remain unstable. The distribution of economic control and political power among multiple ethnically defined peasantries and the dependence of the state on local economies and administration are simply incompatible with the exogenous structure of the state itself and even more so with its aspirations to central control and to a rapidly expanding urban industrial base. It is because of this incompatibility that local organizations remain essential to the maintenance of the state, even though they limit its powers. Local organizations that can focus and communicate peasant protest and demands forcefully enough to make the state listen and to bargain provide linkages between the local and central power systems that can mediate the inevitable struggles between the peasants and the state. Without such linkages, both the peasants and the state will follow their own political and economic imperatives, the state into self-destructive attempts to control more than its limited strength allows, and the peasants into the isolation and uncertainty of self-sufficiency. The state's attempts to increase its own power by eliminating the challenges that peasant organizations make possible actually weaken it much further, as these attempts undermine the only economic base from which the state can extract sufficient revenues to sustain itself.

NOTES

1. This does not mean that predominantly peasant economies per se cannot accumulate economic and social capital for development; there are many examples to the contrary. The point made throughout this study has been rather that a freeholding peasantry with power over its own administrative structure may be able to prevent capital accumulation, which would necessarily be at its own expense and in favor of other sectors of the economy.

2. Note that this new dependency on international credit agencies is still very different from that described in the literature on Latin America. Uganda's debt and its dependency on foreign capital are not so much the result of foreign investment as they are of the various struggles to capture and keep the weak state. Also note the recency of this phenomenon in Uganda's history.

Postscript

In January 1986 Yoweri Museveni led his National Resistance Army into Kampala, wresting control of the state from the military government that had replaced Obote six months earlier. Museveni's well-disciplined army extended its control over the rest of the country with surprising speed and efficiency. His first months in power and his early policy statements suggest that he may be able to reestablish peace and willing to provide the incentives necessary to stimulate peasant production of export crops, but the legacy of corruption, destruction, and violence still poses enormous danger for Uganda's weak and precariously held state.

APPENDIX 1

Arabica Coffee Production in Bugisu/Sebei
Parchment only (lights and buni excluded)
(Weights in long tons)

Season	Tons	Five-year Average to Date	Season	Tons	Five-year Average to Date
1915-16	11	—	1947-48	2,561	2,939
1921-22	20	—	1948-49	2,857	3,045
1926-27	60	—	1949-50	2,852	2,804
1927-28	120	—	1950-51	3,896	3,045
1928-29	130	—	1951-52	2,200	2,873
1929-30	103	—	1952-53	2,307	2,822
1930-31	260	135	1953-54	3,021	3,855
1931-32	264	175	1954-55	6,170	3,519
1932-33	734	298	1955-56	4,098	3,559
1933-34	964	465	1956-57	5,175	4,154
1934-35	1,378	720	1957-58	4,805	4,654
1935-56	2,034	1,075	1958-59	4,912	5,032
1936-37	1,321	1,286	1959-60	5,791	4,956
1937-38	2,079	1,555	1960-61	5,149	5,166
1938-39	1,822	1,717	1961-62	8,409[a]	5,893
1939-40	4,144	2,280	1962-63	3,426[a]	5,817
1940-41	2,165	2,306	1963-64	9,522	6,739
1941-42	3,010	2,644	1964-65	4,521	6,485
1942-43	2,200	2,668	1965-66	13,886	8,233
1943-44	3,679	3,040	1966-67	7,928	8,057
1944-45	2,705	2,752	1967-68	13,128	9,797
1945-46	2,692	2,857	1968-69	7,256	—
1946-47	3,058	2,867			

[a] In addition to the figures shown for 1961-62 and 1962-63, undisclosed quantities were collected by the Bugisu Coffee Marketing Association. It is considered likely that they were 400 tons and 1,000 tons, respectively, for those two seasons, and these figures have been included in the calculation of the five-year averages.

Total Coffee (tons) Purchased and Processed by the Bugisu Cooperative Union, 1970-82

Financial Year	Coffee Purchased	Coffee Processed
1970-71	12,955	12,300
1971-72	12,076	11,103
1972-73	15,097	15,217
1973-74	11,421	12,787
1974-75	12,312	10,762
1975-76	11,634	11,084
1976-77	2,315	4,416
1977-78	652	623
1978-79	5,760	4,007
1979-80	6,965	6,055
1980-81	2,661	3,886
1981-82	19,388[a]	10,764

SOURCE: Bugisu Cooperative Union.

[a] This figure reflects the purchase of coffee stored by farmers and Growers Cooperative Societies from three previous seasons, much of it of low quality.

APPENDIX 2

Coffee Trade Balance in the Bugisu Cooperative Union
(In Pounds)

Year	Surplus	Deficit
1958		118,209
1959	354,286	
1960	409,482	
1961	328,430	
1962	1,226	
1963	48,179	
1964	153,664	
1965	55,390	
1966	15,682	
1967		74,497
1968	228,707	
1969	109,541	
1970	139,093	

SOURCE: Bugisu Cooperative Union.
NOTE: Exact figures for 1955-57 are not available, but there was apparently a surplus.

Operating Balance in the Bugisu Cooperative Union
(In Shillings)

Financial Year	Profit (Loss)
1969-70	4,781,971
1970-71	(1,143,849)
1971-72	(1,306,561)
1972-73	1,008,056
1973-74	(19,003)
1974-75	(978,078)
1975-76	(817,776)
1976-77	(3,224,818)
1977-78	(3,607,401)
1978-79	(5,648,261)

SOURCE: Bugisu Cooperative Union. Accounts for subsequent years have not yet been approved, but have also entailed losses. Prior to 1970-71, the BCU had recorded losses in only two financial years, 1954-55 and 1958-59.

References

Adams, Richard Newbold
  1975   *Energy and Structure: A Theory of Social Power.* Austin: University of Texas Press.

Amin, Samir
  1964   "The Class Struggle in Africa." *Revolution* 1, 9.
  1976   *Unequal Development.* New York: Monthly Review Press.
  1977   *Imperialism and Unequal Development.* New York: Monthly Review Press.

Amman, Victor F.
  1980   "The Cooperative Movement in Uganda." Paper 1 in Working Papers prepared by IADS Agricultural Group in Uganda, Jan.-Feb.

Anderson, Bo, and James D. Cockcroft
  1966   "Control and Cooptation in Mexican Politics." *International Journal of Comparative Sociology* 7, 1 (Mar.):11-28.

Anderson, Perry
  1974   *Lineages of the Absolutist State.* New York: Monthly Review Press.

Balandier, George
  1955   *La Sociologie Actuelle de l'Afrique Noire.* Paris: Presses Universitaires de France.
  1966   "The Colonial Situation: A Theoretical Approach." Pp. 34-61 in Immanuel Wallerstein (ed.), *Social Change: The Colonial Situation.* New York: John Wiley & Sons.
  1970   *Political Anthropology.* New York: Random House.

Bates, Robert H.
  1981   *Markets and States in Tropical Africa: The Political Basis of Agricultural Policies.* Berkeley: University of California Press.

Bates, Robert H., Robert W. Hahn, and John G. Kreag
  1981   "The Reorganization of the Marketing and Processing of Crops in Uganda: Report to the Ministry of Cooperatives and Marketing." University of California, Berkeley: Institute of International Studies, Project for Managing Decentralization.

Bath, C. Richard, and Dilmus D. James
1976 "Dependency Analysis of Latin America; Some Criticisms, Some Suggestions." *Latin American Research Review,* 11, 3:3-54.

BCS (Bugisu Coffee Scheme)
1940-54 Minutes of the Advisory Committee.

BCU (Bugisu Cooperative Union)
1954-71 Annual General Meeting Minutes.

Bettelheim, Charles
1972 Theoretical Comments." Pp. 271-322 in A. Emmanuel, *Unequal Exchange: A Study of the Imperialism of Trade,* Appendix I. New York: Monthly Review Press.

BNA (Bugisu District Native Administration)
1940-71 Annual Report. Mbale. (mimeograph)

Blau, Peter
1964 *Exchange and Power in Social Life.* New York: John Wiley and Sons.

Block, Fred
1977 "The Ruling Class Does Not Rule." *Socialist Revolution* 32:6-28.

Bornschier, Volker, Christopher Chase-Dunn, and Richard Rubinson
1978 "Cross-national Evidence on the Effects of Foreign Investment and Aid on Economic Growth and Inequality: A Survey of Findings and a Reanalysis." *American Journal of Sociology* 84:651-83.

Bornschier, Volker, and Thanh-Huyen Ballmer-Cao
1979 "Income Inequality: A Cross-national Study." *American Sociological Review* 44, 3:487-506.

Bottomore, T. B.
1964 *Elites and Society.* New York: Basic Books.

Brenner, Robert
1977 "The Origins of Capitalist Development: A Critique of Neo-Smithian Marxism." *New Left Review* 104:27-59.

Brett, E. A.
1970 "Problems of Cooperative Development in Uganda." Pp. 95-156 in R. J. Apthorpe (ed.), *Rural Cooperatives and Planned Change in Africa.* Geneva: UNRISDP.
1973 *Colonialism and Underdevelopment in East Africa.* New York: Nok Publishers.

Brock, Beverley
1969 "Land Tenure and Social Change in Bugisu." *Nkanga* 4:13-23.

Brokensha, David, and Charles Erasmus
1969 "African Peasants and Community Development." Pp. 85-100 in David Brokensha and Marion Pearsall (eds.), *The Anthropology of Development in Sub-Saharan Africa.* Lexington: University Press of Kentucky.

Bugisu District Administration
1970 Budget Estimates.

Bugisu District Council.
1952-71 Council Minutes.

Bunker, Stephen G.
1975   "The Uses and Abuses of Power in a Uganda Farmers' Marketing Association—The Bugisu Cooperation Union, Ltd." Doctoral dissertation, Duke University.
1979   "Power Structures and Exchange between Government Agencies in the Expansion of the Agricultural Sector." *Studies in Comparative International Development* 14, 1:56-76.
1981   "Class, Status, and the Small Farmer: Rural Development Programs and the Advance of Capitalism in Uganda and Brazil." *Latin American Perspectives*, 8, 1 (Winter): 89-107.
1983a   "Dependency, Inequality, and Development Policy: A Case from Bugisu, Uganda." *British Journal of Sociology* 34, 2:157-81.
1983b   "Center-Local Struggles for Bureaucratic Control in Bugisu, Uganda." *American Ethnologist* 10, 4 (Nov.):749-69.
1984a   "Modes of Extraction, Unequal Exchange, and the Progressive Underdevelopment of an Extreme Periphery: The Brazilian Amazon, 1600-1980." *American Journal of Sociology*, 89, 5:1017-64.
1984b   "Ideologies of Intervention: The Ugandan State and Local Organization in Bugisu." *Africa* 54, 3:50-71.
1985a   "Peasant Responses to a Dependent State: Uganda, 1983." *Canadian Journal of African Studies* 19, 2:371-86.
1985b   "Property, Protest, and Politics in Bugisu, Uganda." Pp. 267-85 in Donald Crummey (ed.), *Banditry, Rebellion, and Social Protest in Africa*. London: James Currey, Publisher.
Cardoso, Fernando Henrique
1973   "Associated Dependent Development: Theoretical and Practical Implications." Pp. 142-78 in A. Stepan (ed.), *Authoritarian Brazil*. New Haven: Yale University Press.
1977   "The Consumption of Dependency Theory in the United States." *Latin American Research Review* 12, 3:7-24.
Cardoso, Fernando Henrique, and Enzo Faletto
1969   *Dependencia y Desarrollo en America Latina*. Mexico City: Siglo XXI Editores.
Chase-Dunn, Christopher
1975   "The Effects of International Economic Dependence on Development and Inequality." *American Sociological Review* 40: 720-38.
Chilcote, Ronald H.
1974   "A Critical Synthesis of Dependency Theory." *Latin American Perspectives* 1, 1:4-29.
1978   "A Question of Dependency." *Latin American Research Review* 13, 2:55-68.
Cliffe, Lionel
1973   "The Policy of Ujamaa Vijijini and the Class Struggle in Tanzania." Pp. 195-211 in Lionel Cliffe and John Saul (eds.), *Socialism in Tanzania, Volume II: Policies*. Nairobi: East African Publishing House.

Cockcroft, James D.
  1972   "Coercion and Ideology in Mexican Politics." Pp. 245-67 in James D. Cockcroft, Andre Gunder Frank, and Dale L. Johnson (eds.), *Dependence and Underdevelopment*. Garden City: Anchor Books.

Cooper, Frederick
  1981a   "Africa and the World Economy." *African Studies Review* 24, 2/3 (June/Sept.):1-86.
  1981b   "Peasants, Capitalists, and Historians: A Review Article." *Journal of Southern Africa Studies* 7 (Apr.):284-314.

Cutright, Phillipps
  1967   "Inequality: A Cross-National Analysis." *American Sociological Review* 32:562-78.

de Janvry, Alain
  1981   *The Agrarian Question and Reformism in Latin America*. Baltimore: Johns Hopkins University Press.

Domar, Evsey O.
  1970   "The Causes of Slavery and Serfdom: A Hypothesis." *Journal of Economic History* 30 (Mar.):18-32.

dos Santos, Theotonio
  1970   "The Structure of Dependence." *American Economic Review* 60:231-6.

Eckstein, Susan
  1977   *The Poverty of Revolution*. Princeton: Princeton University Press.

Emmanuel, Arghiri
  1972   *Unequal Exchange: A Study in the Imperialism of Trade*. New York: Monthly Review Press.

Fallers, Lloyd
  1955   "The Predicament of the Modern African Chief: An Instance from Uganda." *American Anthropologist* 57:290-305.
  1959   "Despotism, Status Culture, and Social Mobility in an African Kingdom." *Studies in Society and History* 2, 1:11-32.
  1965   *Bantu Bureaucracy: A Century of Political Evolution among the Ba-*
  [1956] *soga of Uganda*. Chicago: University of Chicago Press.

Frank, Andre Gunder
  1967   *Capitalism and Underdevelopment in Latin America: Historical Studies of Chile and Brazil*. New York: Monthly Review Press.
  1969   *Latin America: Underdevelopment or Revolution*. New York: Monthly Review Press.

Furtado, Celso
  1976   *Economic Development of Latin America*. Cambridge: Cambridge University Press.

Gale, H. P.
  1959   *Uganda and the Mill Hill Fathers*. London: Macmillan.

Galtung, J.
  1971   "A Structural Theory of Imperialism." *Journal of Peace Research* 8, 2:81-117.

Gates, R. C.
  1966   *The Principles and Practice of Cooperation: A Brief Textbook for Use in the Primary Cooperatives of Uganda.* 2d ed. Kampala: Uganda Cooperative Central Union Ltd.

Gayer, C. M. A.
  1957   "Report on Land Tenure in Bugisu." Pp. 1-16 in Uganda Protectorate, *Land Tenure in Uganda.* Entebbe: Government Printer.

Gluckman, Max
  1963   *Order and Rebellion in Tribal Africa.* London: Cohen and West.
  1964   *Custom and Conflict in Africa.* New York: Barnes and Noble.

Green, Reginald
  1981   "Magendo in the Political Economy of Uganda: Pathology, Parallel System, or Dominant Sub-mode of Production?" Discussion Paper No. 165, Institute of Development Studies, University of Sussex.

Haydon, E. S.
  1953   "The History of the Bugisu Coffee Scheme." Mbale, Uganda: Bugisu Coffee Board. (Mimeograph)

Hamnett, Brian R.
  1978   *Revolución y Contrarrevolución en Mexico y el Peru.* Mexico: Fondo de Cultura Económica.

Heald, Suzette
  1968   "Casualties of the Social Structure. A Discussion of Ways of Failing and Its Consequences among the Bagisu." University of E. Africa, USSCC paper (limited circulation).
  1982   "Chiefs and Administrators in Bugisu." Pp. 37-52 in A. F. Robertson (ed.), *Uganda's First Republic: Chiefs, Administrators, and Politicians, 1967-71.* Cambridge: Cambridge University African Studies Centre.

Higgott, Richard A.
  1980   "From Modernization Theory to Public Policy: Continuity and Change in the Political Science of Political Development." *Studies in Comparative International Development* 15, 4 (Winter):26-58.

Hindess, Barry, and Paul C. Hirst
  1975   *Pre-capitalist Modes of Production.* London: Routledge and Kegan Paul.

Hirschman, Albert O.
  1970   *Exit, Voice, and Loyalty: Responses to Decline in Firms, Organizations and States.* Cambridge, Mass.: Harvard University Press.

Holmquist, Frank
  1977   "Mechanisms of Internal Dependency: Effects upon East African Agricultural Producers' Cooperatives." Paper presented at the Joint Meeting of the Latin American Studies and African Studies Association, Houston.
  1980   "Defending Peasant Political Space in Independent Africa." *Canadian Journal of African Studies* 14, 1:157-68.

Huntington, Samuel
  1965   "Political Development and Political Decay." *World Politics* 17:386-430.
Hyden, Goran
  1969   "Cooperatives and Rural Development." Economic Commission for Africa. Moshi, Tanzania, 1969.
  1970a   "Cooperatives and Their Socio-Political Environment." Pp. 61-80 in Carl Gosta Widstrand (ed.), *Cooperatives and Rural Development in East Africa.* Uppsala: The Scandinavian Institute of African Studies.
  1970b   "Cooperatives in Kenya, Problems and Prospects." Paper submitted to the Department of Cooperative Development, Nairobi, Kenya.
  1973   *Efficiency vs. Distribution in East African Cooperatives: A Study in Organizational Conflicts.* Nairobi: East African Literature Bureau.
  1980   *Beyond Ujamaa in Tanzania: Underdevelopment and an Uncaptured Peasantry.* Berkeley: University of California Press.
IBRD/World Bank
  1982   *Uganda, Country Economic Memorandum.* Washington, D.C.: The World Bank.
Jacobson, David
  1968   "Friendship and Mobility in the Development of an Urban Elite African Social System." *Southwestern Journal of Anthropology* 24, 2 (Summer 1968):123-38.
  1973   *Itinerant Townsmen.* Menlo Park: Cummings.
Kasfir, Nelson
  1967   "The Administrative Implications of the Cooperative Movement in Uganda." Paper given at Conference on Cooperatives, Makerere University, August 1967.
  1970   "Organizational Analysis and Ugandan Co-operative Unions." Pp. 178-208 in Carl Gosta Widstrand (ed.), *Cooperatives and Rural Development in East Africa.* Uppsala: The Scandinavian Institute of African Studies.
Kelley, Jonathan
  1971   "Social Mobility in Traditional Society: The Toro of Uganda." Ph.D. dissertation, University of California, Berkeley.
Kelley, Jonathan, and Herbert S. Klein
  1981   *Revolution and the Rebirth of Inequality: A Theory Applied to the National Revolution in Bolivia.* Berkeley: University of California Press.
Kerr, A. J.
  1947   Report on the Bugishu Coffee Scheme. Mbale. (Mimeograph)
Kitching, Gavin
  1980   *Class and Economic Change in Kenya: The Making of an African Petite-Bourgeoisie.* New Haven: Yale University Press.

La Fontaine, Jean S.

1957   "The Social Organization of the Gisu of Uganda with Special Reference to Their Initiation Ceremonies." Ph.D. thesis, Cambridge University.

1959a   *The Gisu of Uganda.* London: International African Institute.

1959b   "The Gisu." Pp. 260-77 in Audrey Richards (ed.), *East African Chiefs.* London: Faber & Faber.

1960   "Homicide and Suicide among the Gisu." Pp. 94-129 in Paul Bohannan (ed.), *African Homicide and Suicide.* Princeton: Princeton University Press.

1962   "Gisu Marriage and Affinal Relations." Pp. 88-120 in Meyer Fortes (ed.), *Marriage in Tribal Societies.* Cambridge Papers in Social Anthropology, Vol. III. Cambridge: Cambridge University Press.

1963   "Witchcraft in Bugisu." Pp. 197-220 in J. Middleton and E. H. Winter (eds.), *Witchcraft and Sorcery in East Africa.* London: Routledge and Kegan Paul.

1967   "Parricide in Bugisu: A Study of Inter-generational Conflict." *Man* n.s., 2, 2:249-59.

1969   "Tribalism among the Gisu." Pp. 177-92 in P. H. Gulliver (ed.), *Tradition and Transition in East Africa: Studies of the Tribal Element in the Modern Era.* Berkeley: University of California Press.

Lamb, Geoff

1974   *Peasant Politics.* New York: St. Martin's Press.

Lenin

1939   *Imperialism, the Highest Stage of Capitalism.* New York: International Publishers.

Leys, Colin

1967   *Politicians and Policies: An Essay on Politics in Acholi, Uganda, 1962-65.* Nairobi: East African Publishing.

1971   "Politics in Kenya: The Development of Peasant Society." *British Journal of Political Science* 1, 1 (July):307-37.

1975   *Underdevelopment in Kenya.* London: Heinemann.

1976   "The 'Over-developed' Post-Colonial State: A Re-evaluation." *Review of African Political Economy* 5:39-48.

Long, Norman

1970   "Cooperative Enterprise and Rural Development in Tanzania." Pp. 287-361 in R. J. Apthorpe (ed.), *Rural Cooperatives and Planned Change in Africa.* Geneva: UNRISD.

Lonsdale, John

1981   "States and Social Processes in Africa: A Historiographical Survey." *African Studies Review* 24, 213 (June/Sept.): 139-225.

Lonsdale, John, and Bruce Berman

1979   "Coping with the Contradictions: The Development of the Colonial State in Kenya, 1895-1914." *Journal of African History* 20:487-505.

Lukhobo (Bugisu District Council)
   1949-70   Minutes.
Luxemburg, Rosa
   1951   *The Accumulation of Capital.* London: Routledge and Kegan Paul.
McCoy, Alfred W., and Edilberto de Jesus (eds.)
   1982   *Philippine Social History: Global Trade and Local Transformations.*
            Honolulu: University of Hawaii Press.
Mamdani, Mahmood
   1976   *Politics and Class Formation in Uganda.* New York: Monthly Review
            Press.
Mandel, Ernest
   1975   *Late Capitalism.* London: New Left Review Editions.
Marx, Karl
   1963   *The Eighteenth Brumaire of Louis Bonaparte.* New York: International
            Publishers.
Maquet, Jacques
   1971   *Power and Society in Africa.* Translated by Jeannette Kupfermann.
            New York: McGraw-Hill.
Meillassoux, Claude
   1973   "The Social Organization of the Peasantry." *Journal of Peasant
            Studies* 1, 1:81-90.
Miller, Norman N.
   1968   "The Political Survival of Traditional Leadership." *Journal of Mod-
            ern African Studies* 6, 2:183-201.
Miracle, Marvin P., and Seidman, Ann
   1968   "Agricultural Cooperatives and Quasi-Cooperatives in Ghana, 1951-
            1965." Land Tenure Center, University of Wisconsin, Madison.
   1968   "State Farms in Ghana." Land Tenure Center, University of Wis-
            consin, Madison.
Nadel, S. F.
   1956   "The Concept of Social Elites." UNESCO, *International Social Sci-
            ence Bulletin,* Vol. III, no. 3.
O'Brien, D. C. Cruise
   1975   *Saints and Politicians: Essays on the Organization of a Senegalese
            Peasant Society.* Cambridge: Cambridge University Press.
Okereke, O.
   1970   "The Place of Marketing Cooperatives in the Economy of Uganda."
            Pp. 153-77 in Carl Gosta Widstrand (ed.), *Cooperatives and Rural
            Development in East Africa.* New York: Africana Publishing Cor-
            poration.
Paige, Jeffrey M.
   1975   *Agrarian Revolution.* New York: The Free Press.
Palloix, Christian
   1969   *Problèmes de la Croissance en Economie Ouverte.* Paris: Maspero.

Palmer, Robin, and Neil Parsons (eds.)
  1977   *The Roots of Rural Poverty in East and Central Africa.* Berkeley: University of California Press.
Parkin, David
  1969   *Neighbours and Nationals in an African City Ward.* London: Routledge and Kegan Paul.
Peel, J. D. Y.
  1976   "Inequality and Action: The Forms of Ijesha Social Conflict." *Canadian Journal of African Studies* 14, 3:473-502.
Portes, Alejandro
  1976   "On the Sociology of National Development: Theories and Issues." *American Journal of Sociology* 82, 1 (July): 55-85.
Roscoe, John
  1909   "Notes on the Bageshu." *Journal of the Anthropological Institute* 39:181-90.
  1915   *The Northern Bantu: An Account of Some Central African Tribes of the Uganda Protectorate.* Cambridge: Cambridge University Press.
  1924   *The Bageshu and other Tribes of the Uganda Protectorate: The Third Part of the Report of the Mackie Ethnological Expedition to Central Africa.* Cambridge: Cambridge University Press.
Rubinson, Richard
  1976   "The World-economy and the Distribution of Income within States: A Cross-national Study." *American Sociological Review* 41:638-59.
Rubinson, Richard, and Dan Quinlan
  1977   "Democracy and Social Inequality: A Reanalysis." *American Sociological Review* 42:611-23.
Samoff, Joel
  1979   "The Bureaucracy and the Bourgeoisie: Decentralization and Class Structure in Tanzania." *Comparative Studies in Society and History* 21, 1 (Jan.):30-62.
Saul, John S.
  1969   "Marketing Cooperatives in Tanzania." Paper presented at the Institute of Development Studies, University of Sussex.
  1972   "Class and Penetration in Tanzania." Pp. 118-26 in Lionel Cliffe and John Saul (eds.), *Socialism in Tanzania, Volume I: Politics.* Nairobi: East African Publishing House.
  1974   "The State in Post-Colonial Societies: Tanzania." Pp. 349-72, in *Socialist Register 1974.* London: Merlin Press.
  1976   "The Unsteady State: Uganda, Obote, and General Amin." *Review of African Political Economy,* 5:12-38.
Saul, John S., and Roger Woods
  1971   "African Peasantries." Pp. 103-14 in Teodor Shanin (ed.), *Peasants and Peasant Societies.* Harmondsworth, England: Penguin.
Scott, James C.
  1976   *The Moral Economy of the Peasant: Rebellion and Subsistence in Southeast Asia.* New Haven: Yale University Press.

Seers, D., et al.
1979   *The Rehabilitation of the Economy of Uganda,* vol. 2. London: Commonwealth Secretariat.
Selznick, Philip
1966   *TVA and the Grass Roots.* New York: Harper and Row.
Shanin, Teodor
1972   *The Awkward Class.* London: Oxford University Press.
Shaw, R. Paul
1976   *Land Tenure and the Rural Exodus in Chile, Columbia, Costa Rica, and Peru.* Gainesville: University Presses of Florida.
Shivji, Issa
1976   *Class Struggles in Tanzania.* New York: Monthly Review Press.
Spittler, Gerd
1983   "Administration in a Peasant State." *Sociologia Ruralis* 23:130-44.
Stavenhagen, Rodolfo
1966-67 "Seven Erroneous Theses about Latin America." *New York University Thought* 4 (Winter):25-37.
Steward, Julian
1967   "Perspectives on Modernization: Introduction to the Studies." Pp. 1-55 in Julian Steward (ed.), *Contemporary Change in Traditional Societies,* vol. 1. Urbana: University of Illinois Press.
Swartz, Marc, V. Turner, and Arthur Tuden
1970   *Political Anthropology.* Chicago: Aldine Publishing Company.
Twaddle, M.
1966   "The Founding of Mbale." *Uganda Journal* 30, 1:25-38.
Uchendu, Victor
1969   "Political Primacy and African Economic Development." Paper presented at University Social Sciences Council Conference, Nairobi.
Uganda Government
1963   *The Cooperative Societies Act and Rules.* Entebbe: Government Printer.
1966a   *Work for Progress: Uganda's Second Five Year Plan, 1966-1971.* Entebbe: Government Printer.
1966b   *Census of Agriculture.* Entebbe: Government Printer.
1966c   *The Report of the Committee of Inquiry into the Affairs of all Cooperative Unions in Uganda.* Entebbe: Government Printer.
Uganda Protectorate
1925   "Report on Chiefs' Salaries." Entebbe Secretariat Archives Cg 6025.
1946   *The Cooperative Societies Ordinance.* Entebbe: Government Printer.
1952   Annual Report for Eastern Province.
1952-62 Bugisu District Annual Reports.
1955a   *The Bugisu Coffee Ordinance.* Entebbe: Government Printer.
1955b   *Local Government Ordinances.* Entebbe: Government Printer.
1955c   *Land Tenure Proposals.* Entebbe: Government Printer.
1956   *Annual Report.* Entebbe: Government Printer.

1958a   *Report of the Commission of Inquiry into the Affairs of the Bugisu Cooperative Union Limited* Sessional Paper no. 14. Entebbe: Government Printer.

1958b   *Memorandum by Government on the Future Organization of the Bugisu Coffee Industry* Sessional Paper no. 19. Entebbe: Government Printer.

1959   *Uganda Population Census.* Entebbe: Government Printer.

1960a   *Report of the Commission of Inquiry into Disturbances in the Eastern Provinces.* Entebbe: Government Printer.

1960b   *Report of the Commission of Inquiry into the Affairs of the Bugisu District Council.* Entebbe: Government Printer.

1962   *Report of the Commission Appointed to Review the Boundary between the Districts of Bugisu and Bukedi.* Entebbe: Government Printer.

Uganda, Republic of

1967   *Atlas of Uganda.* Entebbe: Government Printer.

1968   *The Produce Marketing Board Act.* Entebbe: Government Printer.

1969   *Uganda Census* (provisional results).

1969   *Statistical Abstracts.* Entebbe: Government Printer.

1970   *Cooperative Societies Act.* Entebbe: Government Printer.

1970   *Uganda Statistical Abstracts.* Entebbe: Government Printer.

1982   "1982 Recovery Program, 1982-1984". Kampala: mimeograph.

1985   *Background of the Budget, 1985-1986.* Kampala: Ministry of Planning and Economic Development.

United Nations

1981   *Uganda: Country Presentation,* prepared for the United Nations Conference on the Least Developed Nations Country Review Meetings, East Africa. Addis Ababa: Mimeograph.

van Binsbergen, Alfred F. E.

1977   "The Contribution of Small Farmers and Rural Workers to Food Production and Development in Latin America." *Land Reform* 1:15-14.

Vansina, Jan

1973   *The Tio Kingdom of the Middle Kingdom, 1880-1892.* London: Oxford University Press for the International African Institute.

Vincent, Joan

1969   "The Primary Society and the Parish: Problems of Organization, Representation, and Communication." *Nkanga* 4:7-12.

1971   *African Elite.* New York: Columbia University Press.

1982   *Teso in Transformation: The Political Economy of Peasant and Class in Eastern Africa.* Berkeley: University of California Press.

Wallace, I. R.

n.d.   *The World Coffee Situation and the Importance of Quality to Peasant Producers of Arabica Coffee in East Africa.* Kampala, Makerere University, R.D.R. 23.

n.d.   "Some Technical and Economic Aspects of Coffee Production on Peasant Farms in Bugisu/Sebei." Paper for restricted circulation EAISR.

Wallace, I. R., D. G. R. Belshaw, and Beverley Brock
n.d.   "The Bugisu Coffee Industry." Kampala: Makerere Institute of Social Research (bound mimeograph).

Wallerstein, Immanuel
1972   "Social Conflict in Post-independence Black Africa: The Concepts of Race and Status-group Reconsidered." Pp. 207-26 in Ernest Q. Campbell (ed.), *Racial Tensions and National Identity.* Nashville: Vanderbilt University Press.
1974   "The Rise and Future Demise of the World Capitalist System." *Comparative Studies in Society and History* 16(4):387-415.

Wallis, C. A. G.
1953   *Report of an Inquiry into African Local Government in the Protectorate of Uganda.* Entebbe: Government Printer.

Weatherby, J. M.
1962   "Inter-Tribal Warfare on Mount Elgon in the 19th and 20th Centuries." *Uganda Journal* 26:200-212.

Weber, Max
1958   *From Max Weber. Essays in Sociology.* H. H. Gerth and C. Wright Mills (eds.). New York: Oxford University Press.
1968   *Economy and Society.* 3 vols. New York: Bedminister Press.

Wolf, Eric
1956   "Aspects of Group Relations in a Complex Society: Mexico." *American Anthropologist* 58:1065-78.
1969   *Peasant Wars of the Twentieth Century.* New York: Harper and Row.

Wrigley, C. C.
1959   *Crops and Wealth in Uganda: A Short Agrarian History.* Kampala: East African Institute of Social Research.

Young, M. Crawford
1971   "Agricultural Policy in Uganda: Capability and Choice." Pp. 141-64 in Michael Lofchie (ed.), *The State of the Nations.* Berkeley: University of California Press.
1976   *The Politics of Cultural Pluralism.* Madison: University of Wisconsin Press.
1978   "Bugisu: Geography, Social Composition and Traditional Political Organization." In *Uganda: District Government and Politics.* African Studies Program, Madison, University of Wisconsin.
1979   "The State and the Small Urban Center in Africa." Pp. 313-33 in Aidan Southall (ed.), *Small Urban Centers and Rural Development in Africa.* Madison: African Studies Program, University of Wisconsin.

Young, Crawford, Neal P. Sherman, and Tim H. Rose
  1981   *Cooperatives and Development: Agricultural Politics in Ghana and Uganda.* Madison: University of Wisconsin Press.
Zaman, M. A.
  1975   "Bangladesh: The Case for Further Land Reform." *South Asian Review* 8, 2:97-115.

Index

Wealth, 7, 9, 22, 246; access to, 59, 78, 84, 99-100, 105-6, 182-83, 189, 245; and authority, 33-34, 46, 109; changing attitudes toward, 109
Weber, M. (1958), 41
Wolf, E. (1969), 2, 27n
Women, 241; and inheritance, 75n, 78; in agriculture, 67, 79; in marriage alliances, 34, 41, 66, 94-96, 126; in politics, 66, 75n
Woods, R., 123-27

World Bank, 228, 229, 231, 232
World-system, 2, 4, 15, 16, 49, 251-52
World War II, 14, 50, 251; Bagisu participation in, 49; effects on coffee prices, 50
Wrigley, C. C. (1959), 20, 24, 50

Young, M. C., vii; (1971), 5, 1; (1976), 23, 49n, 162n; (1979), 193
Young, M. C. et al. (1981), 23, 24, 55, 180, 190, 199, 240n

Note on the Author

STEPHEN G. BUNKER is a member of the Department of Sociology at Johns Hopkins University. He has degrees from Harvard (B.A.) and Duke (M.A. and Ph.D.) universities. He has previously taught at the University of Illinois at Urbana-Champaign, the Universidade Federal do Pará (Brazil), and at the Universidad del Valle (Guatemala); he was also a research associate at the Makerere Institute of Social Research (Uganda).

Mr. Bunker has studied peasant communities in New Mexico, Guatemala, Uganda, Brazilian Amazonia, and the Peruvian highlands. Many of his articles examine the reasons for the success or failure of peasant groups who seek to defend themselves against dominant landowning classes and modernizing state bureaucracies. The persistence of viable peasant political organizations in Uganda, which he discusses in this book, contrasts sharply with the repeated ecological and social disruptions of peasant communities that he portrays in *Underdeveloping the Amazon: Extraction, Unequal Exchange, and the Failure of the Modern State* (University of Illinois Press, 1985).